**Other books in *Tricycle*'s three-volume collection:
the Beginning Buddhist Practice series . . .**

BREATH SWEEPS MIND
A First Guide to Meditation Practice

A simple, accessible guide to the ancient art of meditation, this
book answers the most basic questions: What is meditation?
Why meditate? and How does one meditate?

EVERYDAY MIND
366 Reflections on the Buddhist Path

First in the series, *Everyday Mind* is a book of daily reflections.
It introduces the novice to the textual foundations and basic steps
of Buddhism, and it serves as a ''Best of'' collection for those
already familiar with Buddhist practice.

Radiant Mind

Essential Buddhist Teachings and Texts

A Tricycle Book

Edited by Jean Smith

Riverhead Books, New York

Riverhead Books
Published by The Berkley Publishing Group
A division of Penguin Putnam Inc.
375 Hudson Street
New York, New York 10014

A continuation of credits appears on pages 330–338.

Published simultaneously in Canada.

First edition: February 1999

Visit our website at
www.penguinputnam.com

Library of Congress Cataloging-in-Publication Data

Radiant mind : essential Buddhist teachings and texts / edited by Jean
Smith.—1st ed.
p.   cm.
"A tricycle book."
ISBN 1-57322-717-X
1. Buddhism—Doctrines.   2. Religious life—Buddhism.   I. Smith,
Jean.
BQ4165.R33   1999
394.3'4—dc21   98-27109
CIP

Printed in the United States of America

10   9   8   7   6

With gratitude, for teachers everywhere

Contents

Contents

VIII

CONTENTS

IX

Wisdom

The Three Refuges / The Triple Treasure

Buddha Nature

CONTENTS

x

Enlightenment

Bodhisattvas

The Self

Karma

The Dhammapada

Contents

Nirvana

Preface

MANY PEOPLE TODAY begin to explore the teachings of the Buddha as an expansion of their meditation practice. In a sense they are emulating the Buddha's own enlightenment experience, in which through meditation he sought—and found—truth. After his enlightenment, in about 528 BCE, he walked from village to village on the Ganges plain and for the next forty-five years taught the truth he had discovered.

In his teachings, the Buddha urged each person to seek the truth from direct and personal experience. Thus, from the Buddha's earliest adherents to contemporary teachers, his followers have examined his teachings within the perspective of their own times and lives, using their own "radiant minds," as described by the Buddha. Sariputta, one of the Buddha's closest disciples, found a simile in the way trackers pursued elephants. Sariputta proclaimed that just as the footprints of all living beings can be placed within the footprint of an elephant, so too can all their conditions be placed within the Buddha's teachings on suffering and the end of suffering through the development of conscious moral conduct, mental discipline, and wisdom. Twenty-five hundred years later, contemporary Vipassana teacher Jack Kornfield found a statement relative to the Buddha's teaching on mental discipline on a sign outside a Las Vegas casino: "You must be present to win."

Here are collected starting points: essential teachings and texts of the Buddha's discourses, accompanied by the commentaries of some seekers who traveled with him on his journey during his lifetime and some who have come since. The earliest recorded teachings make up the Pali canon, the collection of discourses preserved by oral tradition until the first century BCE, when they were written down in the Pali language of the Buddha's day. These teachings are the bedrock of the Theravada tradition. They are marked by a rather standard form of presentation, stereotyped phrases, and extensive repetition—all characteristics of a body of discourses preserved initially by oral tradition. Early in the common era, other discourses were recorded in Sanskrit; these became the foundation of Mahayana, the other major tradition in Buddhism. In this collection of discourses and commentaries, spellings have been retained from the original sources, representing both major traditions. Thus, some terms are expressed in one place in Pali but in other places in Sanskrit—for example, the Pali *Sutta*, *Dhamma*, and *Nibbana* and the Sanskrit *Sutra*, *Dharma*, and *Nirvana*. When teachings from the discourses are given within quotation marks and are not otherwise attributed, the speaker is the Buddha.

THE BUDDHA STRESSED that his teachings are like a raft to get to the other shore—we would be foolish, after crossing over, to pick up the raft and carry it around on our back. The Buddha's teachings, then, are a starting point, to be examined and tested within our personal encounter with reality. His experience of enlightenment is the foundation upon which this search is built, but the search is ours.

Part I

The Buddha
and
Buddhism

The Buddha

The prince born twenty-five hundred years ago who became the historical Buddha was the only founder of a major world religion who claimed to be neither a god nor a messenger of a god. When asked once just what he was, he replied simply, "I am awake."

Although many legends surround his life, we do know approximately when he lived (c. 563–483 BCE) and what his key teachings were. In ancient and modern times, the Buddha's life has been an ideal of conduct and a source of inspiration. One contemporary teacher put it most succinctly when she said, "The Buddha showed us what is possible."

JEAN SMITH
Life of the Buddha

TWENTY-FIVE HUNDRED YEARS ago, a prince was born in the Sakya kingdom, in the southern Nepal foothills of the Himalayas. This prince, Siddhartha Gautama, would become the historic Buddha ("the Enlightened One"). Mysterious stories surround his birth: His mother, Queen Mahamaya, dreamed that her side was pierced by the six tusks of a white elephant and understood the apparition to mean that she had conceived a child. When she told her husband, King Shuddhodana, of the dream, he consulted an astrologer, who foresaw that the child would become either a universal ruler or a fully enlightened being, a buddha.

3

A week after the prince's birth, his mother died, and he was given for care to her sister, Mahaprajapati Gautami, who was also married to Shuddhodana, a known custom of the time. Although all the events leading up to the birth of Siddhartha had been joyful, after Mahamaya's death Shuddhodana feared that he would be heirless if Siddhartha turned to the religious rather than the political life foretold by the seer. From then on, the king did everything in his power to make Siddhartha's life one of pleasure, confined mostly to the palace. The young man—who was said to be physically, intellectually, and spiritually beautiful—was surrounded by luxury. When he was sixteen, he was married to a beautiful and generous-spirited young noblewoman named Yashodara.

Outwardly, little changed for Siddhartha during the next dozen years. On the few occasions when he left the palace, his father tried to control the pleasantness of his experience, to the extent, so the stories say, of having the streets swept and flowers placed along his route and removing anything that might offend Siddhartha's eye. But on these rare outings, Siddhartha had four experiences that would alter his life—and history. It is told that he encountered four heavenly messengers who appeared to him in different guises. On one trip, Siddhartha saw, for the first time, a very old man. His chariot driver, Chandaka, explained that the effects of aging happened to all people. On another, Siddhartha saw, again for the first time, a man suffering horrible ravages of disease, and again Chandaka explained the phenomenon to him. Another time, Siddhartha saw a corpse, surrounded by grief-stricken mourners, and learned from Chandaka that death is the fate awaiting all living beings. So protected had Siddhartha been that he was shocked by the revelation, on each occasion, of common experiences of suffering: illness, old age, and death. The trauma of seeing these sufferings and realizing that he himself was subject to them caused him great despondency. On a fourth excursion, Siddhartha encountered a wandering holy man, an ascetic who had given up all earthly possessions yet somehow seemed greatly at peace.

Siddhartha's mind struggled with the contrast between the artificiality of his life of pleasure and the reality of the suffering that surrounded him in the world. According to legend, one night, as he sat alone in a garden, a deep peace came over him and he resolved to become a buddha, an enlightened one, to find a way to the end of the suffering he saw. Filled with grief and at the same time with resolve, the twenty-nine-year-old Siddhartha left his parents, his wife, and his infant son, Rahula, renouncing his kingdom and all worldly ties.

Siddhartha took his best horse and, accompanied by his charioteer, Chandaka, rode as far from the palace as he could in a night. The next morning, after crossing a small river, he exchanged clothes with a poor hunter, cut off all his hair, and sent Chandaka back to his father's palace with his horse, jewelry, and other belongings. He spent the next six years as a wandering mendicant, spending time with first one then another of the notable teachers in the valley of the Ganges. He mastered their lessons and meditation techniques readily, but still he felt far from his goal of enlightenment. He left these teachers to travel with five other ascetics, living a life of the most severe austerities. Finally, Siddhartha, weak from hunger, realized that the way to enlightenment was not through such extreme deprivation, and he separated from the other ascetics. After taking some nourishment and regaining his strength, Siddhartha sat down in meditation beneath a pipal tree by the river Neranjara, near the town now known as Bodhgaya, and vowed not to arise until he had achieved enlightenment. There he spent the night of the full moon in May—his thirty-fifth birthday—battling Mara, the manifestation of all the demons of his mind. At dawn, reaching down with his right hand and touching the earth as his witness, he understood the nature of suffering and was liberated.

The Buddha walked to Deer Park near Sarnath, where he encountered the five ascetics with whom he had traveled when his search began. It was this group who heard his first sermon and became his first disciples. Liberated from the endless suffering of the wheel of life, samsara, he set in motion the great wheel of the Dharma, his teachings on suffering and the end of suffering. For the next forty-five years, the Buddha traveled with bands of disciples, his sangha, teaching the Dharma to those who gathered around him, regardless of their social background or caste. He died at the age of eighty, near the village of Kushinagara.

JOHN SNELLING

The Teaching Career

SO BEGAN A forty-five-year ministry . . . [c. 528–483 BCE] during which the Buddha wandered between the towns, villages and cities of the middle Ganges plain, mainly in the ancient kingdoms of Magadha and Kosala.

From the start he seems to have possessed a kind of radiance that stirred a deep response in those who met him. He was also a teacher of consummate skill and, though he never set himself up as a competitive rival to other religious teachers or to the brahmin priesthood, all the indications are that he was very concerned to get his message across. For one thing, he wished his teachings to be formulated in the local dialects in which they would be fully accessible to ordinary people and not in the rarefied liturgical language of the times. And it is clear from the accounts that large numbers of people, of all classes and conditions, became enlightened by his teachings.

There are many stories relating to this phase of the Buddha's life, but the story of Kisagotami exemplifies as well as any the Buddha's skill as a teacher.

Kisagotami was a poor widow who had suffered many cruel reversals in life. Then, a final twist of the knife, the beloved baby that was all she had in the world died. She was inconsolable and would not have the child's body cremated. Despairing, some of her fellow villagers suggested she go to see the Buddha. She arrived before him, still clutching the child's corpse in her arms. "Give me some special medicine that will cure my child," she begged.

The Buddha knew at once that the woman could not take the bald truth, so he thought for a while. Then he said, "Yes, I can help you. Go and get me three grains of mustard seed. But they have to come from a house in which no death has ever occurred."

Kisagotami set off with new hope in her heart. But as she went from door to door, she heard one heart-rending tale of bereavement after another. That evening, when she returned to the Buddha, she had learnt that bereavement was not her own personal tragedy but a feature of the human condition—and she had accepted the fact. Sadly, she laid down her dead child's body and bowed to the Buddha.

The Buddha's teachings are not merely for intellectual contemplation. They involve practice: things to do—and things requiring discipline and application. Though many of his early followers were lay-people, there were also those who wished to give up the world and family life in order to devote their time and energy entirely to the Dharma. So emerged the Sangha, the community of Buddhist monks, to which later nuns were admitted. At first the Sangha lived lives of extreme simplicity as homeless mendicants, dressing in rags, living only on alms-food and seeking shelter in caves and beneath the roots of trees. Later, however, thanks to the largesse of wealthy lay benefactors—the Buddha numbered among his devotees kings, aristocrats and rich merchants—they obtained more permanent and comfortable residences during the Monsoon or Rainy Season. These were the beginnings of vihare: Buddhist monasteries.

JOSEPH GOLDSTEIN

The Example of the Buddha

A QUESTION FOR us to consider is whether we can relate to the life of the Buddha, both in our formal practice and in our everyday lives, in a way that is meaningful for us in these times. Can we relate to his life in some way that gives perspective and context to our own? One possibility is to see the Buddha as a particular historical figure, a person who lived in what is now northern India in the fifth and sixth centuries BCE, and who went through a powerful awakening transformation at the age of thirty-five. We can relate in a very human, historical way, understanding his struggles, his quest, his enlightenment, from the perspective of one human being to another.

Another level on which we can relate is to view the Buddha as a fundamental archetype of humanity; that is, as the full manifestation of buddha-nature, the mind that is free of defilement and distortion, and understanding his life story as a great journey representing some basic archetypal aspects of human existence. By viewing the life of the Buddha in both of these ways, as a historical person and as an archetype, it becomes possible to see the unfolding of universal principles within the particular content of his life experience. We can then view the Buddha's life not as an abstract, removed story of somebody who lived twenty-five hundred years ago, but as one that reveals the nature of the universal in us all. This becomes a way of understanding our own experience in a larger and more profound context, one that connects the Buddha's journey with our own. We have undertaken to follow the same path, motivated by the same questions: What is the true nature of our lives? What is the root cause of our suffering?

In his book *Hero with a Thousand Faces* . . . , Joseph Campbell, the great scholar of humanity's myths and archetypes, explores the nature of the hero myth. He speaks of four stages in the great journey of the archetypal hero or heroine, and his discussion of the Buddha's journey in terms of these four stages is a wonderful interweaving of the personal elements of the Buddha's life and the universal principles they embody. Realizing how the events of the Buddha's life relate directly to our own experiences can give tremendous energy and inspiration to our individual journeys. Reflecting upon the life of the Buddha brings a sense of joy to the mind, because in recognizing the power and magnitude of the Buddha's spiritual quest, we reconnect with our own deepest impulses and motivations for practicing the dharma. . . .

Campbell calls the first stage of the hero's journey the call to destiny. According to traditional accounts, the Buddha first heard this call many lifetimes before his birth as Siddhartha Gotama, when he was a forest-dwelling hermit named Sumedha in the time of the previous buddha, Dipankara. One day Sumedha heard that Dipankara Buddha would be passing nearby and he joined the many people who were going to pay their respects. The people were preparing the road for Dipankara and the procession of monks and nuns, and Sumedha was given one small section of the road to prepare and make smooth. He had not quite finished and the road was still muddy when they were about to arrive, so at the last minute Sumedha laid his body down on the road for Dipankara to walk over.

It is said that when he saw Dipankara, Sumedha was so inspired by his presence and nobility that he resolved that he, too, would one day bring to perfection all the qualities of mind of a buddha. Dipankara saw this aspiration in the mind of the hermit and prophesied that many aeons of time in the future, Sumedha would be born a prince named Siddhartha Gotama and in that lifetime would attain to buddhahood. From the moment of hearing and responding to that call to destiny Sumedha was a bodhisattva, a being destined to attain the awakening and perfection of a buddha. . . .

The first stage of the archetypal journey is the call to destiny; the second is the great renunciation, the leaving behind of old patterns and habits, beginning to see our lives in a new way; the third stage is the great struggle with all the forces of delusion; and the fourth stage in this universal journey is the great awakening. After the hosts of Mara were dispersed, the bodhisattva spent the three watches of the night contemplating various aspects of the dharma. In the first watch he surveyed with his power of concentration the succession of births and deaths through countless lifetimes. Through seeing this process stretching back into beginningless time—being born into certain circumstances, going through the dramas of life, dying and being reborn—came a profound understanding of the impermanence and insubstantiality of existence. Life and death are arising and vanishing like bubbles on the surface of a stream. The long-range perspective of the cycles of lifetimes undercuts the seeming solidity and importance our attachments and preferences assume when we are identified with particular situations or experiences.

In the second watch of the night, he contemplated the law of karma. He saw how the karmic force of past actions propels and conditions beings through successive rebirths. Seeing beings driven by ignorance through the whirlwind of differing destinies awoke in him the energy of deep compassion. In the third watch of the night he contemplated the Four Noble Truths and the law of dependent origination. He saw how the mind becomes attached, and how through attachment there is suffering. He understood the possibility of deconditioning that attachment and coming to a place of freedom.

It is said that just at the moment of dawn, when the morning star appeared in the sky, his mind realized the deepest, most complete illumination. After attaining the great enlightenment, the Buddha uttered this verse in his heart:

> *I wandered through the rounds of countless births,*
> *Seeking but not finding the builder of this house.*
> *Sorrowful indeed is birth again and again.*
> *Oh, housebuilder! You have now been seen.*
> *You shall build the house no longer.*
> *All your rafters have been broken,*
> *Your ridgepole shattered.*
> *My mind has attained to unconditioned freedom.*
> *Achieved is the end of craving.*

The Buddha saw that in this world of samsara, of constant appearing and disappearing, being born and dying, there was great suffering. Craving, the builder of this house of suffering (the mind and body), was discovered; the defilements of mind, the rafters, were broken; the force of ignorance, the ridgepole, was shattered, and thus the Buddha realized nirvana, the unconditioned [see also pages 307–314]. It is said that the path to nirvana, the Eightfold Path, is a silent vehicle, like a chariot that drives smoothly and gracefully, without emitting squeaks and clatter.

The people who ride on this chariot, however, those who have realized the truth, may be quite noisy. They are noisy in their songs of praise for this vehicle and for this completion of their journey.

In the *Theragatha* and *Therigatha*—collections of enlightenment verses of the early monks and nuns—we often find the refrain "Done is what had to be done." In attaining the great enlightenment, the bodhisattva experienced the completion and fulfillment of his long journey, a fulfillment of the potential shared by all human beings. He had become the Buddha, the Awakened One. He spent the next seven weeks in the area of the bodhi [pipal] tree, contemplating different aspects of the truth. He had completed his own journey of liberation, and he now wondered whether it was possible to share the profound dharma he had realized with others, blinded as they were by their attachments. . . .

The Buddha continued his teaching travels, and when sixty of his disciples had themselves come to full enlightenment, he sent them out to begin spreading the dharma with this exhortation: "Go forth, O monks, for the good of the many, for the happiness of the many, out of compassion for the world, for the good, benefit, and happiness of people and devas [celestial beings]. Let not two go by one way. Teach the dharma, excellent in the beginning, excellent in the middle, and excellent in the end. Proclaim the noble life, altogether perfect and pure; work for the good of others, those of you who have done your duty."

We can see from this statement of the Buddha that the whole thrust of practice and of understanding is to develop freedom in oneself, compassion for the suffering of the world, and an active sense of service for the welfare of others. Seeing the purification of our own hearts and minds in the context of working for the benefit of others inspires and gives energy to our practice. Practice is never just for oneself; the manifestation of truth is always one of greater connectedness and compassion. . . .

The Buddha was endowed with three accomplishments. The first is called the accomplishment of cause, which refers to the extraordinary effort made by the bodhisattva through innumerable lifetimes to perfect the paramis ["perfections"—generosity, discipline, patience, endeavor, meditative concentration, wisdom]; that is, he accomplished the cause for buddhahood. The second is the accomplishment of result, which refers to his enlightenment and attainment of omniscient knowledge. And the third is the accomplishment of service, seeing to the welfare of others. The Buddha was not complacent with his own awakening, but out of loving care for all beings he set forth to teach, and until he died he shared the dharma with all those who were ready to hear.

The heroic effort made by the bodhisattva to develop the perfections is only possible through the motivation of extraordinary compassion. Yet compassion alone is not enough; for it to bring effective results, compassion must be acted upon, and this demands a discriminating wisdom as to beneficial or harmful actions, knowing which paths will bring happiness and which will not. Great compassion requires great wisdom in order to bear fruit, and great wisdom requires deep compassion as the motivation and impetus for action to be undertaken for the sake of other beings. These two great wings of the dharma were perfectly fulfilled in the Buddha.

It is said that even if one were to combine the love and compassion of all parents on the planet for their children, it would not approach the great compassion of the Buddha. Parents may have a great capacity to love and forgive their children. In the Buddha, these qualities were boundless. Because of his practical compassion, he ceaselessly exhorted beings to follow the path that leads to happiness, well-being, and freedom. . . .

There are innumerable stories of people from all walks of life—beggars, merchants, artisans, courtesans, village people, nobles, kings and queens—each coming to the Buddha with varying degrees of faith and understanding, whom he helped come to freedom and peace through the power of his love, wisdom, and skillful means.

One discourse the Buddha gave that is particularly helpful in understanding the spirit of investigation and discovery in dharma practice is known as the *Kalama Sutta*. He was asked by a village people known as the Kalamas how they could know which among the many different religious teachings and teachers to believe. The Buddha said that they should not blindly believe anyone—not their parents or teachers, not the books or traditions, not even the Buddha himself. Rather, they should look carefully into their own experience to see which things lead to more greed, more hatred, more delusion, and should abandon them; and they should look to see what things lead to greater love, generosity, wisdom, openness, and peace, and should cultivate those things. The Buddha's teachings always encourage us to take responsibility for our own development and to directly investigate the nature of our experience. There was no desire in the Buddha's mind for fame, honor, or disciples. He was motivated by genuine compassion. . . .

As practice deepens and we come to a fuller appreciation and understanding of our own true nature, there develops a wonderful love and respect for the Buddha, both as a historical figure and as the archetype of the buddha-nature potential within us all [see also pages 229–237]. If we reflect on the three great accomplishments of the Buddha's life, we can become filled with a sense of deep appreciation for having the opportunity to walk the path discovered by such a being, a path of the greatest distinction and truest nobility. With mindfulness and insight we can reflect the Buddha's journey in our own.

THE DALAI LAMA

The Buddha's Life

IN THE PAST, erudite Buddhists tried to prove their own version of the historical facts surrounding the Buddha's life mainly through logic and argumentation. Given the nature of the question, however, I think such types of proof can never be conclusive.

Despite conflicting assertions regarding the historical reckoning of his birth, there is a general consensus in the literature as to the key events of the Buddha's life. We know that the Buddha was originally an ordinary person like ourselves, with all the basic faults and weaknesses of a human being. He was born into a royal family, married, and had a son. Later, however, he came into contact with the unsatisfactory suffering nature of life in the form of unexpected encounters with people afflicted by sickness, old age, and death. Deeply disturbed by these sights, the prince eventually left the palace and renounced his comfortable and sheltered princely way of life. His initial reaction to these experiences was to adopt the austere lifestyle of an ascetic, engaging in a spiritual path involving great physical penances. Later, he discovered that the true path out of suffering lies in a middle way between the extremes of strict asceticism and self-indulgent luxury. His single-minded spiritual pursuit ultimately resulted in his full awakening, or enlightenment: buddhahood.

I feel that the story of the Buddha's life holds great significance for us. It exemplifies the tremendous potentials and capacities that are intrinsic to human existence. For me, the events that led to his full enlightenment set an appropriate and inspiring example for his followers. In short, his life makes the following statement: "This is the way that you should pursue your spiritual path. You must bear in mind that the attainment of enlightenment is not an easy task. It requires time, will, and perseverance.'' Therefore, right from the beginning, it is crucial to harbor no illusions of a swift and easy path. As a spiritual trainee, you must be prepared to endure the hardships involved in a genuine spiritual pursuit and be determined to sustain your effort and will. You must anticipate the multiple obstacles that you are bound to encounter along the path and understand that the key to a successful practice is never to lose your determination. Such a resolute approach is very important. The story of the Buddha's personal life, as we have seen, is the story of someone who attained full enlightenment through hard work and un-wavering dedication. It is ironic that sometimes we seem to believe that we, who are following in the footsteps of the Buddha, can somehow realize full enlightenment with greater ease and less effort.

HUANG PO (NINTH CENTURY)

The Real Buddha

THE MASTER SAID to me: All the Buddhas and all sentient beings are nothing but the One Mind, beside which nothing exists. This Mind, which is without beginning, is unborn and indestructible. It is not green, nor yel-low, and has neither form nor appearance. It does not belong to the cate-gories of things which exist or do not exist, nor can it be thought of in terms of new or old. It is neither long nor short, big nor small, for it tran-scends all limits, measures, names, traces, and comparisons. It is that which you see before you—begin to reason about it and you at once fall into error. It is like the boundless void which cannot be fathomed or measured. The One Mind alone is the Buddha, and there is no distinction between the Buddha and sentient things, but that sentient beings are attached to forms and so seek externally for Buddhahood. By their very seeking they lose it, for that is using the Buddha to seek for the Buddha and using mind to grasp Mind. Even though they do their utmost for a full aeon, they will not be able to attain it. They do not know that, if they put a stop to conceptual thought and forget their anxiety, the Buddha will appear before them, for this Mind is the Buddha and the Buddha is all living beings. It is not the less for being manifested in ordinary beings, nor is it greater for being manifested in the Buddhas. . . . If you are not absolutely convinced that the Mind is the Buddha, and if you are attached to forms, practices and meritorious performances, your way of thinking is false and quite incompatible with the Way. The Mind is the Buddha, nor are there any other Buddhas or any other mind. It is bright and spotless as the void, having no form or appearance whatever. To make use of your minds to think conceptually is to leave the substance and attach yourselves to form. The Ever-Existent Buddha is not a Buddha of form or attachment. To practice the six paramitas [generosity, discipline, patience, endeavor, meditative concentration, wisdom] and myriad similar practices with the intention of becoming a Buddha thereby is to advance by stages, but the Ever-Existent Buddha is not a Buddha of stages. Only awake to the One Mind, and there is nothing whatsoever to be attained. This is the real Buddha. The Buddha and all sentient beings are the One Mind and nothing else.

This pure Mind, the source of everything, shines forever and on all with the brilliance of its own perfection. But the people of the world do not awake to it, regarding only that which sees, hears, feels, and knows as mind. Blinded by their own sight, hearing, feeling, and knowing, they do not perceive the spiritual brilliance of the source-substance. If they would only eliminate all conceptual thought in a flash, that source-substance would manifest itself like the sun ascending through the void and illuminating the whole universe without hindrance or bounds. Therefore, if you students of the Way seek to progress through seeing, hearing, feeling, and knowing, when you are deprived of your perceptions, your way to Mind will be cut off and you will find nowhere to enter. Only realize that, though real Mind is expressed in these perceptions, it neither forms part of them nor is separate from them. You should not start reasoning from these perceptions, nor allow them to give rise to conceptual thought; yet nor should you seek the One Mind apart from them or abandon them in your pursuit of the Dharma. Do not keep them nor abandon them nor dwell in them nor cleave to them. Above, below, and around you, all is spontaneously existing, for there is nowhere which is outside the Buddha-Mind.

Buddhism

A sign over a spiritual center in New York City reads: "The Paths Are Many; the Truth Is One." As the paths have radiated from Bodhgaya to all parts of the world, the Buddha's teachings have evolved within the cultures where their seeds were planted by disciples, generals, royalty, immigrants—even, most recently in the United States, by Peace Corps workers returning from assignments in Asia. Today, the many sects in Buddhism can be considered within three main traditions: Theravada, or Hinayana, or Insight Meditation, which has developed primarily in Southeast Asia; Mahayana, which includes Ch'an in China and Zen in Japan; and Mahayana Vajrayana, in Tibet. All are flourishing in the West as well. All are based on the Buddha's core teachings, but each tradition has its own emphases, role of teachers, and methods of teachings, including the use of riddles.

SHERAB CHÖDZIN KOHN
A Short History of Buddhism

THE HISTORY OF the Buddha Dharma begins with the enlightenment of the Buddha, who at the age of thirty-five (probably around 528 BCE) awakened from the sleep of delusion that grips all beings in an endless vicious cycle of ignorance and unnecessary suffering (*samsara*). Having awakened, he decided to "go against the current" and communicate his liberating wakefulness to suffering beings—that is, to teach the Dharma. For forty-five years, he crossed and recrossed India's central Gangetic plain on foot conveying his profound, brilliant wakefulness directly as well as by means of explanations that grew into a great body of spiritual, psychological, and practical doctrine. His enlightenment as well as the doctrine leading to it have been passed down through numerous unbroken lineages of teachers, which have spread to many countries. Many of these lineages still flourish.

At the time of the Buddha's death (ca. 483 BCE), his Dharma was well established in central India. There were many lay followers, but the heart of the Dharma community were the monastics, many of whom were *arhats* ["worthy ones," who attain Nirvana at the end of this lifetime]. Numerous monasteries had already been built round about such large cities as Rajagriha, Shravasti, and Vaishali.

The first to assume the Buddha's mantle, tradition tells, was his disciple Mahakashyapa, who had the duty of establishing an authoritative version of the Buddha's teachings. Thus, during the first rainy season after the Buddha's *parinirvana* [death], Mahakashyapa convoked an assembly of five hundred arhats. At this assembly, it is said, Ananda, the Buddha's personal attendant, recited all of the master's discourses (*sutras*), naming the place where each was given and describing the circumstances. A *bhikshu* [monk] named Upali recited all the rules and procedures the Buddha had established for the conduct of monastic life. Mahakashyapa himself recited the *matrika*, lists of terms organized to provide analytical synopses of the teachings given in the sutras. These three extensive recitations, reviewed and verified by the assembly, became the basis for the Sutra Pitaka (Discourse Basket), the Vinaya Pitaka (Discipline Basket), and Abhidharma Pitaka (Special Teachings Basket), respectively. The Tripitaka (all three together) is the core of the Buddhist scriptures. This assembly, held at Rajagriha with the patronage of the Magadhan king Ajatashatru, is called the First Council.

In the early centuries after the Buddha's death, the Buddha Dharma spread throughout India and became a main force in the life of its peoples. Its strength lay in its realized (arhat) teachers and large monasteries that sheltered highly developed spiritual and intellectual communities. Monks traveled frequently between the monasteries, binding them into a powerful network.

As the Dharma spread to different parts of India, differences emerged, particularly regarding the Vinaya, or rules of conduct. Roughly a hundred years after the First Council, such discrepancies led to a Second Council in Vaishali, in which seven hundred arhats censured ten points of lax conduct on the part of the local monks, notably the acceptance of donations of gold and silver. In spite of this council and other efforts to maintain unity, gradually, perhaps primarily because of size alone, the Sangha divided into divergent schools.

Among the principal schools was a conservative faction, the Sthaviravada (way of the elders), which held firmly to the old monastic ideal with the arhat at its center and to the original teaching of the Buddha as expressed in the Tripitaka. Another school, the Mahasanghikas, asserted the fallibility of arhats. It sought to weaken the authority of the monastic elite and open the Dharma gates to the lay community. In this, as well as in certain metaphysical doctrines, the Mahasanghikas prefigured the Mahayana. Another important school was that of the Sarvastivadins (from Sanskrit *sarva asti,* "all exists"), who held the divergent view that past, present, and future realities all exist. In all, eighteen schools with varying shades of opinion on points of doctrine or discipline developed by the end of the third century BCE. However, all considered themselves part of the spiritual family of the Buddha and in general were accepted as such by the others. It was not rare for monks of different schools to live or travel together.

According to the Sthaviravadin tradition (known in Pali as the Theravada), which continues today in Southeast Asia, a Third Council took place in the time of King Ashoka (r. 276–232 BCE) at which the king declared the Sthaviravadin teachings the standard from which all other schools deviated. Perhaps in reaction to this, the Sarvastivadins gradually migrated to the west. They established a bastion in the city of Mathura, from which their influence continued to spread. Over centuries, they dominated the northwest, including all of Kashmir and much of Central Asia. Today a Sarvastivadin Vinaya lineage still survives in all the schools of Tibetan Buddhism.

King Ashoka was the third emperor of the Mauryan empire, which covered all of the Indian subcontinent but its southern tip. His personal espousal of the Dharma and adoption of its principles for the governance of his immense realm meant a quantum leap in the spread of the Buddha's teaching. The imperial government promulgated the teachings, supported the monasteries, and sent proselytizing missions to the Hellenic states of the northwest and to Southeast Asia. Under King Ashoka, institutions of compassion and nonviolence were established throughout much of India, such as peaceful relations with all neighboring states, hospitals and animal hospitals, special officials to oversee the welfare of local populations, shady rest stops for travelers, and so on. Thus he remains today the paragon of a Buddhist ruler, and his reign is looked back upon by Buddhists as a golden age.

The Mauryan empire soon fragmented, but the Buddha Dharma continued as a dominant force throughout India in the early centuries of the common era. The kings of the Satavahana dynasty of central India followed Ashoka in adopting the Dharma as a civilizing and unifying force in governing disparate peoples. King Kanishka (r. first–second centuries), whose vast Kushan empire, centered on Gandhara, encompassed northern India and large parts of Central Asia, was a champion of the Dharma, hailed as a second Ashoka. Under his patronage, a Fourth

Council was held, at which major new commentaries on the Tripitaka were written, largely under Sarvastivadin influence. Under Kanishka, the Buddha Dharma was firmly planted among the Central Asian peoples whose homelands lay along the Silk Route, whence the way lay open to China. The Kushan empire also saw the flowering of Gandharan art, which under Hellenistic influences produced Buddha images of extraordinary nobility and beauty.

Traditional accounts of the Fourth Council say that the assembly was composed of arhats under the leadership of the arhat Parshva but also under the accomplished bodhisattva Vasumitra. Indeed it was at this time, about the beginning of the second century, that the way of the bodhisattva, or the Mahayana (Great Vehicle), appeared. It was this form of the Buddha Dharma that was to conquer the north, including China, Japan, Korea, Tibet, and Mongolia.

The most visible manifestation of the Mahayana was a new wave of sutras, scriptures claiming to be the word of the Buddha that had remained hidden until then in other realms of existence. The Mahayana replaced the ideal of the arhat with that of the bodhisattva. Whereas arhats sought to end confusion in themselves in order to escape samsara, bodhisattvas vowed to end confusion in themselves yet remain in samsara to liberate all other sentient beings. The vision of spiritual life broadened beyond the controlled circumstances of cloister and study to include the wide-open situations of the world. Correspondingly, the notion of "buddha" was no longer limited to a series of historical personages, the last of whom was Shakyamuni [Siddhartha Gautama], but referred also to a fundamental self-existing principle of spiritual wakefulness or enlightenment. While continuing to accept the old Tripitaka, Mahayanists regarded it as a restricted expression of the Buddha's teaching, and they characterized those who held to it exclusively as Hinayanists (adherents of the Hinayana, the Small Vehicle).

Great masters shaped the Mahayana in the early centuries of the common era. Outstanding among them all was Nagarjuna (fl. second or third century), whose name connects him with the *nagas* (serpent deities) from whose hidden realm he is said to have retrieved the *Prajnaparamita* sutras, foundational Mahayana scriptures [see pages 177–213]. Nagarjuna was born in South India and became the head of Nalanda, the great Buddhist university, a few miles north of Rajagriha, which was a major stronghold of the Dharma for a thousand years. Nagarjuna's commentaries and treatises expounded the teachings of the Madhyamaka (Middle Way), one of the two main Mahayana schools. Another great master was Asanga (fl. fourth century), who founded the other main school, the Yogachara, which focused on experience as the ultimate principle.

Through most of the Gupta period (c. 300–c. 600), the Buddha Dharma flourished unhindered in India. In the sixth century, however, hundreds of Buddhist monasteries were destroyed by invading Huns under King Mihirakula. This was a serious blow, but the Dharma revived and flourished once again, mainly in northeastern India under the Pala kings (eighth–twelfth centuries). These Buddhist kings patronized the monasteries and built new scholastic centers such as Odantapuri near the Ganges some miles east of Nalanda. Though the Hinayana had largely vanished from India by the seventh century, in this last Indian period the Mahayana continued, and yet another form—known as Mantrayana, Vajrayana, or Tantra—became dominant.

Like the Mahayana, the Vajrayana (Diamond Vehicle) was based on a class of scriptures ultimately attributed to the Buddha, in this case known as Tantras. Vajrayanists regarded the Hinayana and Mahayana as successive stages on the way to the tantric level. The Vajrayana leaped yet further than the Mahayana in acceptance of the world, holding that all experiences, including the sensual, are sacred manifestations of awakened mind, the buddha principle. It emphasized liturgical methods of meditation, or *sadhanas,* in which the practitioner identified with deities symbolizing various aspects of awakened mind. The palace of the deity, identical with the phenomenal world as a whole, was known as a *mandala.* In the place of the arhat and the bodhisattva, the Vajrayana placed the *siddha,* the realized tantric master.

By the thirteenth century, largely as a result of violent suppression by Islamic conquerors, the Buddha Dharma was practically extinct in the land of its birth. However, by this time Hinayana forms were firmly ensconced in Southeast Asia, and varieties of Mahayana and Vajrayana in most of the rest of Asia.

China

The Mahayana entered China through Central Asia at the beginning of the common era. At first it was confused with indigenous Taoism, whose terms it had to borrow. The Kuchean monk Kumarajiva (344–413), brought to China as a prisoner of war, created a new level of precision in Chinese Buddhism. His lucid translation and teaching resulted in the formation of the Chinese Madhyamaka school (San-lun, Three Treatises). Paramartha (499–569) was another great translator and teacher. His work made possible the development of the Fa-hsiang, or Chinese Yogachara, school. Buddha Dharma's golden age in China was the T'ang period (618–907). Monasteries were numerous and powerful and had the support of the emperors. During this time the other main Chinese Dharma schools—Hua-yen, T'ien-t'ai, Ch'an, Pure Land, and the tantric Mi-tsung—made their appearance. In 845, however, came a major persecution of the Dharma community, and the monasteries had to be evacuated. Thereafter the Buddha Dharma in China never recovered its former glory.

The Sung period (960–1279) was a time of blending Taoist, Buddhist, and Confucian ideas and methods. Under the Ming dynasty (1368–1662), a fusion of Ch'an and Pure Land opened the way for a strong lay movement. During the Ch'ing period (1663–1908), the Tibetan Vajrayana made its mark on Chinese Buddhism, mainly through the imperial courts. Communist rule in the twentieth century reduced the Dharma community to a remnant, but in Taiwan the Dharma flourished, predominantly in Pure Land and other popular forms.

Korea

Buddha Dharma came to Korea from China in the fourth century CE. It flourished after the Silla unification in the seventh century. By the tenth century there were Korean versions of most Chinese schools. Paramount were Ch'an, Hua-yen, and a Vajrayana form related to the Chinese Mi-tsung. The heyday of Korean Dharma was the Koryo period (932–1392), during which the comprehensive *Tripitaka Koreana* was published. Under the Yi dynasty (1392–1910), Confucianism became the state religion and the Buddha Dharma was forced into the background. A revival came after the end of Japanese rule in 1945, when the Won movement, a popular Buddhism much influenced by Ch'an, came to the fore. Nowadays, a kind of syncretic Buddhism is widespread in Korea.

Japan

The Buddha Dharma was brought to Japan from Korea in 522. It received its major impetus from the regent prince Shotoku (r. 593–621), a Japanese Ashoka. He established Buddhism as the state religion of Japan, founded monasteries, and himself wrote important commentaries on the sutras. Initially, it was primarily the Sanron (San-lun, Madhyamaka) school that spread. In the ninth century, six Japanese schools, originally brought from China—Kosha, Hosso, Sanron, Jojitsu, Ritsu, and Kegon—were officially recognized, with the imperial house adopting the Kegon Dharma. During the latter part of the Heian period (794–1184), the Tendai and tantric Shingon schools became predominant. From the tenth to fourteenth centuries, various Pure Land sects began to prosper. Zen (Ch'an) came to Japan from China toward the end of the twelfth century, and remained a vital force in Japanese cultural life ever after; Soto and Rinzai are its two main schools. After the appearance of the Nichiren school in the thirteenth century, no further movements developed until modern times. All Japanese schools assimilated aspects of indigenous Shinto kami [deities inhabiting nature] and ancestor worship. Since World War II, various modernizing lay movements such as Soka-gakkai and Rissho Kosei-kai have developed. Japan today boasts an unparalleled variety of Buddhist sects.

Tibet

The Buddha Dharma of Tibet (and Himalayan countries such as Sikkim, Bhutan, and Ladakh) preserved and developed the Vajrayana tradition of late Indian Buddhism and joined it with the Sarvastivadin monastic rule. The first spreading of Buddhism was initiated by King Trisong Detsen (755–797), who invited to Tibet the Indian pandit [learned man] Shantarakshita, notable for his brilliant synthesis of the Madhayamaka and Yogachara, and the great Indian *siddha* Padmasambhava. The tradition of the Nyingma school stems from this time. After a period of persecution, a second spreading came in the eleventh century, resulting in the foundation of the Kagyu and Shakya schools. A major part of Indian Buddhist writings were translated to form the Tibetan canon, which included tantric scriptures and commentaries, preserving many texts otherwise lost. In the fourteenth century, a reform movement resulted in the formation of the Gelukpa school, the fourth of the principal schools of Tibetan Buddhism. By the late twentieth century, as a result of Chinese repression Buddhism in Tibet was reduced to a vestige, but it remained in Sikkim and Bhutan. Centers of Tibetan Buddhism also developed in northern India and Nepal as well as in Europe, Australia, and North America.

Mongolia

The Mongols were definitively converted to Tibetan Buddhism in the sixteenth century. Scriptures and liturgies were translated into Mongolian, and the four principal Tibetan schools flourished until the Communist takeover of the twentieth century.

Vietnam

Vietnam lay under Chinese influence, and the Chinese Mahayana sects of Ch'an (Thien) and Pure Land (Tindo) were well established in the country by the end of the first millennium. Theravada was introduced by the Khmers but remained largely confined to areas along the Cambodian border. A modern social-action–oriented movement fusing the two Mahayana sects began in Saigon in 1932. In 1963 Theravadans joined this movement, and a United Buddhist Congregation of Vietnam existed fleetingly. Today Buddhists in Vietnam remain intensely involved in politics and social action.

Burma [Myanmar]

Emissaries sent by King Ashoka in the third century BCE first brought the Dharma to Burma. By the fifth century, the Theravada was well established, and by the seventh century the Mahayana had appeared in regions near the Chinese border. By the eighth century, the Vajrayana was also present, and all three forms continued to coexist until King Anaratha established the Theravada throughout the land in the eleventh century. Pagan, the royal capital in the north, was adorned with thousands upon thousands of Buddhist stupas and temples, and was the principal bastion of Buddha Dharma on earth until sacked by the Mongols in 1287. In succeeding centuries the Theravada continued strong, interacting closely at times with the Dharma centers of Ceylon [Sri Lanka]. The Burmese form of Theravada acquired a unique flavor through its assimilation of folk beliefs connected with spirits of all kinds known as *nats*. Today 85 percent of Burmese are Buddhist, and Buddhism is the official religion of the country.

Cambodia (Kampuchea)

The Buddhism of the Sarvastivadin school spread to Cambodia in the third century BCE and reached a high point in the fifth and sixth centuries. By the end of the eighth century, elements of Mahayana had also appeared. Succeeding centuries brought a fusion of Buddha Dharma with Shaivite Hinduism. In the fourteenth century, however, the Theravada was firmly imposed on the country by the royal house, and it has remained dominant. In 1955 Prince Norodom Sihanouk sought to unite the country under the banner of king, Dharma, and socialism.

Sri Lanka (Ceylon)

In the third century BCE, King Devanampiya Tissa was converted to Theravada Buddhism by King Ashoka's son, Mahinda. The Sinhalese king built the Mahavihara monastery and there enshrined a branch of the

Bodhi Tree that had been brought from India. For more than two millennia since that time, the Mahavihara has been a powerful force in the Buddhism of Ceylon and other countries of Southeast Asia, notably Burma and Thailand. The Theravada in Ceylon remains the oldest continuous Dharma tradition anywhere in the world. Nonetheless, factions reflecting the influence of other Indian or Theravada schools played a significant role. These centered around other great Sinhalese monasteries such as the Abhayagirivihara and the Jetavanavihara. Mahayana and tantric influences are also traceable, and Tamil Hinduism had an ongoing influence outside the monasteries. Associated with the Mahavihara was the preeminent teacher and writer Buddhaghosha (fl. fourth–fifth centuries), whose great *Vishuddimagga* (Path of Purity) gives a definitive account of the Theravada. In the twelfth century King Parakkambahu forcibly imposed the Mahaviharan brand of Theravada on the entire country.

The attempted conversion of the country to Christianity by Portuguese and Dutch colonists in the sixteenth and seventeenth centuries greatly weakened the Dharma in Ceylon but made it a rallying point for Sinhalese nationalism. In the following centuries Sinhalese kings turned to Burma and Thailand to refresh Sinhalese monastic lineages. In the nineteenth and twentieth centuries, many Europeans came to the aid of Sinhalese Buddhism. By the time of independence in 1948, the Theravada was again thriving in Ceylon and exercising significant influence beyond its borders.

Thailand

Some form of Hinayana Buddhism arrived in Thailand from Burma in about the sixth century; however, the Mahayana seems to have been dominant between the eighth and thirteenth centuries. From the eleventh century, Hinduist Khmers were a major factor in many regions of

the country, but in the thirteenth century the Thai royal house established Theravada Buddhism as the national religion. Eventually the
Khmers were converted to Theravada and became strong supporters. In
the nineteenth century, the reformist Dhammayut school, characterized
by strict adherence to Vinaya discipline, arose under royal influence.
Today it remains the dominant element in Thai Buddhism and has also
influenced other countries of Southeast Asia. Ninety-five percent of the
Thai population is Buddhist.

The Western World

Over the last two hundred years many Western intellectuals were
drawn to and influenced by Buddhism. Philosophers like Arthur Scho-
penhauer, Henri Bergson, and others were inspired by the exotic profundity of Buddhist thought. In the twentieth century there has been
considerable attention to Buddha Dharma in academic circles, and fairly
accurate translations of Buddhist texts have gradually become available
since the 1930s. A new level of understanding has come about since the
1950s as authentic Asian meditation masters have established themselves
in Western countries and taken on serious Western students. Theravada
Buddhism has had a significant impact since the 1930s, Zen since the
1950s, and the tantric Buddhism of Tibet since the 1970s. Recently
Westerners have begun assuming leadership in age-old Asian lineages.
Of course, significant numbers of Asian Buddhists have reached the West
as part of immigrant populations, but thus far there has been little cross-
over of Buddha Dharma from this source into host cultures.

JACK KORNFIELD

Theravada / Vipassana Practice

OVER THE YEARS and throughout various cultures, many techniques and systems of Buddhist practice have been developed . . . , but the essence of awakening is always the same: to see clearly and directly the truth of our experience in each moment, to be aware, to be mindful. This practice is a systematic development and opening of awareness called by the Buddha the four foundations of mindfulness: awareness of the body, awareness of feelings, awareness of mental phenomena, and awareness of truths, of the laws of experience [see pages 121–135].

To succeed in the cultivation of mindfulness, said the Buddha, is the highest benefit, informing all aspects of our life. "Sandalwood and tagara are delicately scented and give a little fragrance, but the fragrance of virtue and a mind well trained rises even to the gods."

How are we to begin? *The Path of Purification,* an ancient Buddhist text and guide, was written in answer to a short poem:

The world is entangled in a knot.
Who can untangle the tangle?

It is to untangle the tangle that we begin meditation practice. To disentangle ourselves, to be free, requires that we train our attention. We must begin to see how we get caught by fear, by attachment, by aversion—caught by suffering. This means directing attention to our everyday experience and learning to listen to our bodies, hearts, and minds. We attain wisdom not by creating ideals but by learning to see things clearly, as they are.

What is meditation? It's a good question. There is no shortage of descriptions, theories, manuals, texts, and ideas about it. There are hundreds of schools of meditation, which include prayer, reflection, devotion, visualization, and myriad ways to calm and focus the mind. Insight meditation (and other disciplines like it) is particularly directed to bringing understanding to the mind and heart. It begins with a training of awareness and a process of inquiry in ourselves. From this point of view, asking, "What is meditation?" is really the same as asking, "What is the mind?" or "Who am I?" or "What does it mean to be alive, to be free?"—questions about the fundamental nature of life and death. We must answer these questions in our own experience, through a discovery in ourselves. This is the heart of meditation.

It is a wonderful thing to discover these answers. Otherwise, much of life is spent on automatic pilot. Many people pass through years of life driven by greed, fear, aggression, or endless grasping after security, affection, power, sex, wealth, pleasure, and fame. This endless cycle of seeking is what Buddhism calls samsara. It is rare that we take time to understand this life that we are given to work with. We're born, we grow older, and eventually we die; we enjoy, we suffer, we wake, we sleep—how quickly it all slips away. Awareness of the suffering involved in this process of life, of being born, growing old, and dying led the Buddha to question deeply how it comes about and how we can find freedom. That was the Buddha's question. That is where he began his practice. Each of us has our own way of posing this question. To understand ourselves and our life is the point of insight meditation: to understand and to be free.

There are several types of understanding. One type comes from reading the words of others. We have all read and stored away an enormous amount of information, even about spiritual matters. Although this kind of understanding is useful, it is still someone else's experience.

Similarly there is the understanding that comes from being told by someone wise or experienced: "It's this way, friend." That too can be useful.

There is a deeper understanding based on our own consideration and reflection: "I've seen this through thoughtful analysis. I understand how it works." A tremendous amount can be known through thought. But is there a level deeper than that? What happens when we begin to ask the most fundamental questions about our lives? What is love? What is freedom? These questions cannot be answered by secondhand or intellectual ways of understanding. What the Buddha discovered, and what has been rediscovered by generation after generation of those who have practiced his teachings in their lives, is that there is a way to answer these difficult and wonderful questions. They are answered by an intuitive, silent knowing, by developing our own capacity to see clearly and directly.

How are we to begin? Traditionally this understanding grows through the development of three aspects of our being: a ground of conscious conduct, a steadiness of the heart and mind, and a clarity of vision or wisdom.

Conscious Conduct: The Five Training Precepts

The first aspect, conscious conduct or virtue, means acting harmoniously and with care toward the life around us. For spiritual practice to develop, it is absolutely essential that we establish a basis of moral conduct in our lives. If we are engaged in actions that cause pain and conflict to ourselves and others, it is impossible for the mind to become settled, collected, and focused in meditation; it is impossible for the heart to open. To a mind grounded in unselfishness and truth, concentration and wisdom develop easily.

The Buddha outlined five areas of basic morality that lead to a conscious life [see also pages 103–120]. These training precepts are given to all students who wish to follow the path of mindfulness. They are not given as absolute commandments; rather, they are practical guidelines to help us live in a more harmonious way and develop peace and power of mind. As we work with them, we discover that they are universal precepts that apply to any culture, in any time. They are a part of basic mindfulness practice and can be cultivated in our spiritual life.

The first precept is to refrain from killing. It means honoring all life, not acting out of hatred or aversion in such a way as to cause harm to any living creature. We work to develop a reverence and caring for life in all its forms. In the Eightfold Path [see pages 85–102] this is called one aspect of right action.

Even though it sounds obvious, we still manage to forget it. There was a cartoon in the *New Yorker* magazine some years ago during the hunting season. One deer turns to the other and says, "Why don't they thin their own goddamn herds?" We get into formulating excuses: "Well, there are too many deer." As we become more conscious and connected with life, it becomes clear that we shouldn't harm others, because it hurts us to kill. And they don't like it; even the tiniest creatures don't wish to die. So in practicing this precept we learn to stop creating pain for others and pain for ourselves.

The second precept asks us to refrain from stealing, meaning not to take what is not ours. Not to steal is called basic nonharming. We need to let go of being greedy and not take too much. More positively, it means to use things with sensitivity and care, to develop our sense of sharing this life, this planet. To live, we need plants, we need animals, and we need insects. This whole world has to share its resources. It is a boat of a certain size with so many beings living on it. We're connected with the bees and the insects and the earthworms. If there weren't earthworms to aerate the soil, and if there weren't bees to pollinate the crops, we'd starve. We need bees; we need insects. We're all inter-woven. If we can learn to love the earth, we can be happy whatever we do, with a happiness born of contentment. This is the source of genuine ecology. It's a source of world peace, when we see that we're not separate from the earth but that we all come out of it and are connected with one another. From this sense of connectedness we can commit ourselves to share, to live a life of helpfulness and generosity for the world. To cultivate generosity directly is another fundamental part of living a spiritual life. Like the training precepts and like our inner meditations, generosity can actually be practiced. With practice, its spirit forms our actions, and our hearts will grow stronger and lighter. It can lead us to new levels of letting go and great happiness. The Buddha emphasized the importance of generosity when he said, "If you knew what I know about the power of giving, you would not let a single meal pass without sharing it in some way."

Traditionally there are described three kinds of giving, and we are encouraged to begin developing generosity at whatever level we find it arising in our heart. At first we find tentative giving. This is where we take an object and think, "Well, I'm probably not going to use this anyway. Maybe I should give it away. No, I should save it for next year. No, I'll give it away." Even this level is positive. It creates some joy for us and it helps someone else. It's a sharing and a connecting.

The next level of generosity to discover is friendly giving. It's like relating to a brother or sister. "Please share what I have; enjoy this as I do." Sharing openly of our time, our energy, the things we have, feels even better. It's lovely to do. The fact is that we do not need a lot of possessions to be happy. It is our relationship to this changing life that determines our happiness or sorrow. Happiness comes from the heart.

The third level of giving is kingly or queenly giving. It's where we take something—our time or our energy or an object that is the best we have—and give it to someone happily and say, "Please, would you enjoy this too." We give to the other person and take our joy in that sharing. This level of giving is a beautiful thing to learn.

As we start to learn to be more generous, to give more of our time, our energy, our goods, our money, we can find a way to do it not just to fit a self-image or please an external authority, but because it is a source of genuine happiness in our lives. Of course this doesn't mean giving everything away. That would be excessive, because we have to be compassionate and care for ourselves as well. Yet to understand the power of practicing this kind of openness is very special. It is a privilege to be able to bring this generosity into our lives.

The third precept of conscious conduct is to refrain from false speech. The Eightfold Path calls this right speech. Don't lie, it says. Speak only what is true and useful; speak wisely, responsibly, and appropriately. Right speech really poses a question. It asks us to be aware of how we actually use the energy of our words. We spend so much of our lives talking and analyzing and discussing and gossiping and planning. Most of this talk is not very conscious or aware. It is possible to use speech to become awake. We can be mindful of what we are doing when we speak, of what the motivation is and how we are feeling. We can also be mindful in listening. We can align our speech to the principles of what is truthful and what is most kind or helpful. In practicing mindfulness we can begin to understand and discover the power of speech.

Once a master was called to heal a sick child with a few words of prayer. A skeptic in the crowd observed it all and expressed doubts about such a superficial way of healing. The master turned to him and said, "You know nothing of these matters; you are an ignorant fool!" The skeptic became very upset. He turned red and shook with anger.

Before he could gather himself to reply, however, the master spoke again, asking, "When one word has the power to make you hot and angry, why should not another word have the power to heal?"

Our speech is powerful. It can be destructive or enlightening, idle gossip or compassionate communication. We are asked to be mindful and let our speech come from the heart. When we speak what is true and helpful, people are attracted to us. To be mindful and honest makes our minds quieter and more open, our hearts happier and more peaceful.

The fourth precept, to refrain from sexual misconduct, reminds us not to act out of sexual desire in such a way as to cause harm to another. It requires that we be responsible and honest in sexual relations. Sexual energy is very powerful. In these times of rapidly changing relationships and sexual values, we are asked to become conscious of our use of this power. If we associate this energy in our lives with grasping and greed, exploitation and compulsion, we will perform actions that bring harm to ourselves and others, such as adultery. There is great suffering consequent to these actions and great joy in the simplicity that comes in their absence.

The spirit of this precept asks us to look at the motivation behind our actions. To pay attention in this way allows us (as lay people) to discover how sexuality can be connected to the heart and how it can be an expression of love, caring, and genuine intimacy. We have almost all been fools at some time in our sexual life, and we have also used sex to try to touch what is beautiful, to touch another person deeply. Conscious sexuality is an essential part of living a mindful life.

To refrain from the heedless use of intoxicants is the fifth precept. It means to avoid taking intoxicants to the point of making the mind cloudy and to devote our lives instead to developing clarity and alertness. We have just one mind, so we must take care of it. In our country there are millions of alcoholics and others who have abused drugs. Their unconsciousness and fearful use of intoxicants has caused great pain to themselves, their families, and all those they touch. To live consciously is not easy—it means we often must face fears and pains that challenge our heart. Abuse of intoxicants is clearly not the way.

To enter the human realm, to establish a ground for spiritual life, requires that we bring awareness to all the actions in our world, to our use of intoxicants, our speech, to all of our actions. Establishing a virtuous and harmonious relationship to the world brings ease and lightness to the heart and steadfast clarity to the mind. A foundation of virtue brings great happiness and liberation in itself and is the precondition for wise meditation. With it we can be conscious and not waste the extraordinary opportunity of a human birth, the opportunity to grow in compassion and true understanding in our life.

Concentration of Mind

Out of a foundation of conscious conduct, the first steps of the mindful way, grows the second aspect of the path, which is called the development of samadhi, or steadiness and concentration of mind. As we bring the grace and harmony of virtue into our outer lives, so we can begin to establish an inner order, a sense of peace and clarity. This is the domain of formal meditation, and it begins with training the heart and mind in concentration. It means collecting the mind or bringing together the mind and body, focusing one's attention on one's experience in the present moment. Skill in concentrating and steadying the mind is the basis for all types of meditation and is in truth a basic skill for any endeavor—for art or athletics, computer programming or self-knowledge. In meditation, the development of the power of concentration comes through systematic training and can be done by using a variety of objects, such as the breath, visualization, a mantra, or a particular feeling such as loving kindness. . . . Most fundamentally [concentrating the mind] is a simple process of focusing and steadying attention on an object like the breath and bringing the mind back to that object again and again. It requires that we let go of thoughts about the past and future, of fantasies and attachment, and bring the mind back to what is actually happening: the actual moment of feeling, of touching the breath as it is. Samadhi doesn't just come of itself; it takes practice. What is wonderful is the discovery made by the Buddha and all great yogis that the mind can actually be trained.

There is a sign outside a casino in Las Vegas that says, "You must be present to win." The same is true in meditation. If we want to see the nature of our lives, we must actually be present, aware, awake. Developing samadhi is much like polishing a lens. If we are looking to see the cells and workings of the body with a lens that has not been ground sufficiently, we will not see clearly. In order to penetrate the nature of the mind and body we must collect and concentrate our resources and observe with a steady, silent mind. This is exactly what the Buddha did: he sat, concentrated his mind, and looked within. To become a yogi, an explorer of the heart and mind, we must develop this capacity as well.

Wisdom

Built on the foundation of concentration is the third aspect of the Buddha's path of awakening: clarity of vision and the development of wisdom. In our lives there is much we don't see. We are too busy to see, or we forget or haven't learned about our capacity to see in new ways. Our steady and careful observation of the body, heart, and mind can bring about the growth of understanding and wisdom.

Wisdom comes from directly observing the truth of our experience.

We learn as we become able to live fully in the moment, rather than being lost in the dreams, plans, memories, and commentaries of the thinking mind. There is a big difference between drinking a cup of tea while being there completely, and drinking a cup of tea while thinking about five other things. There is a big difference between taking a walk in the woods and really being there, and taking a walk and spending the whole time thinking about visiting Disneyland or what you are going to cook for dinner, or imagining all the stories you can tell your friends about what a great walk in the woods you had. It is only by being fully in the moment that the fundamental questions of the heart can be answered; it is only in the timeless moment that we can come to that intuitive, silent knowing of the truth. It is the intuitive wisdom that liberates us.

Inquiry and Observation

Wisdom grows out of our clear seeing in each moment. Seeing the arising and passing of our experience and how we relate to it. It arises through our gentle and careful inquiry into the workings of the body and mind and through an open inquiry into how this body and mind relate to the whole world around us. For insight to develop, this spirit of observation and deep questioning must be kept in the forefront. We can collect and quiet the mind, but then we must observe, examine, see its ways and its laws.

As we meditate we can learn more about desire, see what its root is, see whether it is pleasant or painful, see how it arises and affects our life. We can equally well observe moments of stillness and contentment. We can also begin to observe the inner workings of cause and effect, the laws of karma [see pages 289–300]. Similarly, the law of impermanence can reveal itself under our attention, how it operates, and whether there is anything in our experience that does not change. As things change, we can also observe how attachment works and see how tension and grasping are created in our body and mind. We can see what closes our heart, and how it can open. Over time we may discover new levels of stillness in ourselves or find lights or visions or a whole array of new inner experiences. We can also discover our shadow and bring our awareness to the fears and pains and deep feelings we have long suppressed in our lives. Insights about the psychological patterns we live by will arise, and we can see the functioning of the level we call the personality. When we bring the same spirit of inquiry and awareness to our relation with the whole world around us, our observation can also show us the illusions of our boundaries and how to truly connect the inner and the outer.

Beyond these, our inquiry can lead us to most fundamental spiritual questions, the nature of our own self. If everything we see is changing, what can we identify in this process as ourself? We can see what concepts or body image or deep sense of self we hold as "me" or "mine," as who we are, and begin to question this whole structure. And perhaps, in deep stillness, we can come to that which goes beyond our limited sense of self, that which is silent and timeless and universal.

Wisdom is not one particular experience, nor a series of ideas or knowledge to be collected. It is an ongoing process of discovery that unfolds when we live with balance and full awareness in each moment. It grows out of our sincerity and genuine openness, and it can lead us to a whole new world of freedom.

Insight meditation [Vipassana] is a path of discovery. It is straightforward and direct, with no frills or gimmicks. It is simple, though not easy. Although the forms vary, the genuine practice of insight meditation is this single quest: to establish a foundation of harmonious action, to collect and concentrate the mind and body, and to see the laws of life by our own true, careful, and direct observation. After understanding the way of practice and realizing that meditative life involves this whole process of awakening, there is only one thing left to do. We have to undertake it ourselves.

THE DALAI LAMA
Mahayana / Vajrayana Practice

I USUALLY CONSIDER the teachings of the Buddha under two headings: activity and view. *Activity* means refraining from harming others. This is something that is universally helpful, something that all people appreciate, whether they are religious or not. *View* refers to the principle of interdependence. Happiness and suffering, and the beings who experience them, do not arise without cause nor are they caused by some eternal creator. In fact, all things arise from causes corresponding to them. This idea is upheld by all schools of Buddhism, and so I usually say that our view is that of interdependence.

The view of interdependence makes for a great openness of mind. In general, instead of realizing that what we experience arises from a complicated network of causes, we tend to attribute happiness or sadness, for example, to single, individual sources. But if this were so, as soon as we came into contact with what we consider to be good, we would be automatically happy, and conversely, in the case of bad things, invariably sad. The causes of joy and sorrow would be easy to identify and target. It would all be very simple, and there would be good reason for our anger and attachment. When, on the other hand, we consider that everything we experience results from a complex interplay of causes and conditions, we find that there is no single thing to desire or resent, and it is more difficult for the afflictions of attachment or anger to arise. In this way, the view of interdependence makes our minds more relaxed and open.

By training our minds and getting used to this view, we change our way of seeing things, and as a result we gradually change our behavior and do less harm to others. As it says in the sutras:

> Abandon evildoing;
> Practice virtue well;
> Subdue your mind:
> This is the Buddha's teaching.

We should avoid even the smallest negative actions, and we should perform even the most insignificant positive actions without underestimating their value. The reason for this is that the happiness we all want and the suffering we all try to avoid are produced precisely by our actions, or *karma*. Everything we experience is, as it were, programmed by our actions, and these in turn depend on our attitude. Whatever we do, say, and think in our youth is the cause of the happiness and suffering we experience in our old age. Moreover, what we do in this life will determine the happiness and suffering of the next life. And the actions of this kalpa [eon] will result in the experiences of future kalpas. This is what we mean by the law of karma, the law of cause and effect.

On this basis, an action is called negative or evil if it results in suffering, which is something we wish to avoid. It is called positive or virtuous if it results in happiness, which is something we want. We consider an action positive or negative not on its own account but according to whether it leads to joy or sorrow. This all depends on motivation, and so the text says, "Subdue your mind." A mind that is not disciplined will experience suffering, but a mind that is under control will be happy and at peace.

It is important to know all the methods for subduing the mind through the instructions of the vast and profound path. The antidote to hatred is meditation on love. To overcome attachment, we should meditate on the ugliness of what attracts us. The antidote to pride is meditation on the *skandhas,* or aggregates. To counteract ignorance we should concentrate on the movement of the breath and on interdependence. The root of the mind's turmoil is in fact ignorance, on account of which we fail to understand the true nature of things. The mind is brought under control by purifying our mistaken notion of reality. This is the teaching of the Buddha. It is through training the mind that we can transform the way in which we act, speak, and think.

It would be helpful at this point to say something about the Buddha's teaching in general. According to the Mahayana, after attaining enlightenment, the Buddha turned the Wheel of the Dharma, setting forth his teaching in three stages. First he taught the Four Noble Truths [see pages 65–79], on which the entire Buddhist doctrine is based. These are the truth of suffering, the truth of the origin of suffering, the truth of the cessation of suffering, and the truth of the path. With the second (or middle) turning, he gave the teachings on emptiness and the profound and detailed aspects of the path, which make up the *Prajnaparamita Sutras* [see pages 177–213]. With the third turning of the wheel, he presented the teachings on emptiness in a more accessible fashion. In sutras such as the *Sutra of Buddha Nature,* he spoke of an absolute nature that is devoid of the dualistic concept of subject and object. This is also the subject of the *Sublime Continuum.*

The origin of suffering—namely, negative emotions—may be understood with varying degrees of subtlety, and this requires an understanding of the nature of phenomena. In the second turning of the wheel, the Buddha explained in detail the truth of the cessation of suffering. He showed that an increasingly subtle analysis of phenomena leads to a greater understanding of the negative emotions and finally to an ever more refined insight into the nature of emptiness. This in turn leads to more profound understanding of the truth of the path.

In the third turning we find a detailed explanation of the path for attaining enlightenment. It emphasizes the potential that we all have for future enlightenment. This potential, called *Tathagatagarbha,* or Buddha nature [see pages 229–237], is something we have always had, from time without beginning. When we talk about the truth of the path, we are not talking about something completely foreign to our nature, which might suddenly appear like a mushroom, as though without a seed or cause. It is because we have this foundation or capacity for ultimate omniscience that we are able to attain enlightenment.

The texts belonging to the second turning demonstrate the empty nature of phenomena, while the *Sutra of Buddha Nature* and other teachings relating to the third turning emphasize wisdom, the clear and luminous aspect of the mind.

The Buddha taught the Four Noble Truths first, as the foundation of his whole doctrine. As he elaborated his teachings, he adapted his words to suit different needs and mental capacities. The way he taught varied considerably, and what he said was more or less profound, depending on those he was addressing. It is important, therefore, to know which teachings express the ultimate sense and which have been adapted to the particular capacities of his disciples. If, on analysis, we find that the Buddha's words, taken literally, appear illogical or lead to contradictions, we should understand that such teachings are a relative expression of the truth necessarily adapted to the comprehension of particular beings. On the other hand, if his words can be taken literally and are without any contradictions or flaws, we can accept these teachings as expressing the ultimate truth.

Faith is very important in Buddhism, but wisdom is even more so. True faith has to be based on reasoning. Simply to say, "I take refuge," or "I am devoted," blindly and without reflection, is of no value. Without rational investigation, it is impossible to distinguish whether the Buddha was speaking in an adapted, or relative, sense or whether his words are to be taken literally as expressing the ultimate meaning. This is why the sutras mention the *four reliances:*

Do not rely on individuals, rely on the teachings.
Do not rely on the words, rely on the meaning.
Do not rely on the adapted meaning, rely on the ultimate meaning.
Do not rely on intellectual knowledge, rely on wisdom.

In contrast to ordinary intellectual understanding, the true nature of the mind is clear and knowing and has never been veiled by obscurations. The practice of the Mahayana is entirely based on this understanding.

In Tibet, all the teachings of the Buddha, from the Four Noble Truths up to the highest yoga *tantras,* have been preserved, and are practiced in the following traditional order. The first stage is the Shravakayana, or Fundamental Vehicle, the path of the Four Noble Truths. Beginning with the Vinaya, which teaches the training of discipline, one progresses through the thirty-seven practices leading to enlightenment, thereby developing the two trainings of concentration and wisdom. These three trainings are the basis for the two other vehicles.

The second stage is the Mahayana, or Great Vehicle, and consists of the practice of the six *paramitas:* generosity, discipline, patience, endeavor, meditative concentration, and wisdom. The third stage is the

Vajrayana, the vehicle of the secret mantras, which sets out the extraordinary means for realizing profound concentration through the union of mental calm and clear insight (*shamatha* and *vipashyana*) and for progression through the four tantra classes: kriya, upa, yoga, and anuttara.

Buddhism has flourished for centuries in many countries, but it was in Tibet that all three paths, the Shravakayana, Mahayana, and Vajrayana, were preserved completely. It is, in fact, possible to go through all these stages of practice in the course of a single session. Moreover, Tibetan scholars never ignored the practice aspect, and experienced practitioners did not neglect to study. This seems to me a very good way of doing things.

In the course of time, different lineages appeared within this complete tradition, influenced by extraordinary masters who, at different times and in different places, expressed the teachings in slightly different ways. We therefore have the ancient tradition of the Nyingma and the newer traditions of the Kadam, Sakya, and Kagyu. The present Gelug tradition evolved from the Kadam lineage. Despite the differences between these lineages, they all incorporate the Buddha's teachings in full, combining the practices of the Sutrayana and the Mahayana. The Bon tradition, which had existed in Tibet before the arrival of Buddhism, also came to possess a complete set of the Buddha's teachings.

D. T. SUZUKI

Mahayana/Zen Practice

ZEN IN ITS essence is the art of seeing into the nature of one's own being, and it points the way from bondage to freedom. By making us drink right from the foundation of life, it liberates us from all the yokes under which we finite beings are usually suffering in this world. We can say that Zen liberates all the energies properly and naturally stored in each of us, which are in ordinary circumstances cramped and distorted so that they find no adequate channel for activity.

This body of ours is something like an electric battery in which a mysterious power latently lies. When this power is not properly brought into operation, it either grows moldy and withers away or is warped and expresses itself abnormally. It is the object of Zen, therefore, to save us from going crazy or being crippled. This is what I mean by freedom, giving free play to all the creative and benevolent impulses inherently lying in our hearts. Generally, we are blind to this fact, that we are in possession of all the necessary faculties that will make us happy and loving towards one another. All the struggles that we see around us come from this ignorance. Zen, therefore, wants us to open a "third eye," as Buddhists call it, to the hitherto undreamed-of region shut away from us through our own ignorance. When the cloud of ignorance disappears, the infinity of the heavens is manifested, where we see for the first time into the nature of our own being. We now know the signification of life, we know that it is not blind striving, nor is it a mere display of brutal forces, but that while we know not definitely what the ultimate purport of life is, there is something in it that makes us feel infinitely blessed in the living of it and remain quite contented with it in all its evolution, without raising questions or entertaining pessimistic doubts.

When we are full of vitality and not yet awakened to the knowledge of life, we cannot comprehend the seriousness of all the conflicts involved in it which are apparently for the moment in a state of quiescence. But sooner or later the time will come when we have to face life squarely and solve its most perplexing and most pressing riddles. . . .

Life, as most of us live it, is suffering. There is no denying the fact. As long as life is a form of struggle, it cannot be anything but pain. Does not a struggle mean the impact of two conflicting forces, each trying to get the upper hand of the other? If the battle is lost, the outcome is death, and death is the fearsomest thing in the world. Even when death is conquered, one is left alone, and the loneliness is sometimes more unbearable than the struggle itself. One may not be conscious of all this, and may go on indulging in those momentary pleasures that are afforded by the senses. But this being unconscious does not in the least alter the facts of life. However insistently the blind may deny the existence of the sun, they cannot annihilate it. The tropical heat will mercilessly scorch them, and if they do not take proper care they will all be wiped away from the surface of the earth.

The Buddha was perfectly right when he propounded his "Fourfold Noble Truths" [see pages 65–79], the first of which is that life is pain. Did not every one of us come to this world screaming and in a way protesting? To come out into cold and prohibitive surroundings after a soft, warm motherly womb was surely a painful incident, to say the least. Growth is always attended with pain. Teething is more or less a painful process. Puberty is usually accompanied by a mental as well as a physical disturbance. The growth of the organism called society is also marked with painful cataclysms. . . .

How does Zen solve the problem of problems?

In the first place, Zen proposes its solution by directly appealing to facts of personal experience and not to book-knowledge. The nature of one's own being where apparently rages the struggle between the finite and the infinite is to be grasped by a higher faculty than the intellect. . . .

By personal experience [Zen] is meant to get at the fact at first hand and not through any intermediary, whatever this may be. Its favourite analogy is: to point at the moon a finger is needed, but woe to those who take the finger for the moon; a basket is welcome to carry our fish home, but when the fish are safely on the table why should we eternally bother ourselves with the basket? Here stands the fact, and let us grasp it with the naked hands lest it should slip away—this is what Zen proposes to do. As nature abhors a vacuum, Zen abhors anything coming between the fact and ourselves. According to Zen there is no struggle in the fact itself such as between the finite and the infinite, between the flesh and the spirit. These are idle distinctions fictitiously designed by the intellect for its own interest. Those who take them too seriously or those who try to read them into the very fact of life are those who take the finger for the moon. When we are hungry we eat; when we are sleepy we lay ourselves down; and where does the infinite or the finite come in here? Are not we complete in ourselves and each in himself? Life as it is lived suffices. It is only when the disquieting intellect steps in and tries to murder it that we stop to live and imagine ourselves to be short of or in something. Let the intellect alone, it has its usefulness in its proper sphere, but let it not interfere with the flowing of the life-stream. If you are at all tempted to look into it, do so while letting it flow. The fact of flowing must under no circumstances be arrested or meddled with; for the moment your hands are dipped into it, its transparency is disturbed, it ceases to reflect your image which you have had from the very beginning and will continue to have to the end of time.

Almost corresponding to the "Four Maxims" of the Nichiren Sect, Zen has its own four statements:

> *A special transmission outside the Scriptures;*
> *No dependence upon words and letters;*
> *Direct pointing to the soul of man;*

*Seeing into one's nature and the attainment of
Buddhahood.*

This sums up all that is claimed by Zen as religion.

SHUNRYU SUZUKI
Mahayana / Zen Practice

PEOPLE SAY THAT practicing Zen is difficult, but there is a misunderstanding as to why. It is not difficult because it is hard to sit in the cross-legged position, or to attain enlightenment. It is difficult because it is hard to keep our mind pure and our practice pure in its fundamental sense. The Zen school developed in many ways after it was established in China, but at the same time, it became more and more impure. But I do not want to talk about Chinese Zen or the history of Zen. I am interested in helping you keep your practice from becoming impure.

In Japan we have the phrase *shoshin,* which means "beginner's mind." The goal of practice is always to keep our beginner's mind. Suppose you recite the Prajna Paramita Sutra [see pages 192–195] only once. It might be a very good recitation. But what would happen to you if you recited it twice, three times, four times, or more? You might easily lose your original attitude towards it. The same thing will happen in your other Zen practices. For a while you will keep your beginner's mind, but if you continue to practice one, two, three years or more, although you may improve some, you are liable to lose the limitless meaning of original mind.

For Zen students the most important thing is not to be dualistic. Our "original mind" includes everything within itself. It is always rich and sufficient within itself. You should not lose your self-sufficient state of mind. This does not mean a closed mind, but actually an empty mind and a ready mind. If your mind is empty, it is always ready for anything; it is open to everything. In the beginner's mind there are many possibilities; in the expert's mind there are few.

If you discriminate too much, you limit yourself. If you are too demanding or too greedy, your mind is not rich and self-sufficient. If we lose our original self-sufficient mind, we will lose all precepts. When your mind becomes demanding, when you long for something, you will end up violating your own precepts: not to tell lies, not to steal, not to kill, not to be immoral, and so forth. If you keep your original mind, the precepts will keep themselves.

In the beginner's mind there is no thought, "I have attained something." All self-centered thoughts limit our vast mind. When we have no thought of achievement, no thought of self, we are true beginners. Then we can really learn something. The beginner's mind is the mind of compassion. When our mind is compassionate, it is boundless. Dogen-zenji [1200–53], the founder of our school, always emphasized how important it is to resume our boundless original mind. Then we are always true to ourselves, in sympathy with all beings, and can actually practice.

So the most difficult thing is always to keep your beginner's mind. There is no need to have a deep understanding of Zen. Even though you read much Zen literature, you must read each sentence with a fresh mind. You should not say, "I know what Zen is," or "I have attained enlightenment." This is also the real secret of the arts: always be a beginner. Be very very careful about this point. If you start to practice zazen [meditation], you will begin to appreciate your beginner's mind. It is the secret of Zen practice.

B. ALAN WALLACE

Teachers / Mentors

IN THE MAHAYANA tradition we take refuge in three things: in the Buddha, in the Dharma (his teachings), and in the Sangha (the spiritual community . . .) [see pages 215–228]. We also take refuge in our spiritual mentors. Most of our own teachers may not be fully enlightened. Like ourselves they are travelers on the spiritual path, although they may have attained a greater degree of insight. They are competent teachers who are able to lead us farther along the path, and knowing this, we take refuge in them and rely on them.

. . . [T]he individual vehicle the teacher is regarded as a representative of the Buddha who guides us to the experience of nirvana. In the Mahayana tradition the view of the spiritual mentor is very different, a difference rooted in the idea of dharmakaya, the transcendent consciousness of the Buddha. From this point of view a spiritual mentor is a vessel for the expression of dharmakaya. Insofar as a spiritual mentor expresses the dharmakaya within, that person is a manifestation of true Buddhahood.

The idea of dharmakaya is especially useful when we have to deal with the possible faults of our teacher. The subtle but significant distinction here is that we are not saying all spiritual mentors are realized Buddhas, but rather we are regarding them as if they were windows through which we glimpse the dharmakaya.

This has several implications. For one thing, if we should ever become aware of a teacher's faults, we must remember that the teacher is not a static object but a matrix of experienced events, inextricably linked to our own perceptions and conceptions. When we realize this, we may have to take some responsibility for the failings we see in others. There is growth and understanding here, when we start to look deeply at the question of how much a teacher's seeming faults come from his or her side at all, and how much they come from our own side.

If we took upon the spiritual mentor as if he or she were expressing dharmakaya, then when we see a fault, say narrow-mindedness, we can recognize it for what it is. For one thing, as stated above, we can realize that the quality may be within us also, and learn from the way we perceive it in someone else. Or upon deeper reflection, we may conclude that the judgment of narrow-mindedness was purely our own projection, stemming from our own confusion.

Do we have to stand in judgment on our teacher? The answer is no. Our task is to transform and awaken our own minds for the sake of all sentient beings. Our teacher's apparent imperfections, within the context of an understanding of dharmakaya, are simply tools we can use to complete that task.

D. T. SUZUKI

Teachers/Koans

WHAT IS A koan?

A koan, according to one authority, means "a public document setting up a standard of judgment," whereby one's Zen understanding is tested as to its correctness. A koan is generally some statement made by an old Zen master, or some answer of his given to a questioner. The following are some that are commonly given to the uninitiated:

1. A monk asked Tung-shan, "Who is the Buddha?" "Three *chin* of flax."

2. Yun-men was once asked, "When not a thought is stirring in one's mind, is there any error here?" "As much as Mount Sumeru."

3. Chao-chou answered, *"Wu!"* (*mu* in Japanese) to a monk's question, "Is there Buddha-nature in a dog?" *Wu* literally means "not" or "none," but when this is ordinarily given as a koan, it has no reference to its literal signification; it is *"Wu"* pure and simple.

4. When Ming the monk overtook the fugitive Hui-neng, he wanted Hui-neng to give up the secret of Zen. Hui-neng replied, "What are your original features which you have even prior to your birth?"

5. A monk asked Chao-chou, "What is the meaning of the First Patriarch's visit to China?" "The cypress tree in the front courtyard."

6. When Chao-chou came to study Zen under Nan-ch'uan, he asked, "What is the Tao (or the Way)?" Nan-ch'uan replied, "Your everyday mind, that is the Tao."

7. A monk asked, "All things are said to be reducible to the One, but where is the One to be reduced?" Chao-chou answered, "When I was in the district of Ch'ing I had a robe made that weighed seven *chin*."

8. When P'ang the old Zen adept first came to Ma-tsu in order to master Zen, he asked, "Who is he who has no companion among the ten thousand things of the world?" Ma-tsu replied, "When you swallow up in one draught all the water in the Hsi Ch'iang, I will tell you."

When such problems are given to the uninitiated for solution, what is the object of the master? The idea is to unfold the Zen psychology in the mind of the uninitiated, and to reproduce the state of consciousness, of which these statements are the expression. That is to say, when the koans are understood the master's state of mind is understood, which is satori [enlightenment] and without which Zen is a sealed book.

In the beginning of Zen history a question was brought up by the pupil to the notice of the master, who thereby gauged the mental state of the questioner and knew what necessary help to give him. The help thus given was sometimes enough to awaken him to realization, but more frequently than not puzzled and perplexed him beyond description, and the result was an ever-increasing mental strain or "searching and contriving" on the part of the pupil. . . . In actual cases, however, the master would have to wait for a long while for the pupil's first question, if it were coming at all. To ask the first question means more than half the way to its own solution, for it is the outcome of a most intense mental effort for the questioner to bring his mind to a crisis. The question indicates that the crisis is reached and the mind is ready to leave it behind. An experienced master often knows how to lead the pupil to a crisis and to make him successfully pass it. This was really the case before the koan exercise came in vogue, as was already illustrated by the examples of Lin-chi, Nan-yueh, and others.

As time went on there grew up many "questions and answers" (*mondo* in Japanese) which were exchanged between masters and pupils. And with the growth of Zen literature it was perfectly natural now for Zen followers to begin to attempt an intellectual solution or interpretation of it. The "questions and answers" ceased to be experiences and intuitions of Zen consciousness, and became subjects of logical inquiry. This was disastrous, yet inevitable. Therefore the Zen master who wished for the normal development of Zen consciousness and the vigorous growth of Zen tradition would not fail to recognize rightly the actual state of things, and to devise such a method as to achieve finally the attainment of the Zen truth.

The method that would suggest itself in the circumstances was to select some of the statements made by the old masters and to use them as pointers. A pointer would then function in two directions: (1) To check the working of the intellect, or rather to let the intellect see by itself how far it can go, and also that there is a realm into which it as such can never enter; (2) To effect the maturity of Zen consciousness which eventually breaks out into a state of satori.

When the koan works in the first direction there takes place what has been called "searching and contriving." Instead of the intellect, which taken by itself forms only a part of our being, the entire personality, mind and body, is thrown out into the solution of the koan. When this extraordinary state of spiritual tension, guided by an experienced master, is made to mature, the koan works itself out into what has been designated as the Zen experience. An intuition of the truth of Zen is now attained, for the wall against which the Yogin [Yogi] has been beating hitherto to no purpose breaks down, and an entirely new vista opens before him. Without the koan the Zen consciousness loses its pointer, and there will never be a state of satori. A psychological impasse is the necessary antecedent of satori. Formerly, that is, before the days of the koan exercise, the antecedent pointer was created in the consciousness of the Yogin by his own intense spirituality. But when Zen became systematized owing to the accumulation of Zen literature in the shape of "questions and answers" the indispensability of the koan had come to be universally recognized by the masters.

The worst enemy of Zen experience, at least in the beginning, is the intellect, which consists and insists in discriminating subject from object. The discriminating intellect, therefore, must be cut short if Zen consciousness is to unfold itself, and the koan is constructed eminently to serve this end.

On examination we at once notice that there is no room in the koan to insert an intellectual interpretation. The knife is not sharp enough to cut the koan open and see what are its contents. For a koan is not a logical proposition but the expression of a certain mental state resulting from the Zen discipline. For instance, what logical connection can there be between the Buddha and "three *chin* of flax"? or between the Buddha-nature and *"Wu"*? or between the secret message of Bodhidharma and "a cypress tree"? In a noted Zen textbook known as *Hekiganshu* (*Pi-yen-chi* in Chinese) Yuan-wu gives the following notes concerning the "three *chin* of flax," showing how the koan was interpreted by those pseudo-Zen followers who failed to grasp Zen:

"There are some people these days who do not truly understand this koan; this is because there is no crack in it to insert their intellectual teeth. By this I mean that it is altogether too plain and tasteless. Various answers have been given by different masters to the question, 'What is the Buddha?' One said, 'He sits in the Buddha Hall.' Another said, 'The one endowed with the thirty-two marks of excellence.' Still another, 'A bamboo-root whip.' None, however, can excel Tung-shan's 'three *chin* of flax' as regards its irrationality, which cuts off all passage of speculation. Some comment that Tung-shan was weighing flax at the moment, hence the answer. Others say that it was a trick of equivocation on the part of Tung-shan; and still others think that as the questioner was not conscious of the fact that he was himself the Buddha, Tung-shan answered him in this indirect way.

"Such [commentators] are all like corpses, for they are utterly unable to comprehend the living truth. There are still others, however, who take the 'three *chin* of flax' as the Buddha [thus giving it a pantheistic interpretation]. What wild and fantastic remarks they make! As long as they are beguiled by words, they can never expect to penetrate into the heart of Tung-shan, even if they live to the time of Maitreya Buddha [the Buddha of the future]. Why? Because words are merely a vehicle on which the truth is carried. Not comprehending the meaning of the old master, they endeavor to find it in his words only, but they will find therein nothing to lay their hands on. The truth itself is beyond all description, as is affirmed by an ancient sage, but it is by words that the truth is manifested.

"Let us, then, forget the words when we gain the truth itself. This is done only when we have an insight through experience into that which is indicated by words. The 'three *chin* of flax' is like the royal thoroughfare to the capital; when you are once on it every step you take is in the right direction. When Yun-men was once asked what was the teaching that went beyond the Buddhas and the patriarchs, he said, 'Dumpling.' Yun-men and Tung-shan are walking the same road hand in hand. When you are thoroughly cleansed of all the impurities of discrimination, without further ado the truth will be understood. Later the monk who wanted to know what the Buddha was went to Chih-men and asked him what Tung-shan meant by 'three *chin* of flax.' Said Chih-men, 'A mass of flowers, a mass of brocade.' He added, 'Do you understand?' The monk replied, 'No.' 'Bamboos in the South, trees in the North,' was the conclusion of Chih-men."

Technically speaking, the koan given to the uninitiated is intended "to destroy the root of life," "to make the calculating mind die," "to root out the entire mind that has been at work since eternity," etc. This may sound murderous, but the ultimate intent is to go beyond the limits of intellection, and these limits can be crossed over only by exhausting oneself once for all, by using up all the psychic powers at one's command. Logic then turns into psychology, intellection into conation and intuition. What could not be solved on the plane of empirical consciousness is now transferred to the deeper recesses of the mind. So, says a Zen master, "Unless at one time perspiration has streamed down your back, you cannot see the boat sailing before the wind." "Unless once you have been thoroughly drenched in a perspiration you cannot expect to see the revelation of a palace of pearls on a blade of grass."

The koan refuses to be solved under any easier conditions. But once solved the koan is compared to a piece of brick used to knock at a gate; when the gate is opened the brick is thrown away. The koan is useful as long as the mental doors are closed, but when they are opened it may be forgotten. What one sees after the opening will be something quite unexpected, something that has never before entered even into one's imagination. But when the koan is re-examined from this newly acquired point of view, how marvelously suggestive, how fittingly constructed, although there is nothing artificial here!

Part II

Teachings
and
Texts

The Four Noble Truths

The Buddha said, "I teach one thing and one thing only: suffering and the end of suffering," which is the ultimate goal of Buddhism. In his first sermon at Deer Park, he taught the Four Noble Truths of the existence of suffering, the cause of suffering, that the cause of suffering can end, and the path to the end of suffering. This doctrine, expounded by the Buddha in his major discourses and expanded upon in expositions by his closest disciples, underlies the basic Buddhist teachings that have evolved since his time.

WALPOLA RAHULA, TRANS.
The First Sermon of the Buddha

THUS HAVE I heard. The Blessed One was once living in the Deer Park at Isipatana (the Resort of Seers) near Baranasi (Benares). There he addressed the group of five bhikkhus [monks]:

"Bhikkhus, these two extremes ought not to be practiced by one who has gone forth from the household life. What are the two? There is devotion to the indulgence of sense-pleasures, which is low, common, the way of ordinary people, unworthy and unprofitable; and there is devotion to self-mortification, which is painful, unworthy and unprofitable.

"Avoiding both these extremes, the Tathagata ["Thus-Perfected One"] has realized the Middle Path: It gives vision, it gives knowledge,

65

and it leads to calm, to insight, to enlightenment, to Nibbana [Sanskrit Nirvana]. And what is that Middle Path . . . ? It is simply the Noble Eightfold Path, namely, right view, right thought, right speech, right action, right livelihood, right effort, right mindfulness, right concentration. This is the Middle Path realized by the Tathagata, which gives vision, which gives knowledge, and which leads to calm, to insight, to enlightenment, to Nibbana.

"The Noble Truth of suffering (*Dukkha*) is this: Birth is suffering; aging is suffering; sickness is suffering; death is suffering; sorrow and lamentation, pain, grief and despair are suffering; association with the unpleasant is suffering; dissociation from the pleasant is suffering; not to get what one wants is suffering—in brief, the five aggregates of attachment are suffering.

"The Noble Truth of the origin of suffering is this: It is this thirst (craving) which produces re-existence and re-becoming, bound up with passionate greed. It finds fresh delight now here and now there, namely, thirst for sense-pleasures; thirst for existence and becoming; and thirst for non-existence (self-annihilation).

"The Noble Truth of the Cessation of suffering is this: It is the complete cessation of that very thirst, giving it up, renouncing it, emancipating oneself from it, detaching oneself from it.

"The Noble Truth of the Path leading to the Cessation of suffering is this: It is simply the Noble Eightfold Path, namely right view; right thought; right speech; right action; right livelihood; right effort; right mindfulness; right concentration. . . ."

BHIKKHU NANAMOLI AND BHIKKHU BODHI, TRANS.

The Exposition of the Four Noble Truths

THE VENERABLE SARIPUTTA said this:

"At Benares [Sarnath], friends, in the Deer Park at Isipatana the Tathagata, accomplished and fully enlightened, set rolling the matchless Wheel of the Dhamma . . . and exhibiting of the Four Noble Truths. Of what four?

"The announcing . . . and exhibiting of the noble truth of suffering . . . of the noble truth of the origin of suffering . . . of the noble truth of the cessation of suffering . . . of the noble truth of the way leading to the cessation of suffering.

"And what, friends, is the noble truth of suffering? Birth is suffering; ageing is suffering; death is suffering; sorrow, lamentation, pain, grief, and despair are suffering; not to obtain what one wants is suffering; in short, the five aggregates affected by clinging are suffering.

"And what, friends, is birth? The birth of beings into the various orders of beings, their coming to birth, precipitation [in a womb], generation, the manifestation of the aggregates, obtaining the bases for contact—this is called birth.

"And what, friends, is ageing? The ageing of beings in the various orders of beings, their old age, brokenness of teeth, greyness of hair, wrinkling of skin, decline of life, weakness of faculties—this is called ageing.

"And what, friends, is death? The passing of beings out of the various orders of beings, their passing away, dissolution, disappearance, dying, completion of time, dissolution of aggregates, laying down of the body—this is called death.

"And what, friends, is sorrow? The sorrow, sorrowing, sorrowfulness, inner sorrow, inner sorriness, of one who has encountered some misfortune or is affected by some painful state—this is called sorrow.

"And what, friends, is lamentation? The wail and lament, wailing and lamenting, bewailing and lamentation, of one who has encountered some misfortune or is affected by some painful state—this is called lamentation.

"And what, friends, is pain? Bodily pain, bodily discomfort, painful, uncomfortable feeling born of bodily contact—this is called pain.

"And what, friends, is grief? Mental pain, mental discomfort, painful, uncomfortable feeling born of mental contact—this is called grief.

"And what, friends, is despair? The trouble and despair, the tribulation and desperation, of one who has encountered some misfortune or is affected by some painful state—this is called despair.

"And what, friends, is 'not to obtain what one wants is suffering'? To beings subject to birth there comes the wish: 'Oh, that we were not subject to birth! That birth would not come to us!' But this is not to be obtained by wishing, and not to obtain what one wants is suffering. To beings subject to ageing . . . subject to sickness . . . subject to death . . . subject to sorrow, lamentation, pain, grief, and despair, there comes the wish: 'Oh, that we were not subject to sorrow, lamentation, pain, grief, and despair! That sorrow, lamentation, pain, grief, and despair would not come to us!' But this is not to be obtained by wishing, and not to obtain what one wants is suffering.

"And what, friends, are the five aggregates affected by clinging that, in short, are suffering? They are: the material form aggregate affected by clinging, the feeling aggregate affected by clinging, the perception aggregate affected by clinging, the [mental] formations aggregate affected by clinging, and the consciousness aggregate affected by clinging. These are the five aggregates affected by clinging that, in short, are suffering. This is called the noble truth of suffering.

"And what, friends, is the noble truth of the origin of suffering? It is craving, which brings renewal of being, is accompanied by delight and lust, and delights in this and that; that is, craving for sensual pleasures, craving for being, and craving for non-being. This is called the noble truth of the origin of suffering.

"And what, friends, is the noble truth of the cessation of suffering? It is the remainderless fading away and ceasing, the giving up, relinquishing, letting go, and rejecting of that same craving. This is called the noble truth of the cessation of suffering.

"And what, friends, is the noble truth of the way leading to the cessation of suffering? It is just this Noble Eightfold Path; that is, right view, right intention, right speech, right action, right livelihood, right effort, right mindfulness, and right concentration.

"And what, friends, is right view? Knowledge of suffering, knowledge of the origin of suffering, knowledge of the cessation of suffering, and knowledge of the way leading to the cessation of suffering—this is called right view.

"And what, friends, is right intention? Intention of renunciation, intention of non–ill will, and intention of non-cruelty—this is called right intention.

"And what, friends, is right speech? Abstaining from false speech, abstaining from malicious speech, abstaining from harsh speech, and abstaining from idle chatter—this is called right speech.

"And what, friends, is right action? Abstaining from killing living beings, abstaining from taking what is not given, and abstaining from misconduct in sensual pleasures—this is called right action.

"And what, friends, is right livelihood? Here a noble disciple, having abandoned wrong livelihood, earns his living by right livelihood—this is called right livelihood.

"And what, friends, is right effort? Here a bhikkhu awakens zeal for the non-arising of unarisen evil unwholesome states, and he makes effort, arouses energy, exerts his mind, and strives. He awakens zeal for the abandoning of arisen evil unwholesome states, and he makes effort, arouses energy, exerts his mind, and strives. He awakens zeal for the arising of unarisen wholesome states, and he makes effort, arouses energy, exerts his mind, and strives. He awakens zeal for the continuance, non-disappearance, strengthening, increase, and fulfilment by development of arisen wholesome states, and he makes effort, arouses energy, exerts his mind, and strives. This is called right effort.

"And what, friends, is right mindfulness? Here a bhikkhu abides contemplating the body as a body, ardent, fully aware, and mindful, having put away covetousness and grief for the world. He abides contemplating feelings as feelings, ardent, fully aware, and mindful, having put away covetousness and grief for the world. He abides contemplating mind as mind, ardent, fully aware, and mindful, having put away covetousness and grief for the world. He abides contemplating mind-objects as mind-objects, ardent, fully aware, and mindful, having put away covetousness and grief for the world. This is called right mindfulness.

"And what, friends, is right concentration? Here, quite secluded from sensual pleasures, secluded from unwholesome states, a bhikkhu enters upon and abides in the first jhana [meditation], which is accompanied by applied and sustained thought, with rapture and pleasure born of seclusion. With the stilling of applied and sustained thought, he enters upon and abides in the second jhana, which has self-confidence and singleness of mind without applied and sustained thought, with rapture and pleasure born of concentration. With the fading away as well of rapture, he abides in equanimity, and mindful and fully aware, still feeling pleasure with the body, he enters upon and abides in the third jhana, on account of which noble ones announce: 'He has a pleasant abiding who has equanimity and is mindful.' With the abandoning of pleasure and pain, and with the previous disappearance of joy and grief, he enters upon and abides in the fourth jhana, which has neither-pain-nor-pleasure and purity of mindfulness due to equanimity. This is called right concentration.

"This is called the noble truth of the way leading to the cessation of suffering.

"At Benares, friends, in the Deer Park at Isipatana the Tathagata, accomplished and fully enlightened, set rolling the matchless Wheel of the Dhamma, which cannot be stopped by any recluse or brahmin or god or Mara or Brahma or anyone in the world—that is, the announcing, teaching, describing, establishing, revealing, expounding, and exhibiting of these Four Noble Truths."

Bhikkhu Bodhi

Impermanence and the Four Noble Truths

[T]HE FOUR NOBLE Truths structure the entire teaching of the Buddha, containing its many other principles just as the elephant's footprint contains the footprints of all other animals.

The pivotal notion around which the truths revolve is that of *dukkha,* translated here as "suffering." The Pali word originally meant simply pain and suffering, a meaning it retains in the texts when it is used as a quality of feeling: in these cases it has been rendered as "pain" or "painful." As the first noble truth, however, dukkha has a far wider significance, reflective of a comprehensive philosophical vision. While it draws its affective colouring from its connection with pain and suffering, and certainly includes these, it points beyond such restrictive meanings to the inherent unsatisfactoriness of everything conditioned. This unsatisfactoriness of the conditioned is due to its impermanence, its vulnerability to pain, and its inability to provide complete and lasting satisfaction.

The notion of impermanence (*aniccata*) forms the bedrock for the Buddha's teaching, having been the initial insight that impelled the Bodhisattva to leave the palace in search of a path to enlightenment. Impermanence, in the Buddhist view, comprises the totality of conditioned existence, ranging in scale from the cosmic to the microscopic. At the far end of the spectrum the Buddha's vision reveals a universe of immense dimensions evolving and disintegrating in repetitive cycles throughout beginningless time. . . . In the middle range the mark of impermanence comes to manifestation in our inescapable mortality, our condition of being bound to ageing, sickness, and death, of possessing a body that is subject "to being worn and rubbed away, to dissolution and disintegration." And at the close end of the spectrum, the Buddha's teaching discloses the radical impermanence uncovered only by sustained attention to experience in its living immediacy: the fact that all the constituents of our being, bodily and mental, are in constant process, arising and passing away in rapid succession from moment to moment without any persistent underlying substance. In the very act of observation they are undergoing "destruction, vanishing, fading away, and ceasing."

This characteristic of impermanence that marks everything conditioned leads directly to the recognition of the universality of dukkha or suffering. The Buddha underscores this all-pervasive aspect of dukkha when, in his explanation of the first noble truth, he says, "In short, the five aggregates affected by clinging are suffering." The five aggregates affected by clinging . . . are a classificatory scheme that the Buddha had devised for demonstrating the composite nature of personality. The scheme comprises every possible type of conditioned state, which it distributes into five categories—material form, feeling, perception, mental formations, and consciousness. The aggregate of material form (*rupa*) includes the physical body with its sense faculties as well as external material objects. The aggregate of feeling (*vedanda*) is the affective element in experience, either pleasant, painful, or neutral. Perception (*sanna*), the third aggregate, is the factor responsible for noting the qualities of things and also accounts for recognition and memory. The formations aggregate (*sankhara*) is an umbrella term that includes all volitional, emotive, and intellective aspects of mental life. And consciousness (*vinnana*), the fifth aggregate, is the basic awareness of an object indispensable to all cognition. As the venerable Sariputta shows in his masterly analysis of the first noble truth, representatives of all five aggregates are present on every occasion of experience, arising in connection with each of the six sense faculties and their objects.

The Buddha's statement that the five aggregates are dukkha thus reveals that the very things we identify with and hold to as the basis for happiness, rightly seen, are the basis for the suffering that we dread. Even when we feel ourselves comfortable and secure, the instability of the aggregates is itself a source of oppression and keeps us perpetually exposed to suffering in its more blatant forms. The whole situation becomes multiplied further to dimensions beyond calculation when we take into account the Buddha's disclosure of the fact of rebirth. All beings in whom ignorance and craving remain present wander on in the cycle of repeated existence, *samsara*, in which each turn brings them the suffering of new birth, ageing, illness, and death. All states of existence within samsara, being necessarily transitory and subject to change, are incapable of providing lasting security. Life in any world is unstable, it is swept away, it has no shelter and protector, nothing of its own. . . . Inextricably tied up with impermanence and suffering is a third principle intrinsic to all phenomena of existence. This is the characteristic of non-self (*anatta*) [see pages 275–286], and the three together are called the three marks or characteristics (*tilakkhana*).

WALPOLA RAHULA

Functions Regarding the Four Noble Truths

WITH REGARD TO the Four Noble Truths we have four functions to perform:

The First Noble Truth is *Dukkha,* the nature of life, its suffering, its sorrows and joys, its imperfection and unsatisfactoriness, its impermanence and insubstantiality. With regard to this, our function is to understand it as a fact, clearly and completely (*parinneya*).

The Second Noble Truth is the Origin of *Dukkha,* which is desire, "thirst," accompanied by all other passions, defilements and impurities. A mere understanding of this fact is not sufficient. Here our function is to discard it, to eliminate, to destroy and eradicate it (*pahatabba*).

The Third Noble Truth is the Cessation of *Dukkha,* Nirvana, the Absolute Truth, the Ultimate Reality. Here our function is to realize it (*sacchikatabba*).

The Fourth Noble Truth is the Path leading to the realization of

Nirvana. A mere knowledge of the Path, however complete, will not do. In this case, our function is to follow it and keep to it (*bhavetabba*).

THE DALAI LAMA

The Four Noble Truths

ACCORDING TO POPULAR legend, following his full enlighten-ment the Buddha remained silent and did not give any teachings for forty-nine days. The first public teaching he gave was to the five ascetics who had been his colleagues when he was leading the life of a mendicant. Having realized that asceticism does not lead to freedom from suffering, the Buddha—then called Siddhartha Gautama—had given up his pen-ances and parted company with his fellows. His five colleagues had re-sented what they saw as a betrayal and vowed never to associate with him. For them, this change in Siddhartha had indicated a failure to sustain his commitment to the life of asceticism. However, when they met him after his enlightenment, they felt spontaneously drawn toward him. It was to these five former colleagues that the Buddha gave his first public teaching at Deer Park in Sarnath.

In this discourse, which became known as the first turning of the wheel of Dharma [Buddhist teachings], the Buddha taught the principles of the Four Noble Truths: . . . the truth of suffering, the truth of the origin of suffering, the truth of the cessation of suffering, and the truth of the path leading to this cessation.

According to the sutra [discourse] concerning the first turning, when the Buddha taught the Four Noble Truths, he taught them within the context of three factors: the nature of the truths themselves, their specific functions, and their effects, or complete attainment. The first factor describes the nature of the individual truths. The second explains the importance of comprehending the specific significance of each for the practitioner: namely, suffering must be recognized, and its origin, eliminated; and the cessation of suffering must be actualized, and the path to cessation, realized. In the context of the third factor, the Buddha explained the ultimate result, or complete attainment, of the Four Noble Truths—that is, the completed recognition of suffering, the completed abandonment of the origin of suffering, the completed realization of the cessation of suffering, and the completed actualization of the path to cessation. I personally find the teaching on the Four Noble Truths to be very profound. This teaching lays down the blueprint for the entire body of Buddhist thought and practice, thus setting up the basic framework of an individual's path to enlightenment. . . .

What we desire and seek is to have happiness and overcome suffering. This yearning to have happiness and avoid pain and suffering is innate to all of us and needs no justification for its existence or validity. However, happiness and suffering do not arise from nowhere. They arise as consequences of causes and conditions. In brief, the doctrine of the Four Noble Truths states the principle of causality. Keeping this crucial point in mind, I sometimes remark that all of Buddhist thought and practice can be condensed into the following two principles: (1) adopting a world view that perceives the interdependent nature of phenomena, that is, the dependently originated nature of all things and events, and (2) based on that, leading a non-violent and non-harming way of life.

Buddhism advocates the conduct of non-violence on the basis of two simple and obvious premises: (1) as sentient beings, none of us wants suffering, and (2) suffering originates from its causes and conditions. The Buddhist teachings further assert that the root cause of our pain and suffering lies in our own ignorant and undisciplined state of mind. Therefore, if we do not desire suffering, the logical step to take is to refrain from destructive actions, which naturally lead to consequent experiences of pain and suffering. Pain and suffering do not exist in isolation; they come about as the results of causes and conditions. It is in understanding the nature of suffering and its relation to causes and conditions that the principle of dependent origination plays a crucial role. In essence, the principle of dependent origination states that an effect is dependent upon its cause. So, if you don't want the result, you should strive to put an end to its cause.

Within the Four Truths, we find two distinct sets of cause and result operating: suffering is the result, and the origin of suffering is its cause; in like manner, the true cessation of suffering is peace, the result, and the path leading to it is the cause of that peace.

The happiness we seek, a genuine lasting peace and happiness, can be attained only through the purification of our minds. This is possible if we cut the root cause of all suffering and misery—our fundamental ignorance. This freedom from suffering, the true cessation, can come about only when we have successfully seen through the illusion created by our habitual tendency to grasp at the intrinsic existence of phenomena and, thereby, gained insight that penetrates into the ultimate nature of reality. To attain this, however, the individual must perfect the three higher trainings [ethics, concentration, and wisdom]. The training in insight, or wisdom, acts as the actual antidote to ignorance and its derivative delusions. However, it is only when training in higher insight is conjoined with a highly developed faculty of single-pointedness of the mind that all of one's energy and mental attention can be focused on a chosen object of meditation without distraction. Hence, the training in higher concentration is an indispensable factor in advanced stages of application of the wisdom gained through insight. However, in order for both the trainings in higher concentration and higher insight to be successful, the practitioner must first establish a stable foundation of morality by adopting an ethically sound way of life.

AYYA KHEMA

Dukkha

THE VERY FIRST thing [the Buddha] said was, "There is the Noble Truth of *dukkha*." This is often misunderstood to mean that the Buddha's teaching is pessimistic, or that it stresses only the suffering, pain and unhappiness which are inherent in us. But it is just the opposite. His teaching shows us realistically what is unsatisfactory and how to overcome it.

It is often thought that the Buddha's doctrine teaches us that suffering will disappear if one has meditated long enough, or if one sees everything differently. It is not that at all. Suffering isn't going to go away; the one who suffers is going to go away. That is the way of transcendental dependent arising.

The Buddha said, "There is the deed but no doer, there is suffering but no sufferer, there is the path but no one to enter, there is *nibbana* but no one to attain it." If "I" want *nibbana,* it is out of reach. The saying may sound like a Zen-inspired paradox, but it will become quite clear as we go along.

All of us experience the reality of the unsatisfactoriness of existence, since we are rarely totally satisfied with our life. There will have been occasions in the past we would rather not have had happen. There are others which we will have desired, but which didn't come about. The best way to look at *dukkha* is with gratitude, that it is happening in order to teach us some very important lesson. It is useless to want *dukkha* to go away. It is impermanent, it will go away anyway, but if we don't learn the lesson that it is trying to teach us, it will come back in exactly the same manner. If we learn one particular lesson, *dukkha* will return in a different form, until we see it for what it is, namely universal existence, nothing else. None of us has a monopoly on *dukkha*. None of us is picked out to have a particular *dukkha*. It just is.

The acceptance of "it just is" is the first step towards realizing this path. *Dukkha is.* There are people who live very pleasant lives yet who can still realize it. There are others who live very unpleasant lives and don't realize it at all, but blame circumstances. They blame the government, or sometimes the atom bomb, or at other times the economy. People have all sorts of ideas about what can be blamed. Yet they could see in their own lives that there is a need to learn and grow. Every day we have an opportunity to learn, as there is hardly a human being without some daily *dukkha*.

Dukkha need not necessarily be physical, although that aspect in particular helps us to see the connection between the first and second Noble Truth, so that one may actually practise within these guidelines. The connection is the wanting, the desire either to have or to eliminate. In all our experiences of unpleasantness, that is the underlying cause. Once we are aware of the cause, we can investigate what it is that compels us either to want this or not want that. We can learn to drop these responses, which will help our lives to flow with far more ease and will set much latent energy free for the practice of this path. While we are still using our mental capacities to want certain things and reject others, we are not free to use our energy to practise with great determination.

JOSEPH GOLDSTEIN

Dependent Origination

IT IS BECAUSE of the mystery of birth, old age and death that Buddhas arise in the world. There is no realm of existence in which these realities do not exist, and it is the sole purpose of the Buddha's enlightenment to penetrate into their root causes. Perhaps the most profound part of the Buddha's teaching is the description of how this wheel of life, death and rebirth continues rolling on. The insight into all the links of the chain of existence is expressed in what is called the Law of Dependent Origination.

There are twelve links in this Law of Dependent Origination. The first two have to do with causes in the last life which condition birth in this one. The first of these links is ignorance. Ignorance means not knowing the truth, not understanding the Dharma, ignorance of the four noble truths. Because we do not perceive things clearly, because we do not perceive the fact of suffering and its cause and the way out, that force of ignorance conditions the next link in the chain: volitional actions of body, speech, and mind motivated by wholesome or unwholesome mental factors. Volitional activity is conditioned by ignorance; because we don't understand the truth, we are involved in all kinds of actions. And the karmic force of these actions conditions the third link in the chain.

The third link is rebirth consciousness; that is, the first moment of consciousness in this life. Because ignorance conditioned the energy of karmic activity in our last life, rebirth consciousness arises at the moment of conception. Volition or intention is like the seed; rebirth conscious-ness, like the sprouting of that seed—a cause and–effect conditioned relationship. Because of ignorance there were all kinds of actions, all kinds of karmic formations. Because of karmic formations arises rebirth consciousness, the beginning of this life. Because of the first moment of consciousness in this life arise the whole mind-body phenomena, all the elements of matter, all the factors of mind. Because of the mind-body phenomena arising, the sense spheres develop. This is during development of the embryo, before birth.

Rebirth consciousness at the moment of conception conditions the arising of mind-body phenomena. Because of that arise all the six spheres of the senses, the five physical senses and the mind, which in turn conditions the arising of contact, contact between the sense organ and its appropriate object: the eye and color, the ear and sound, nose and smell, tongue and taste, body and sensation, mind and thoughts or ideas. Contact involves the coming together of an object through its appropriate sense door and the consciousness of either seeing, hearing, smelling, tasting, touching, or thinking. Conditioned by the senses, contact comes into being. Because of the contact between the eye and color, the ear and sound, and the other senses and their objects, there arises feeling. Feeling means the quality of pleasantness, unpleasantness, or neither pleasantness nor unpleasantness involved in every mind moment, in every moment of contact. Whether it is contact through the five physical sense doors or through the mind, feeling is always present, and is called, therefore, a common mental factor. Conditioned by contact, there arises feeling; that is, the quality of pleasantness, unpleasantness or neutrality.

Because of feeling arises craving. Craving means desiring, hankering after objects. What is it that we desire? We desire pleasant sights and sounds, pleasant tastes and smells, pleasant touch sensations and thoughts, or we desire to get rid of unpleasant objects. Desire arises because of feelings. We start hankering after, or wishing to avoid, these six different objects in the world. Feeling conditions desire. Desire conditions grasping. Because we have a desire for the objects of the six senses, mind included, we grasp, we latch on to, we become attached. Grasping is conditioned by desire.

Because of grasping, again we get involved in karmic formations, repeating the kinds of volitions which, in our past life, produced the rebirth consciousness of this life. Feeling conditions desire, desire conditions grasping, and grasping conditions the continual actions of becoming, creating the energy which is the seed for rebirth consciousness in the next life. Because of these karmic actions resulting from grasping, again there is birth.

Because there is birth, there is disease, there is sorrow. There is decay, there is pain. There is suffering. There is death. And so the wheel goes on and on, an impersonal chain of causality.

The Buddha's problem, and the problem of us all, is to discover the way out of this cycle of conditioning. It is said that on the night of his enlightenment he worked backward through the Law of Dependent Origination, seeking the place of release. Why is there old age, disease and death? Because of birth. Why is there birth? Because of all the actions of becoming, all the volitional activities motivated by greed, hatred and delusion. Why are we involved in these kinds of activities? Because of grasping. Why is there grasping? Because of desire in the mind. Why is there desire? Because of feeling, because the quality of pleasantness or unpleasantness arises. Why is there feeling? Because of contact. Why is there contact? Because of the sense-spheres and the whole mind-body phenomena.

But there's nothing we can do now about being a mind-body process. That is conditioned by past ignorance and having taken birth. So there is no way to avoid contact. There's no possible way of closing off all the sense organs even if that were desirable. If there's contact, there's no way of preventing feeling from arising. Because of contact, feeling will be there. It's a common factor of mind. But, it is right at this point that the chain can be broken.

Understanding the Law of Dependent Origination, how because of one thing something else arises, we can begin to break the chain of conditioning. When pleasant things arise, we don't cling. When unpleasant things arise, we don't condemn. When neutral things arise, we're not forgetful. The Buddha said that the way of forgetfulness is the way of death. And that the way of wisdom and awareness is the path to the deathless. We are free to break this chain, to free ourselves from conditioned reactions. It takes a powerful mindfulness in every moment not to allow feelings to generate desire.

When there's ignorance in the mind, feeling conditions desire. If there's something pleasant, we want it; something unpleasant, we desire to get rid of it. But if instead of ignorance in the mind there is wisdom and awareness, then we experience feeling but don't compulsively or habitually grasp or push away. If the feelings are pleasant, we experience them mindfully without clinging. If unpleasant, we experience them mindfully without condemning. No longer do feelings condition desire; instead, there is mindfulness, detachment, letting go. When there is no desire, there's no grasping; without grasping, there's no volitional activity of becoming. If we are not generating that energy, there's no rebirth, no disease, no old age, no death. We become free. No longer driven on by ignorance and desire, the whole mass of suffering is brought to an end.

Every moment of awareness is a hammer stroke on this chain of conditioning. Striking it with the force of wisdom and awareness, the chain gets weaker and weaker until it breaks. What we are doing here is penetrating into the truth of the Law of Dependent Origination, and freeing our minds from it.

The Noble Eightfold Path

Within the Fourth Noble Truth is found the guide to the end of suffering: the Noble Eightfold Path. The eight parts of the path to liberation are grouped into three essential elements of Buddhist practice—moral conduct (Right Speech, Right Action, Right Livelihood); mental discipline (Right Effort, Right Mindfulness, Right Concentration); and wisdom (Right Understanding, Right Thought)—discussed further in the following sections of this book. The Buddha taught the Eightfold Path in virtually all his discourses, and his directions are as clear and practical to his followers today as they were when he first gave them.

WALPOLA RAHULA

The Eightfold Path

1. Right Understanding (*Samma ditthi*)

2. Right Thought (*Samma sankappa*)

3. Right Speech (*Samma vaca*)

4. Right Action (*Samma kammanta*)

5. Right Livelihood (*Samma ajiva*)

6. Right Effort (*Samma vayama*)

7. Right Mindfulness (*Samma sati*)

8. Right Concentration (*Samma samadhi*)

Practically the whole teaching of the Buddha, to which he devoted himself during 45 years, deals in some way or other with this Path. He explained it in different ways and in different words to different people, according to the stage of their development and their capacity to understand and follow him. But the essence of those many thousand discourses scattered in the Buddhist Scriptures is found in the Noble Eightfold Path.

It should not be thought that the eight categories or divisions of the Path should be followed and practised one after the other in the numerical order as given in the usual list above. But they are to be developed more or less simultaneously, as far as possible according to the capacity of each individual. They are all linked together and each helps the cultivation of the others.

These eight factors aim at promoting and perfecting the three essentials of Buddhist training and discipline: namely: (a) Ethical Conduct (*Sila*), (b) Mental Discipline (*Samadhi*) and (c) Wisdom (*Panna*). It will therefore be more helpful for a coherent and better understanding of the eight divisions of the Path if we group them and explain them according to these three heads.

Ethical Conduct (*Sila*) [see also pages 103–120] is built on the vast conception of universal love and compassion for all living beings, on which the Buddha's teaching is based. It is regrettable that many scholars forget this great ideal of the Buddha's teaching, and indulge in only dry philosophical and metaphysical divagations when they talk and write about Buddhism. The Buddha gave his teaching "for the good of the many, for the happiness of the many, out of compassion for the world". . . .

According to Buddhism, for a man to be perfect there are two qualities that he should develop equally: compassion (*karuna*) on one side, and wisdom (*panna*) on the other. Here compassion represents love, charity, kindness, tolerance and such noble qualities on the emotional side, or qualities of the heart, while wisdom would stand for the intellectual side or the qualities of the mind. If one develops only the emotional, neglecting the intellectual, one may become a good-hearted fool; while to develop only the intellectual side [and] neglecting the emotional may turn one into a hard-hearted intellect without feeling for others. Therefore, to be perfect one has to develop both equally. That is the aim of the Buddhist way of life: in it wisdom and compassion are inseparably linked together, as we shall see later.

Now, in Ethical Conduct (*Sila*), based on love and compassion, are included three factors of the Noble Eightfold Path: namely, Right Speech, Right Action and Right Livelihood. (Nos. 3, 4 and 5 in the list).

Right speech means abstention (1) from telling lies, (2) from back-biting and slander and talk that may bring about hatred, enmity, disunity and disharmony among individuals or groups of people, (3) from harsh, rude, impolite, malicious and abusive language, and (4) from idle, useless and foolish babble and gossip. When one abstains from these forms of wrong and harmful speech one naturally has to speak the truth, has to use words that are friendly and benevolent, pleasant and gentle, meaningful and useful. One should not speak carelessly: speech should be at the right time and place. If one cannot say something useful, one should keep "noble silence."

Right Action aims at promoting moral, honourable and peaceful conduct. It admonishes us that we should abstain from destroying life, from stealing, from dishonest dealings, from illegitimate sexual intercourse, and that we should also help others to lead a peaceful and honourable life in the right way.

Right Livelihood means that one should abstain from making one's living through a profession that brings harm to others, such as trading in arms and lethal weapons, intoxicating drinks or poisons, killing animals, cheating, etc., and should live by a profession which is honourable, blameless and innocent of harm to others. One can clearly see here that Buddhism is strongly opposed to any kind of war, when it lays down that trade in arms and lethal weapons is an evil and unjust means of livelihood.

These three factors (Right Speech, Right Action and Right Livelihood) of the Eightfold Path constitute Ethical Conduct. It should be realized that the Buddhist ethical and moral conduct aims at promoting a happy and harmonious life both for the individual and for society. This moral conduct is considered as the indispensable foundation for all higher spiritual attainments. No spiritual development is possible without this moral basis.

Next comes Mental Discipline [see also pages 121–175], in which are included three other factors of the Eightfold Path: namely, Right Effort, Right Mindfulness (or Attentiveness) and Right Concentration. (Nos. 6, 7 and 8 in the list).

Right Effort is the energetic will (1) to prevent evil and unwholesome states of mind from arising, and (2) to get rid of such evil and unwholesome states that have already arisen within a man, and also (3) to produce, to cause to arise, good and wholesome states of mind not yet arisen, and (4) to develop and bring to perfection the good and wholesome states of mind already present in a man.

Right Mindfulness (or Attentiveness) is to be diligently aware, mindful and attentive with regard to (1) the activities of the body (*kaya*), (2) sensations or feelings (*vedana*), (3) the activities of the mind (*citta*) and (4) ideas, thoughts, conceptions and things (*dhamma*).

The practice of concentration on breathing (*anapanasati*) is one of the well-known exercises, connected with the body, for mental development. There are several other ways of developing attentiveness in relation to the body as modes of meditation.

With regard to sensations and feelings, one should be clearly aware of all forms of feelings and sensations, pleasant, unpleasant and neutral, of how they appear and disappear within oneself.

Concerning the activities of mind, one should be aware whether one's mind is lustful or not, given to hatred or not, deluded or not, distracted or concentrated, etc. In this way one should be aware of all movements of mind, how they arise and disappear.

As regards ideas, thoughts, conceptions and things, one should know their nature, how they appear and disappear, how they are developed, how they are suppressed, and destroyed, and so on.

These four forms of mental culture or meditation are treated in detail in the *Satipatthana-sutta* (Setting-up of Mindfulness [pages 121–133]).

The third and last factor of Mental Discipline is Right Concentration, leading to the four stages of *Dhyana*, generally called trance or *recueillement*. In the first stage of *Dhyana*, passionate desires and certain unwholesome thoughts like sensuous lust, ill-will, languor, worry, restlessness, and sceptical doubt are discarded, and feelings of joy and happiness are maintained, along with certain mental activities. In the second stage, all intellectual activities are suppressed, tranquillity and "one-pointedness" of mind developed, and the feelings of joy and happiness are still retained. In the third stage, the feeling of joy, which is an active sensation, also disappears, while the disposition of happiness still remains in addition to mindful equanimity. In the fourth stage of

Dhyana, all sensations, even of happiness and unhappiness, of joy and sorrow, disappear, only pure equanimity and awareness remaining.

Thus the mind is trained and disciplined and developed through Right Effort, Right Mindfulness, and Right Concentration.

The remaining two factors, namely Right Thought and Right Understanding, go to constitute Wisdom [see also pages 177–213].

Right Thought denotes the thoughts of selfless renunciation or detachment, thoughts of love and thoughts of non-violence, which are extended to all beings. It is very interesting and important to note here that thoughts of selfless detachment, love and non-violence are grouped on the side of wisdom. This clearly shows that true wisdom is endowed with these noble qualities, and that all thoughts of selfish desire, ill-will, hatred and violence are the result of a lack of wisdom in all spheres of life whether individual, social, or political.

Right Understanding is the understanding of things as they are, and it is the Four Noble Truths that explain things as they really are. Right Understanding therefore is ultimately reduced to the understanding of the Four Noble Truths. This understanding is the highest wisdom which sees the Ultimate Reality. According to Buddhism there are two sorts of understanding: What we generally call understanding is knowledge, an accumulated memory, an intellectual grasping of a subject according to certain given data. This is called "knowing accordingly" (*anubodha*). It is not very deep. Real deep understanding is called "penetration" (*pativedha*), seeing a thing in its true nature, without name and label. This penetration is possible only when the mind is free from all impurities and is fully developed through meditation.

From this brief account of the Path, one may see that it is a way of life to be followed, practised and developed by each individual. It is self-discipline in body, word and mind, self-development and self-purification. It has nothing to do with belief, prayer, worship or ceremony. In that sense, it has nothing which may popularly be called "religious." It is a Path leading to the realization of Ultimate Reality, to complete freedom, happiness and peace through moral, spiritual and intellectual perfection.

JOSEPH GOLDSTEIN
Noble Eightfold Path

WE HAVE ALL begun a journey. A journey into our minds. A journey of discovery and exploration of who and what we are. Taking the first step is difficult, and in the first days of practice there is often restlessness, or sleepiness, some boredom, laziness, doubt, and perhaps regret about getting involved at all. The first step is difficult for everyone. Spinoza, at the end of one of his important philosophical works, wrote, "All noble things are as difficult as they are rare." The spiritual quest we are embarking upon is a rare and precious undertaking, so be gentle yet persevering through any beginning difficulties.

A beautiful allegory for this journey is the book *Mount Analogue*. The story is of a group of people searching for a mountain. The base of the mountain is on the earth while the summit represents the highest possible spiritual attainment. Initially, the pilgrims are faced with a great obstacle: under ordinary circumstances the mountain is invisible, and considerable struggle and hardship is undergone just to locate it. After much effort, they find the mountain and are able to approach its base. The rest of the book describes all the preparations, difficulties, struggles and excitement of beginning the ascent to the top.

We're on this very same journey, ascending the mountain of spiritual insight. We have already discovered the secret of its invisibility: the fact that the truth, the law, the Dharma, is within us, not outside of ourselves, and that we begin from where we are.

The path up the mountain, the path to freedom, has been well-mapped by the many people who have walked upon it. One of the clearest of these descriptions is found in the teachings of the Buddha, expressed as the noble eightfold path. It is a map, and a guide pointing the way to enlightenment.

The first step of this path up the mountain is right understanding. It is, in fact, both the first step and the last. It is because of some degree of understanding we begin the journey in the first place; and that understanding is brought to completion, to perfection, at the summit when we penetrate to the very deepest levels of our mind. In the beginning, right understanding deals with certain natural laws which govern our everyday lives. One of the most important of these is the law of karma, the law of cause and effect [see also pages 289–300]. Every action brings a certain result. Things are not happening to us by chance or accident. Whenever we act motivated by greed, hatred or delusion, pain and suffering come back to us. When our actions are motivated by generosity, love or wisdom, the results are happiness and peace. If we integrate this understanding of the law of karma into our lives, we can begin more consciously to cultivate and develop wholesome states of mind.

The Buddha often stressed the power and importance of generosity. Giving is the expression in action of non-greed in the mind. The whole spiritual path involves letting go, not grasping, not clinging, and generosity is the manifestation of that non-attachment.

Another part of right understanding is acknowledging the special relationship, the unique karma, we have with our parents, and the responsibilities and obligations we have to them. Our parents cared for us when we were unable to care for ourselves, and it is due to their concern at a time when we were helpless that we now have the opportunity to practice the Dharma. The Buddha said that there is no way of repaying this debt, that we could carry our parents about on our shoulders for an entire lifetime and still we would not have fulfilled our obligation. The only way of repaying our parents is to help establish them in the Dharma, in the truth, in right understanding. Generally, we spend a great deal of time and energy freeing ourselves psychologically from our parents, which certainly has its value, but in that space of freedom, we should recognize our responsibility towards them.

Right understanding also involves a profound and subtle knowledge of our true nature. In the course of meditation practice it becomes increasingly clear that everything is impermanent. All the elements of mind and body exist in a moment and pass away, arising and vanishing continuously. The breath comes in and goes out, thoughts arise and pass away, sensations come into being and vanish. All phenomena are in constant flux. There is no lasting security to be had in this flow of impermanence. And deep insight into the selfless nature of all elements begins to offer a radically different perspective on our lives and the world. The mind stops grasping and clinging when the microscopic transience of everything is realized, and when we experience the process of mind and body without the burden of self. This is the kind of right understanding that is developed in meditation through careful and penetrating observation.

The second step of the eightfold path is right thought. This means thoughts free of sense desire, free of ill will, free of cruelty. As long as the mind is attached to sense desire, it will seek after external objects, external fulfillments which, because of their impermanent nature, cannot be finally satisfying. There is a momentary experience of pleasure and then craving returns for more. The endless cycle of desire for sense pleasures keeps the mind in turbulence and confusion. Freeing thought from sense desires does not mean suppressing them and pretending they are not there. If a desire is suppressed, it will usually manifest in some other way. Equally unskillful is identifying with each desire as it arises and compulsively acting on it. Right thought means becoming aware of sense desires and letting them go. The more we let go, the lighter the mind becomes. Then there is no disturbance, no tension, and we begin to free ourselves from our storehouse of conditioning, from our bondage to sense desires.

Freedom from ill will means freedom from anger. Anger is a burning in the mind, and when expressed causes great suffering to others as well. It is helpful to be able to recognize anger and to let it go. Then the mind becomes light and easy, expressing its natural lovingkindness.

Thoughts free of cruelty mean thoughts of compassion, feeling for the suffering of others and wanting to alleviate it. We should develop thoughts which are completely free of cruelty towards any living thing.

The next steps on the path up the mountain have to do with how we relate in the world; how we relate to our environment, to other people. They are a prescription for putting us into harmony with our surroundings, for establishing a proper ecology of mind so that we're not in discord with others or with nature around us. The first aspect of relating to the world in this way is right speech. Right speech means not speaking what is untrue, or using slanderous, abusive or harsh language; rather, speaking words which are honest and helpful, creating a vibration of peace and harmony.

There is a story told of the Buddha returning after his enlightenment to the city where his family was still living. Many relatives and friends, inspired by his presence, by his love and compassion and wisdom, joined the order of monks. At that time, Rahula, his son, also became a novice in the order. There is one famous discourse called *Advice to Rahula* [see pages 136–143] in which the Buddha, speaking to his son, said that under no circumstances, either for his own benefit or for the benefit of others, should he speak that which is untrue. So important is the commitment to truth. It makes our relationships easy and uncomplicated. Honesty in speech also reflects back to honesty with ourselves. There are many things in our mind and body, tensions of all kinds, unpleasantness, things we don't like to look at, things about which we're untruthful with ourselves. Truthfulness in speech becomes the basis for being honest in our own minds, and that is when things begin to open up. We then begin to see clearly, working through all the neuroses of mind.

The fourth step of the path up the mountain is right action. This means not killing, minimizing the amount of pain we inflict on other beings; not stealing, that is, not taking what isn't given; and not committing sexual misconduct, which in the context of our daily life can be most basically understood as not causing suffering to others out of greed or desire for pleasant sensations. . . .

Because we're not always able to see the far-reaching consequences of each of our acts, we should take care not to create disturbances in the environment but to emanate peacefulness and gentleness, love and compassion.

The next step of the eightfold path involving our relationships in the world is right livelihood. This means doing that kind of work for support and maintenance which is not harmful to others; not having work which involves killing, stealing or dishonesty. There is a traditional list of occupations which are unskillful, such as dealing in weapons or intoxicants, hunting or fishing, all causing suffering to others. The Dharma is not just sitting. Sitting is a powerful tool for understanding, but wisdom and understanding have to be integrated into our lives. Right livelihood is an important part of the integration: "To walk in a sacred manner as was the American Indian way. To make an art of life." To do what we do in a sacred manner. To do what we do with awareness.

The next three steps on the path have to do primarily with the practice of meditation. The first of these is in many respects the most important: right effort. Unless we make the effort, nothing happens. It is said in the Abhidharma, the Buddhist psychology, that effort is the root of all achievement, the foundation of all attainment. If we want to get to the top of the mountain and just sit at the bottom thinking about it, it's not going to happen. It is through the effort, the actual climbing of the mountain, the taking of one step after another, that the summit is reached. Ramana Maharishi, a great sage of modern India, wrote, "No one succeeds without effort. Mind control is not your birthright. Those who succeed owe their success to their perseverance." But effort has to be balanced. Being very tense and anxious is a great hindrance. Energy has to be balanced with tranquillity. It is as if you are trying to tune the strings on a guitar. If they are too tight or too loose, the sound is not right. In our practice also, we have to be persistent and persevering but with a relaxed and balanced mind, making the effort without forcing. There is so much to discover in ourselves, so many levels of mind to understand. By making effort, the path unfolds. No one is going to do it for us. No one can enlighten another being. The Buddha's enlightenment solved his problem, it didn't solve ours . . . except to point out the way. We each have to walk the path for ourselves.

Mindfulness is the seventh step in this noble eightfold path, and it means being aware of what is happening in the present moment. It means noticing the flow of things: when walking, to be aware of the movement of the body; in observing the breath, to be aware of the sensations of the in-out or rising-falling; to notice thoughts or feelings as they arise. As expressed by one Zen master, "When you walk, walk; when you run, run; above all, don't wobble." Whatever the object is, to notice it, to be aware of it, without grasping, which is greed, without condemning, which is hatred, without forgetting, which is delusion; just observing the flow, observing the process. When mindfulness is cultivated it becomes very rhythmic and the whole day becomes a dance. Mindfulness brings the qualities of poise, equilibrium and balance to the mind, keeping it sharply focused, with the attitude of sitting back and watching the passion show.

The last step on the path up the mountain is right concentration. This is one-pointedness of mind, the ability of the mind to stay steady on an object. The first days of this journey may seem difficult because concentration is not yet well developed. To climb a mountain, you need a certain physical strength. If you are not yet very strong, in the beginning you will feel tired and uncomfortable. But as the body gets stronger, climbing becomes easier. It is the same in meditation. As concentration is developed, it becomes less difficult to stay in the moment. The hindrances that are faced in the beginning of practice are then easily overcome.

If you put a kettle on the stove and every few minutes take the lid off, it will take a longer time for the water to boil. If you put the kettle on the stove and leave it there, the water will heat up very quickly. . . .

The journey that we are on combines right relationship in the world with a deepening understanding and insight into our own nature. There is appropriate advice in *Mount Analogue* about ascending this path of wisdom: "Keep your eye fixed on the path to the top. But don't forget to look right in front of you. The last step depends upon the first. Don't think that you're there just because you see the summit. Watch your footing. Be sure of the next step. But don't let that distract you from the highest goal. The first step depends upon the last."

Being grounded in the present, cultivating awareness of the moment, and trusting our vision of freedom.

SYLVIA BOORSTEIN

"The Eightfold Circle"

SUPPOSE WE USE a traveling metaphor for the universal spiritual quest. The main map the Buddha offered for the trip to happiness and contentment is called the Eightfold Path, but I have often thought it should be called the Eightfold Circle. A path goes from here to there, and the nearer you are to *there,* the farther you are from *here.* A path is progressive, like a ladder, and, just as you cannot suddenly leap onto the fifth rung of a ladder and start climbing, on a genuine path you would need to start at the beginning and proceed in a linear way until the end. With a circle, you can join in anywhere, and it's the same circle.

When the Buddha taught his path, he said it had a specific number of constituent parts; people could be sure they were going the right way if they saw any one of eight special markers. These signposts are: Right Understanding, Right Aspiration, Right Action, Right Speech, Right Livelihood, Right Effort, Right Concentration, and Right Mindfulness. Travelers seeing any of the signposts will know they are headed in the direction of happiness.

The order in which the traveler sees the signs doesn't matter. If we look at any sign closely, it becomes apparent that each one has all of the others hidden inside it. Even a tiny bit of Right Understanding, the *suspicion* that it is possible to be contented even when we aren't pleased, arouses Right Aspiration to make a lot of Right Effort to develop more Right Understanding. Anyone who decides to practice Right Speech, making sure every single thing she says is both truthful and helpful, discovers it cannot be done without Right Mindfulness. Right Mindfulness means paying attention in every moment, and those who do that soon discover they have Right Concentration as well. Even if a person said, "Eightfold is too complicated. I just want to do a onefold practice," it wouldn't work. It's all connected.

On the journey to happiness, you start anywhere. You start wherever you are. I have only one hesitation about calling the practice a circle. Even a small circle takes up space, and space creates the idea of a *here* and a *there*. There isn't any *there*. When we wake up to happiness, we get to be more *here* than we ever were before. But, since waking up does happen and practice does work, we need to call it something. I guess it's more like the Eightfold Dot.

SHUNRYU SUZUKI
Right Effort

THE MOST IMPORTANT point in our practice is to have right or perfect effort. Right effort directed in the right direction is necessary. If your effort is headed in the wrong direction, especially if you are not aware of this, it is deluded effort. Our effort in our practice should be directed from achievement to non-achievement.

Usually when you do something, you want to achieve something, you attach to some result. From achievement to non-achievement means to be rid of the unnecessary and bad results of effort. If you do something in the spirit of non-achievement, there is a good quality in it. So just to do something without any particular effort is enough. When you make some special effort to achieve something, some excessive quality, some extra element is involved in it. You should get rid of excessive things. If your practice is good, without being aware of it you will become proud of your practice. That pride is extra. What you do is good, but something more is added to it. So you should get rid of that something which is extra. This point is very, very important, but usually we are not subtle enough to realize it, and we go in the wrong direction.

Because all of us are doing the same thing, making the same mistake, we do not realize it. So without realizing it, we are making many mistakes. And we create problems among us. This kind of bad effort is called being "Dharma-ridden," or "practice-ridden." You are involved in some idea of practice or attainment, and you cannot get out of it. When you are involved in some dualistic idea, it means your practice is not pure. By purity we do not mean to polish something, trying to make some impure thing pure. By purity we just mean things as they are. When something is added, that is impure. When something becomes dualistic, that is not pure. If you think you will get something from practicing zazen, already you are involved in impure practice. It is all right to say there is practice, and there is enlightenment, but we should not be caught by the statement. You should not be tainted by it. When you practice zazen, just practice zazen. If enlightenment comes, it just comes. We should not attach to the attainment. The true quality of zazen is always there, even if you are not aware of it, so forget all about what you think you may have gained from it. Just do it. The quality of zazen will express itself; then you will have it.

People ask what it means to practice zazen with no gaining idea, what kind of effort is necessary for that kind of practice. The answer is: effort to get rid of something extra from our practice. If some extra idea comes, you should try to stop it; you should remain in pure practice. That is the point towards which our effort is directed.

We say, "To hear the sound of one hand clapping." Usually the sound of clapping is made with two hands, and we think that clapping with one hand makes no sound at all. But actually, one hand is sound. Even though you do not hear it, there is sound. If you clap with two hands, you can hear the sound. But if sound did not already exist before you clapped, you could not make the sound. Before you make it there is sound. Because there is sound, you can make it, and you can hear it. Sound is everywhere. If you just practice it, there is sound. Do not try to listen to it. If you do not listen to it, the sound is all over. Because you try to hear it, sometimes there is sound, and sometimes there is no sound. Do you understand? Even though you do not do anything, you have the quality of zazen always. But if you try to find it, if you try to see the quality, you have no quality.

You are living in this world as one individual, but before you take the form of a human being, you are already there, always there. We are always here. Do you understand? You think before you were born you were not here. But how is it possible for you to appear in this world, when there is no you? Because you are already there, you can appear in the world. Also, it is not possible for something to vanish which does not exist. Because something is there, something can vanish. You may think that when you die, you disappear, you no longer exist. But even though you vanish, something which is existent cannot be non-existent. That is the magic. We ourselves cannot put any magic spells on this world. The world is its own magic. If we are looking at something, it can vanish from our sight, but if we do not try to see it, that something cannot vanish. Because you are watching it, it can disappear, but if no one is watching, how is it possible for anything to disappear? If someone is watching you, you can escape from him, but if no one is watching, you cannot escape from yourself.

So try not to see something in particular; try not to achieve anything special. You already have everything in your own pure quality. If you understand this ultimate fact, there is no fear. There may be some difficulty, of course, but there is no fear. If people have difficulty without being aware of the difficulty, that is true difficulty. They may appear very confident, they may think they are making a big effort in the right direction, but without knowing it, what they do comes out of fear. Something may vanish for them. But if your effort is in the right direction, then there is no fear of losing anything. Even if it is in the wrong direction, if you are aware of that, you will not be deluded. There is nothing to lose. There is only the constant pure quality of right practice.

Moral Conduct/The Precepts

As we have seen, the Noble Eightfold Path may be considered within three categories: moral conduct, mental discipline, and wisdom. The broad category of moral conduct has been codified throughout the history of Buddhism, beginning in the Buddha's time, into precepts for conduct. The number of precepts for the behavior of monks has run into the hundreds in some sects; for laypeople, the Theravada tradition has five precepts, which have common elements with most of the descriptions of moral conduct in the other major traditions. Some aspects, especially the precept to refrain from taking life, have been a continuing focus of attention throughout the history of Buddhism, and we shall explore them in depth through teachings from between the fifth and the twentieth centuries.

BUDDHAGHOSA
(FOURTH CENTURY),
EDWARD CONZE, TRANS.

The Five Precepts

I undertake to observe the rule to abstain from taking life;
to abstain from taking what is not given;
to abstain from sensuous misconduct;
to abstain from false speech;
to abstain from intoxicants as tending to cloud the mind.

(1) "Taking life" means to murder anything that lives. It refers to the striking and killing of living beings. "Anything that lives"—ordinary people speak here of a "living being," but more philosophically we speak of "anything that has the life-force." "Taking life" is then the will to kill anything that one perceives as having life, to act so as to terminate the life-force in it, in so far as the will finds expression in bodily action or in speech. With regard to animals it is worse to kill large ones than small. Because a more extensive effort is involved. Even where the effort is the same, the difference in substance must be considered. In the case of humans the killing is the more blameworthy the more virtuous they are. Apart from that, the extent of the offense is proportionate to the intensity of the wish to kill. Five factors are involved: a living being, the perception of a living being, a thought of murder, the action of carrying it out, and death as a result of it. And six are the ways in which the offense may be carried out: with one's own hand, by instigation, by missiles, by slow poisoning, by sorcery, by psychic power.

(2) "To take what is not given" means the appropriation of what is not given. It refers to the removing of someone else's property, to the stealing of it, to theft. "What is not given" means that which belongs to someone else. "Taking what is not given" is then the will to steal anything that one perceives as belonging to someone else, and to act so as to appropriate it. Its blameworthiness depends partly on the value of the property stolen, partly on the worth of its owner. Five factors are involved: someone else's belongings, the awareness that they are someone else's, the thought of theft, the action of carrying it out, the taking away as a result of it. This sin, too, may be carried out in six ways. One may also distinguish unlawful acquisition by way of theft, robbery, underhand dealings, stratagems, and the casting of lots.

(3) "Sensuous misconduct"— here "sensuous" means "sexual,"

and "misconduct" is extremely blameworthy bad behavior. "Sensuous misconduct" is the will to transgress against those whom one should not go into, and the carrying out of this intention by unlawful physical action. By "those one should not go into," first of all men are meant. And then also twenty kinds of women. Ten of them are under some form of protection, by their mother, father, parents, brother, sister, family, clan, co-religionists, by having been claimed from birth onwards, or by the king's law. The other ten kinds are: women bought with money, concubines for the fun of it, kept women, women bought by the gift of a garment, concubines who have been acquired by the ceremony which consists in dipping their hands into water, concubines who once carried burdens on their heads, slave girls who are also concubines, servants who are also concubines, girls captured in war, temporary wives. The offense is the more serious, the more moral and virtuous the person transgressed against. Four factors are involved: someone who should not be gone into, the thought of cohabiting with that one, the actions which lead to such cohabitation, and its actual performance. There is only one way of carrying it out: with one's own body.

(4) "False"—this refers to actions of the voice, or actions of the body, which aim at deceiving others by obscuring the actual facts. "False speech" is the will to deceive others by words or deeds. One can also explain: "False" means something which is not real, not true. "Speech" is the intimation that that is real or true. "False speech" is then the volition which leads to the deliberate intimation to someone else that something is so when it is not so. The seriousness of the offense depends on the circumstances. If a householder, unwilling to give something, says that he has not got it, that is a small offense; but to represent something one has seen with one's own eyes as other than one has seen it, that is a serious offense. If a mendicant has on his rounds got very little oil or ghee [butter], and if he then exclaims, "What a magnificent river flows

along here, my friends!'' that is only a rather stale joke, and the offense is small; but to say that one has seen what one has not seen, that is a serious offense. Four factors are involved: something which is not so, the thought of deception, an effort to carry it out, the communication of the falsehood to someone else. There is only one way of doing it: with one's own body.

"To abstain from"—one crushes or forsakes sin. It means an abstention which is associated with wholesome thoughts. And it is three-fold: (I) one feels obliged to abstain, (II) one formally undertakes to do so, (III) one has lost all temptation not to do so.

(I) Even those who have not formally undertaken to observe the precepts may have the conviction that it is not right to offend against them. So it was with Cakkana, a Ceylonese boy. His mother was ill, and the doctor prescribed fresh rabbit meat for her. His brother sent him into the field to catch a rabbit, and he went as he was bidden. Now a rabbit had run into a field to eat of the corn, but in its eagerness to get there had got entangled in a snare, and gave forth cries of distress. Cakkana followed the sound, and thought—"This rabbit has got caught there, and it will make a fine medicine for my mother!" But then he thought again: "It is not suitable for me that, in order to preserve my mother's life, I should deprive someone else of his life." And so he released the rabbit, and said to it: "Run off, play with the other rabbits in the wood, eat grass and drink water!" On his return he told the story to his brother, who scolded him. He then went to his mother, and said to her: "Even without having been told, I know quite clearly that I should not deliberately deprive any living being of life." He then fervently resolved that these truthful words of his might make his mother well again, and so it actually happened.

(II) The second kind of abstention refers to those who not only have formally undertaken not to offend against the precepts, but who in addition are willing to sacrifice their lives for that. This can be illustrated by a layman who lived near Uttaravarddhamana. He had received the precepts from Buddharakkhita, the Elder. He then went to plow his field, but found that his ox had got lost. In his search for the ox he climbed up the mountain, where a huge snake took hold of him. He thought of cutting off the snake's head with his sharp knife, but on further reflection he thought to himself: "It is not suitable that I, who have received the precepts from the venerable Guru, should break them again." Three times he thought, "My life I will give up, but not the precepts!" and then he threw his knife away. Thereafter the huge viper let him go, and went somewhere else.

(III) The last kind of abstention is associated with the Holy Path. It does not even occur to the Holy Persons to kill any living being.

DAININ KATAGIRI

The Three Collective Pure Precepts

THE THREE COLLECTIVE Pure Precepts, refraining from all that is evil, practicing all that is good, purifying one's mind, are the teachings of all the buddhas. The first two lines, refraining from all evil and practicing all good, are precepts. The third line, purifying one's mind, is having pure faith in the Triple Treasure [see also pages 215–228]. Taking refuge in the Buddha, Dharma and Sangha is purifying one's mind.

Buddhist precepts are not moral or ethical imperatives or orders given by someone that people must follow. They are the ground of

Buddha's world, through which we can manifest ourselves as buddhas. We are already enlightened and the precepts are already enlightened words. Each word is Buddha's mind completely beyond our speculation. If we take the precepts as Buddha's mind, Buddha's teaching, we can each behave as a buddha. But if we take them in the moral sense we become moral people. It is very difficult to understand this with our usual mind, so very naturally we think we are obeying Buddha's teaching in the moral sense. That's all right. Just keep going, accepting the precepts as the Buddha's teaching.

In the beginning, even though you understand the precepts as a moral teaching, all you have to do is take the precepts continually, and learn them in your everyday life. This applies to the precepts and to whatever else you may do. Practice everything you do like this. Before you are conscious of it, that teaching penetrates your life.

If we want to practice calligraphy, we should study the teaching of that art from a textbook written by a great master rather than from one by an ordinary person. Unfortunately, when the characters we have drawn do not look like the calligraphy written by the teacher, we become frustrated and decide we don't like the textbook. We want to have a book in which the calligraphy is similar to our calligraphy. But if we use a book like that, we will never progress. Even though we don't know how long it will take to master this calligraphy, we should take the book by the great teacher and learn. If we practice it continually, we will experience that where no evil is produced the true strength of practice is actualized. Very naturally, sooner or later we will master the calligraphy before we are conscious of it. At that time no particular effort is needed. The brush moves naturally, and the calligraphy matches the teacher's calligraphy exactly. . . .

In order to achieve the perfection of this faith and the precepts we have to sever three ties: the first is selfishness, the second is doubt or wrong view, and the third is wrong religious belief or, in other words, superstition or dogmatism.

In order to sever the tie of doubt or wrong view, we cannot attach to excessive, one-sided ideas. We have to see the human world, human life, in the light of the teaching of impermanence and the law of causation [see also pages 289–300]. This is a very contradictory situation. If everything is impermanent there is nothing to grasp and hold on to. But, on the other hand, there is the law of causation. If you do something, very naturally there will be a result. These two teachings are contradictory, and so, we are confused by the human world, by human life. But impermanence is a very basic teaching of existence. Impermanence is that which causes change to occur. It doesn't have any form or color or smell. Impermanence itself is a kind of energy, moving, functioning, working dynamically, appearing, disappearing, always supporting our life. Only through change can we see it and understand it. Through change we can see the depth of human life based on impermanence. . . .

Next, we have to be free from selfishness. Selfishness means always attaching to the self first. It's very difficult to be free from self. Do you know the children's story of the tortoise and the hare? The tortoise is one of the slowest creatures in this world. Common sense tells us that he would never win a race with a hare. But actually he did it. In order to win, can you imagine how much effort this tortoise made? He made an enormous effort. In order to make this enormous effort he had to be completely free from the label of the slowest creature or the fastest creature. In the race he just made every possible effort to keep moving. It is important to give quality to the effort, instead of expecting the result of the effort. All you have to do is just make your best effort, being free from a label or judgment that you are capable or not or that you are good or not. Forget it and just make an enormous effort.

If while making this effort you are also competing with somebody else or with an idea of how to become a buddha, it's very difficult to give quality to your effort. We always think that we are deluded, ordinary people who will never become a buddha. Such an idea is also competition. If we practice like that it's very hard; our zazen [meditation practice] becomes "hell" zazen. If someone else attains enlightenment that is their story, not yours. If someone stumbles, help them; don't think about being first. Don't compete and don't expect results. This is the best way to be free from selfishness. This is called the practice of egolessness. This is our practice.

The third tie to sever is wrong religious belief. In Buddhism we take refuge in the Triple Treasure. Refuge in Buddhism is not someplace we go in order to escape from the human world. Refuge is a place where everyone has to go, like the terminal station. If you take the train of human life you have to go to the terminal station. And then from the terminal station you can go anywhere else. So it is an end but it's also a beginning. In Buddhism, that terminal station is referred to as the Triple Treasure: Buddha, Dharma and Sangha. Buddha is one who understands human life based on impermanence and the law of causation. His effort is going on continuously and if we participate in it, we are called buddha. But in everyday life it is very difficult to do this because we already have preconceptions, we have our own customs and inherited traits. That's why we have to come back to this way constantly, doing the same thing Buddha did. Every day we have to come back, a hundred, a thousand, a million times, to the Buddha's teaching. We have to come back again and again to the teaching, without a sense of competition or expectation. We have to follow this teaching that is given to us by a person who understands the human world, who lives his own life on the basis of impermanence and the law of causation. We have to grow by ourselves, but we need help. This is to take refuge in the Buddha, the Dharma and the Sangha.

Even though we have Buddha and the Dharma, we need human beings who exist now, who are practicing together. That is Sangha. People come together and practice Buddha's way, Buddha's teaching, and grow and become buddha in the same way that Shakyamuni Buddha did. Then we can transmit that teaching to future generations. We can make human history, we can make human culture. Without human beings who exist now we cannot transmit Buddha's teaching to future generations. We need all of us and we need a place where we practice the Buddha Way together. Buddha, Dharma and Sangha are the terminal station we have to reach. And then we can see our lives extending everywhere. We can see our life from the universal perspective.

The word for "precept" in Sanskrit, *sila,* means to form a habit. Habit, in the usual sense, may last for only a lifetime and there is attachment to self or an object or individual desire involved. Forming a habit of living in a way that is based on Buddha's teaching is the practice of spiritual life and is called "vow." Vow is continually going on in the realm of eternity beyond time and space, life after life. There is no sense of self-attachment, no desire, no individual interest. We have to put this vow into practice in our everyday life. . . . Every day, constantly, we have to form the habit of living in the way that is based on Buddha's teaching.

The deep meaning of precept is that it is Buddha-nature or Truth. To receive the precepts is to awaken to the Buddha-nature [see also pages 229–237]. Even though we don't understand what Buddha-nature or Truth is, to receive the precepts is awareness. For example, if we don't understand the value of a diamond, but somebody gives us one and we receive the diamond in our hand, there is already awareness of the value of the diamond. We may not be conscious of it, but more or less it affects our life in many ways. That's why it's important to receive the precepts. We always try to understand something in terms of our intellect, according to our individual knowledge, our individual education. And then we either receive it or we decide we don't want to receive it. But in spiritual life, regardless of whether we understand it or not, to receive the precepts means to receive Buddha-nature, Truth. In order to help our true nature grow we have to receive the diamond again and again, even though we don't understand what has been given to us. Receive it every day. This practice helps the seed of true nature grow. It is a simple practice. Our consciousness is always grumbling and complaining. Then life appears to be very complicated. But actually, spiritual life is a very simple life. Regardless of whether we understand or not, we receive the diamond as it is in order to help the seed of Buddha-nature grow. . . .

Buddhist precepts are difficult to understand. But it's not necessary to try to understand. Just receive them and form a habit of living them as a vow. It is important to have the guidance of Buddha's teaching, of the ancestors and of living teachers, all walking hand in hand with us, because we don't know how to practice, how to maintain the habit of a way of living based on Buddha's Way.

The main purpose of Buddhism is to form the habit of practice as a vow forever. This is just taking a journey in the universe, day by day, step by step. It is like walking in a mist. We don't know what the mist is, we don't know where we are walking or why; all we have to do is just walk. This is Buddha's practice. (in a nutshell)

EDITORS OF *TRICYCLE*

The First Precept

TO REFRAIN FROM killing is the first Buddhist precept. The Theravada tradition of Southeast Asia interprets this precept in terms that parallel a Western sense of morality: there is a clear-cut distinction between killing and not killing in which the existence of a breathing, moving being either comes to its end—or doesn't. In this view, there is a killer, a separate entity that is killed, and the activity of killing. Compassion is expressed by not harming others, and many followers honor this precept by choosing a vegetarian diet.

In Zen and other Mahayana traditions in East Asia, there is a tendency to translate this precept into the more unfamiliar concept of non-killing. This view emphasizes a nondualistic reality in which there is no killer and no killed. From the Mahayana perspective, all apparent separations are illusions. The meaning of "life" in these traditions extends beyond biological definition; maintaining a non-dual consciousness supports life, and not maintaining such awareness is considered a form of killing. For example, the spiritual goal of the practice is the complete extinction of craving—which Mahayana sees as killing, as does Zen. Zen Master Bodhidharma defines killing as "nursing a view of extinction," which means, in part, defining spiritual practice in terms of the elimination or eradication of some aspect of life perceived as negative. If this is killing, then nirvana itself (usually defined as extinction) is killing. The Mahayana Lotus Sutra [see pages 268–272] makes this point by saying that the nirvana of extinction is not the "true nirvana." The "sword of compassion" in Mahayana teachings is used to cut through the illusion of separation, of self and other, of this or that. Compassion may be understood to be the functioning of an interconnected, interdependent reality.

Vajrayana Buddhism incorporates both Theravada and Mahayana views. The practice of the precepts begins with those rules and regulations of daily conduct that were systematized after the death of Shakyamuni Buddha and unfolds as a mindful response to an ever-changing present. In Vajrayana, as spiritual practice matures, there is less dependency on codified ethics and more on personal guidance from an authentic teacher.

The advent of Buddhism in the United States—1950 to the early 1970s—was dominated by Japanese Zen. In Japan, precept study (largely comprised of koans on the precepts) is introduced at the end of training—a strategy designed to prevent students from blindly embracing rules and regulations. According to Zen adepts, adherence to rules of ethics without some uncovering of Buddha nature (the universal consciousness that knows no duality) produces false piety and jeopardizes what they consider true moral action—action born not of rules but of nondualistic consciousness. This gave rise to a misconception about Buddhist practice in the early days of Buddhism in America—namely, that Buddhists were unconcerned with ethics. Today many American Zen teachers choose not to wait until the end of training to initiate a modified, more discursive form of precept study that uses rational discussion (rather than koans) to explore the precepts. All American Buddhists—no matter which tradition they adhere to—face the challenge of adapting the moral guidelines Shakyamuni created twenty-five hundred years ago to modern life.

BUDDHAGHOSA (FOURTH CENTURY)

The First Precept

With respect to the unprofitable course of action known as killing living things, (a) abandoning is virtue; (b) abstention is virtue; (c) volition is virtue; (d) restraint is virtue; and (e) non-transgression is virtue. . . . And here there is no state called abandoning other than the non-arising of the killing of living things. But the abandoning of a given unprofitable state upholds a given profitable state in the sense of providing a foundation for it, and concentrates it by preventing wavering, so it is called "virtue" (sila) in the sense of composing (silana), reckoned as upholding and concentrating. . . .

EIHEI DOGEN

(THIRTEENTH CENTURY)

The First Precept

Life is non-killing. The seed of Buddha grows continuously. Maintain the wisdom-life of Buddha and do not kill life.

BODHIDHARMA

(FIFTH–SIXTH CENTURY)

The First Precept

*The ten Dharma Worlds are the body and mind. In the sphere of the
everlasting dharma,*
Not nursing a view of extinction
Is called the precept of refraining from killing.

BERNARD GLASSMAN

The First Precept

FROM THE INTRINSIC standpoint—one of body, of Buddha-
nature—non-killing means that there is nothing being born and nothing
dying. The very notions of "birth" and "death" are extra. Life does
not divide up into things to be killed or not killed; it is just this one
body, constantly changing. From the subjective standpoint, there are
two criteria involved: one is compassion and the other is a radically
relative and completely intuitive sense of "rightness." Compassion in
the context of non-killing would mean encouraging or nurturing
life. . . ."Rightness" is defined in terms of four aspects of judgment:
time, place, the people involved, and the quantity or extent. . . .
Whereas the literal perspective sees this precept in absolute terms of
either killing or not-killing, maintaining both the literal and the subjec-

tive standpoints requires the compromise of minimizing the destruction of life. . . . The powerful irony at the heart of Zen practice is that the strongest way to follow this precept of non-killing is by killing the self! If we can kill—that is, truly forget—the self, we are at that very moment the infinite life of the Buddha, and are thus nurturing and fostering life in the fullest, most genuine manner possible.

KELSANG GYATSO

The First Precept

THERE IS NO moral concept that a bodhisattva fails to practice and observe. However, circumstances can arise in which it is better to commit certain normally non-virtuous actions than it is to bind ourselves to a specific moral code. Of course, it takes wisdom to determine when it is appropriate to relax our moral discipline and when it is better to be strict. If we keep our *bodhicitta* [mind of enlightenment] motivation in mind, however, we shall find it much easier to make the correct discriminations. Our basic consideration should be: "What is more beneficial for others? What is the best way of dealing with the situation so that they receive the most good?" [Here] is [a] traditional example used to explain how a bodhisattva can even commit murder if this is beneficial to others. In a previous life, Shakyamuni Buddha was an oarsman and one day he was ferrying 500 merchants across the sea. With his powers of clairvoyance he realized that one of the merchants was planning to kill all the others. He thought to himself, "If he follows out his plan he will not only cause 499 people to lose their lives but will also create the cause for being reborn in the lower realms." The oarsman realized that if he killed the would-be assassin he could prevent all 500 people from being harmed. Therefore, with the motivation of great compassion, he killed the merchant. As a result of this selfless action, the oarsman purified much negative karma accumulated through many eons and also collected limitless merit. This story illustrates the range of a bodhisattva's actions, but most of us are not able to practice like this at the moment. We should be aware of our level of attainment and understand our limitations for, as the saying goes, if a jackal tries to jump where a tiger leaps he will only break his neck!

SULAK SIVARAKSA

The First Precept

ALL BUDDHISTS ACCEPT the five precepts (*panca-sila*) as their basic ethical guidelines.

Using these as a handle, we know how to deal with many of the real issues of our day. The first precept is "I vow to abstain from taking life." We promise not to destroy, cause to be destroyed, or sanction the destruction of any living being. Through accepting this precept, we recognize our relationship to all life and realize that harming any living creature harms oneself. The Buddha said, "Identifying ourselves with others, we can never slay or cause to slay."

This precept applies to all creatures, irrespective of size. We do not sacrifice living beings for worship, convenience, or food. Instead, we try to sacrifice our own selfish motives. Mahayana Buddhists may, however, commit acts that harm themselves if, in doing so, they genuinely help other living beings. The Vietnamese monks who burned themselves, for example, felt that their acts would help bring about the end of the Vietnam War. According to the Theravada Buddhist tradition, purity is essential for wisdom and compassion to be possible, and serious Theravadins do not condone killing at all. For Theravada monks, to cut trees or cultivate land is killing. However, most of us have to compromise. Alan Watts once said that he chose to be a vegetarian because cows cry louder than cabbages. Mahayana monks can generally be vegetarians, since they are permitted to till their own land. Theravada monks depend entirely on lay supporters for food, so they must eat whatever is offered to them, including meat. But if they suspect that an animal has been killed specifically for them, they cannot eat it.

Killing animals and eating meat may be appropriate for a simple agrarian society or village life, but once complicated marketing comes into existence, one has to reexamine the first Buddhist precept carefully. In industrial society, meat is treated as just another product. Is the mass production of meat respectful of the lives of animals? If people in meat-eating countries could discourage the breeding of animals for consumption, it would not only be compassionate toward the animals, but also toward the humans living in poverty who need grains to survive.

Buddhists must also be aware that there is enough food in the world now to feed us all adequately. Hunger is caused only by unequal economic and power structures that do not allow food to end up where it is needed, even when those who are in need are the food producers. And we must look at the sales of arms and challenge these structures, which are responsible for murder. Killing permeates our modern way of life—wars, racial conflicts, breeding animals to serve human markets, and using harmful insecticides. How can we resist this and help create a non-violent society? How can the first precept and its ennobling virtues be used to shape a politically just and merciful world? I do not attempt to answer these questions. I just want to raise them for us to contemplate.

Mental Discipline

The second of the three essential elements addressed within the Noble Eightfold Path—along with moral conduct and wisdom—is mental discipline. In his Greater Discourse on the Foundations of Mindfulness, the Buddha describes in detail the methods of developing the awareness that leads to liberation. As different traditions have evolved in the history of Buddhism, so too have practices of mental discipline, including Vipassana, or insight, meditation; zazen; Tibetan Buddhist meditation; and the concentration practice known as metta.

MAURICE WALSHE, TRANS.

The Greater Discourse on the Foundations of Mindfulness

1. Thus have I heard. Once the Lord was staying among the Kurus. There is a market-town of theirs called Kammasadhamma. And there the Lord addressed the monks: "Monks!" "Lord," they replied, and the Lord said:

"There is, monks, this one way to the purification of beings, for the overcoming of sorrow and distress, for the disappearance of pain and sadness, for the gaining of the right path, for the realisation of Nibbana:—that is to say the four foundations of mindfulness.

"What are the four? Here, monks, a monk abides contemplating

body as body, ardent, clearly aware and mindful, having put aside hankering and fretting for the world; he abides contemplating feelings as
feelings . . . ; he abides contemplating mind as mind . . . ; he abides
contemplating mind-objects as mind-objects, ardent, clearly aware and
mindful, having put aside hankering and fretting for the world.''

(CONTEMPLATION OF THE BODY)
(1. Mindfulness of Breathing)

2. ''And how, monks, does a monk abide contemplating the body
as body? Here a monk, having gone into the forest, or to the root of a
tree, or to an empty place, sits down cross-legged, holding his body
erect, having established mindfulness before him. Mindfully he breathes
in, mindfully he breathes out. Breathing in a long breath, he knows that
he breathes in a long breath, and breathing out a long breath, he knows
that he breathes out a long breath. Breathing in a short breath, he knows
that he breathes in a short breath, and breathing out a short breath, he
knows that he breathes out a short breath. He trains himself, thinking:
'I will breathe in, conscious of the whole body.' He trains himself,
thinking: 'I will breathe out, conscious of the whole body.' He trains
himself, thinking: 'I will breathe in, calming the whole bodily process.'
He trains himself, thinking: 'I will breathe out, calming the whole bodily
process.' Just as a skilled turner, or his assistant, in making a long turn,
knows that he is making a long turn, or in making a short turn, knows
that he is making a short turn, so too a monk, in breathing in a long
breath, knows that he breathes in a long breath . . . and so trains himself, thinking: 'I will breathe out, calming the whole bodily process.' ''

(INSIGHT)

"So he abides contemplating body as body internally, contemplating body as body externally, contemplating body as body both internally and externally. He abides contemplating arising phenomena in the body, he abides contemplating vanishing phenomena in the body, he abides contemplating both arising and vanishing phenomena in the body. Or else, mindfulness that 'there is body' is present to him just to the extent necessary for knowledge and awareness. And he abides independent, not clinging to anything in the world. And that, monks, is how a monk abides contemplating body as body."

(2. The Four Postures)

3. "Again, a monk, when walking, knows that he is walking, when standing, knows that he is standing, when sitting, knows that he is sitting, when lying down, knows that he is lying down. In whatever way his body is disposed, he knows that that is how it is.

"So he abides contemplating body as body internally, externally, and both internally and externally . . . And he abides independent, not clinging to anything in the world. And that, monks, is how a monk abides contemplating body as body."

(3. Clear Awareness)

4. "Again, a monk, when going forward or back, is clearly aware of what he is doing, in looking forward or back he is clearly aware of what he is doing, in bending and stretching he is clearly aware of what he is doing, in carrying his inner and outer robe and his bowl he is clearly aware of what he is doing, in eating, drinking, chewing and savouring he is clearly aware of what he is doing, in passing excrement or urine he is clearly aware of what he is doing, in walking, standing,

sitting, falling asleep and waking up, in speaking or in staying silent, he is clearly aware of what he is doing.

"So he abides contemplating body as body internally, externally, and both internally and externally . . . And he abides independent, not clinging to anything in the world. And that, monks, is how a monk abides contemplating body as body."

(4. Reflection on the Repulsive: Parts of the Body)

5. "Again, a monk reviews this very body from the soles of the feet upwards and from the scalp downwards, enclosed by the skin and full of manifold impurities: 'In this body there are head-hairs, body-hairs, nails, teeth, skin, flesh, sinews, bones, bone-marrow, kidneys, heart, liver, pleura, spleen, lungs, mesentery, bowels, stomach, excrement, bile, phlegm, pus, blood, sweat, fat, tears, tallow, saliva, snot, synovic fluid, urine.' Just as if there were a bag, open at both ends, full of various kinds of grain such as hill-rice, paddy, green gram, kidney-beans, sesame, husked rice, and a man with good eyesight were to open the bag and examine them, saying: 'This is hill-rice, this is paddy, this is green gram, these are kidney-beans, this is sesame, this is husked rice,' so too a monk reviews this very body: "In this body there are head-hairs, . . . urine.'

"So he abides contemplating body as body internally, externally, and both internally and externally . . . And he abides independent, not clinging to anything in the world. And that, monks, is how a monk abides contemplating body as body."

(5. The Four Elements)

6. "Again, a monk reviews this body, however it may be placed or disposed, in terms of the elements: 'There are in this body the earth-element, the water-element, the fire-element, the air-element.' Just as

if a skilled butcher or his assistant, having slaughtered a cow, were to sit at a crossroads with the carcass divided into portions, so a monk reviews this very body . . . in terms of the elements: "There are in this body the earth-element, the water-element, the fire-element, the air-element.'

"So he abides contemplating body as body internally . . . And he abides independent, not clinging to anything in the world. And that, monks, is how a monk abides contemplating body as body."

(6. The Nine Charnel-Ground Contemplations)

7. "Again, a monk, as if he were to see a corpse thrown aside in a charnel-ground, one, two or three days dead, bloated, discoloured, festering, compares this body with that, thinking: 'This body is of the same nature, it will become like that, it is not exempt from that fate.'

"So he abides contemplating body as body internally, externally, and both internally and externally. And he abides independent, not clinging to anything in the world. And that, monks, is how a monk abides contemplating body as body.

8. "Again, a monk, as if he were to see a corpse in a charnel-ground, thrown aside, eaten by crows, hawks or vultures, by dogs or jackals, or various other creatures, compares this body with that, thinking: 'This body is of the same nature, it will become like that, it is not exempt from that fate.'

9. "Again, a monk, as if he were to see a corpse in a charnel-ground, thrown aside, a skeleton with flesh and blood, connected by sinews, . . . a fleshless skeleton smeared with blood, connected by sinews, . . . a skeleton detached from the flesh and blood, connected by sinews, . . . randomly connected bones, scattered in all directions, a hand-bone here, a foot-bone there, a shin-bone here, a thigh-bone there,

a hip-bone here, a spine here, a skull there, compares this body with that . . .

10. "Again, a monk, as if he were to see a corpse in a charnel-ground, thrown aside, the bones whitened, looking like shells . . . , the bones piled up, a year old . . . , the bones rotted away to a powder, compares this body with that, thinking: 'This body is of the same nature, will become like that, is not exempt from that fate.'"

(INSIGHT)

"So he abides contemplating body as body internally, contemplating body as body externally, abides contemplating body as body both internally and externally. He abides contemplating arising phenomena in the body, contemplating vanishing phenomena in the body, he abides contemplating both arising and vanishing phenomena in the body. Or else, mindfulness that 'there is body' is present to him just to the extent necessary for knowledge and awareness. And he abides independent, not clinging to anything in the world. And that, monks, is how a monk abides contemplating body as body."

(CONTEMPLATION OF FEELINGS)

11. "And how, monks, does a monk abide contemplating feelings as feelings? Here, a monk feeling a pleasant feeling knows that he feels a pleasant feeling; feeling a painful feeling he knows that he feels a painful feeling; . . . feeling a feeling that is neither-painful-nor-pleasant he knows that he feels a feeling that is neither-painful-nor-pleasant; feeling a pleasant sensual feeling he knows that he feels a pleasant sensual feeling; feeling a pleasant non-sensual feeling he knows that he feels a pleasant non-sensual

feeling; feeling a painful sensual feeling . . . ; feeling a painful non-sensual feeling . . . ; feeling a sensual feeling that is neither-painful-nor-pleasant . . . ; feeling a non-sensual feeling that is neither-painful-nor-pleasant, he knows that he feels a non-sensual feeling that is neither painful-nor-pleasant.''

(INSIGHT)

"So he abides contemplating feelings as feelings internally. He abides contemplating feelings as feelings externally . . . He abides contemplating arising phenomena in the feelings, vanishing phenomena and both arising and vanishing phenomena in the feelings. Or else, mindfulness that 'there is feeling' is present to him just to the extent necessary for knowledge and awareness. And he abides independent, not clinging to anything in the world. And that, monks, is how a monk abides contemplating feelings as feelings.''

(CONTEMPLATION OF MIND)

12. "And how, monks, does a monk abide contemplating mind as mind? Here, a monk knows a lustful mind as lustful, a mind free from lust as free from lust; a hating mind as hating, a mind free from hate as free from hate; a deluded mind as deluded, an undeluded mind as undeluded; a contracted mind as contracted, a distracted mind as distracted; a developed mind as developed, an undeveloped mind as undeveloped; a surpassed mind as surpassed, an unsurpassed mind as unsurpassed; a concentrated mind as concentrated, an unconcentrated mind as unconcentrated; a liberated mind as liberated, an unliberated mind as unliberated.''

(INSIGHT)

"So he abides contemplating mind as mind internally. He abides contemplating mind as mind externally . . . He abides contemplating arising phenomena in the mind . . . Or else, mindfulness that 'there is mind' is present just to the extent necessary for knowledge and awareness. And he abides detached, not grasping at anything in the world. And that, monks, is how a monk abides contemplating mind as mind."

(CONTEMPLATION OF MIND-OBJECTS)

13. "And how, monks, does a monk abide contemplating mind-objects as mind-objects?"

(1. The Five Hindrances)

"Here, a monk abides contemplating mind-objects as mind-objects in respect of the five hindrances. How does he do so? Here, monks, if sensual desire is present in himself, a monk knows that it is present. If sensual desire is absent in himself, a monk knows that it is absent. And he knows how unarisen sensual desire comes to arise, and he knows how the abandonment of arisen sensual desire comes about, and he knows how the non-arising of the abandoned sensual desire in the future will come about.

"If ill-will is present in himself, a monk knows that it is present . . . And he knows how the non-arising of the abandoned ill-will in the future will come about.

"If sloth-and-torpor is present in himself, a monk knows that it is present . . . And he knows how the non-arising of the abandoned sloth-and-torpor in the future will come about.

"If worry-and-flurry is present in himself, a monk knows that it is present . . . And he knows how the non-arising of the abandoned worry-and-flurry in the future will come about.

"If doubt is present in himself, a monk knows that it is present. If doubt is absent in himself, he knows that it is absent. And he knows how unarisen doubt comes to arise, and he knows how the abandonment of arisen doubt comes about, and he knows how the non-arising of the abandoned doubt in the future will come about."

(INSIGHT)

"So he abides contemplating mind-objects as mind-objects internally . . . He abides contemplating arising phenomena in mind-objects . . . Or else, mindfulness that 'there are mind-objects' is present just to the extent necessary for knowledge and awareness. And he abides detached, not grasping at anything in the world. And that, monks, is how a monk abides contemplating mind-objects as mind-objects in respect of the five hindrances."

(2. The Five Aggregates)

14. "Again, monks, a monk abides contemplating mind-objects as mind-objects in respect of the five aggregates of grasping. How does he do so? Here, a monk thinks: 'Such is form, such the arising of form, such the disappearance of form; such is feeling, such the arising of feeling, such the disappearance of feeling; such is perception, such the arising of perception, such the disappearance of perception; such are the mental formations, such the arising of the mental formations, such the disappearance of the mental formations; such is consciousness, such the arising of consciousness, such the disappearance of consciousness."

(INSIGHT)

"So he abides contemplating mind-objects as mind-objects internally . . . And he abides detached, not grasping at anything in the
world. And that, monks, is how a monk abides contemplating mind-
objects as mind-objects in respect of the five aggregates of grasping."

(3. The Six Internal and External Sense-Bases)

15. "Again, monks, a monk abides contemplating mind-objects as
mind-objects in respect of the six internal and external sense-bases. How
does he do so? Here a monk knows the eye, knows sight-objects, and
he knows whatever fetter arises dependent on the two. And he knows
how an unarisen fetter comes to arise, and he knows how the abandonment of an arisen fetter comes about, and he knows how the non-arising
of the abandoned fetter in the future will come about. He knows the
ear and knows sounds . . . He knows the nose, and knows smells . . .
He knows the tongue and knows tastes . . . He knows the body and
knows tangibles . . . He knows the mind and knows mind-objects, and
he knows whatever fetter arises dependent on the two. And he knows
how an unarisen fetter comes to arise, and he knows how the abandonment of an arisen fetter comes about, and he knows how the non-arising
of the abandoned fetter in the future will come about."

(INSIGHT)

"So he abides contemplating mind-objects as mind-objects internally . . . And he abides detached, not grasping at anything in the world.
And that, monks, is how a monk abides contemplating mind-objects as
mind-objects in respect of the six internal and external sense-bases."

(4. The Seven Factors of Enlightenment)

16. "Again, monks, a monk abides contemplating mind-objects as mind-objects in respect of the seven factors of enlightenment. How does he do so? Here, monks, if the enlightenment-factor of mindfulness is present in himself, a monk knows that it is present. If the enlightenment-factor of mindfulness is absent in himself, he knows that it is absent. And he knows how the unarisen enlightenment-factor of mindfulness comes to arise, and he knows how the complete development of the enlightenment-factor of mindfulness comes about. If the enlightenment-factor of investigation-of-states is present in himself . . . If the enlightenment-factor of energy is present in himself . . . If the enlightenment-factor of delight is present in himself . . . If the enlightenment-factor of tranquillity is present in himself . . . If the enlightenment-factor of concentration is present in himself . . . If the enlightenment-factor of equanimity is present in himself, a monk knows that it is present. If the enlightenment-factor of equanimity is absent in himself, he knows that it is absent. And he knows how the unarisen enlightenment-factor of equanimity comes to arise, and he knows how the complete development of the enlightenment-factor of equanimity comes about."

(INSIGHT)

"So he abides contemplating mind-objects as mind-objects internally . . . And he abides detached, not grasping at anything in the world. And that, monks, is how a monk abides contemplating mind-objects as mind-objects in respect of the seven factors of enlightenment."

(5. The Four Noble Truths [see pages 74–75 for full text])

17. "Again, monks, a monk abides contemplating mind-objects as mind-objects in respect of the Four Noble Truths. How does he do so?

Here, a monk knows as it really is: 'This is suffering'; he knows as it really is: 'This is the origin of suffering'; he knows as it really is: 'This is the cessation of suffering'; he knows as it really is: 'This is the way of practice leading to the cessation of suffering' ''. . . .

21. "And what, monks, is the Noble Truth of the Way of Practice Leading to the Cessation of Suffering? It is just this Noble Eightfold Path [see also pages 85–102 for full text], namely: Right View, Right Thought; Right Speech, Right Action, Right Livelihood; Right Effort, Right Mindfulness, Right Concentration. . . .

(INSIGHT)

"So he abides contemplating mind-objects as mind-objects internally, contemplating mind-objects as mind-objects externally, contemplating mind-objects as mind-objects both internally and externally. He abides contemplating arising phenomena in mind-objects, he abides contemplating vanishing phenomena in mind-objects, he abides contemplating both arising and vanishing phenomena in mind-objects. Or else, mindfulness that 'there are mind-objects' is present just to the extent necessary for knowledge and awareness. And he abides detached, not grasping at anything in the world. And that, monks, is how a monk abides contemplating mind-objects as mind-objects in respect of the Four Noble Truths."

(CONCLUSION)

22. "Whoever, monks, should practise these four foundations of mindfulness for just seven years may expect one of two results: either Arahantship in this life or, if there should be some substrate left, the

state of a Non-Returner. Let alone seven years—whoever should practise them for just six years . . . five years . . . four years . . . three years . . . two years . . . one year may expect one of two results . . . ; let alone one year—whoever should practise them for just seven months . . . six months . . . five months . . . four months . . . three months . . . two months . . . one month . . . half a month may expect one of two results . . . ; let alone half a month—whoever should practise these four foundations of mindfulness for just one week may expect one of two results: either Arahantship in this life or, if there should be some substrate left, the state of a Non-Returner.

"It was said: 'There is, monks, this one way to the purification of beings, for the overcoming of sorrow and distress, for the disappearance of pain and sadness, for the gaining of the right path, for the realisation of Nibbana—that is to say the four foundations of mindfulness,' and it is for this reason that it was said."

Thus the Lord spoke, and the monks rejoiced and were delighted at his words.

Stephen Batchelor

Foundations of Mindfulness

The origins of [mindful awareness] practice are found in Gautama's own discourse on the "Foundations of Mindfulness" (*Satipatthana Sutta*) in the Pali Canon. It has been described as "the most important discourse ever given by the Buddha on mental development," and as such is highly revered in all Theravada Buddhist countries of Asia. The Buddha opened the discourse by declaring:

> *There is, monks, this way that leads only to the purification of beings, to the overcoming of sorrow and distress, to the disappearance of pain and sadness, to the gaining of the right path, to the realization of Nirvana—that is to say the four foundations of Mindfulness.*

These four foundations are the four areas of life to which mindful awareness needs to be applied: body, feelings, mind and objects of mind. In other words, the totality of experience.

The Buddha recommends that a person retire to a forest, the root of a tree or a solitary place, sit cross-legged with body erect and then turn his or her attention to their breath. Then, "mindfully he breathes in, mindfully he breathes out. Breathing in a long breath, he knows that he breathes in a long breath, and breathing out a long breath, he knows that he breathes out a long breath." There is no attempt to control the breath or in any way interfere with the immediacy of experience as it unfolds. If the breath is long, one recognizes it to be long; if short, one recognizes it to be short.

Yet for many this seemingly straightforward exercise turns out to be remarkably tricky. One finds that no matter how sincere one's intention to be attentive and aware, the mind rebels against such instructions and races off to indulge in all manner of distractions, memories and fantasies. One is forced to confront the sobering truth that one is only notionally "in charge" of one's psychological life. The comforting illusion of personal coherence and continuity is ripped away to expose only fragmentary islands of consciousness separated by yawning gulfs of unawareness. Similarly, the convenient fiction of a well-adjusted, consistent personality turns out to be merely a skillfully edited and censored version of a turbulent psyche. The first step in this practice of mindful awareness is radical self-acceptance.

Such self-acceptance, however, does not operate in an ethical vacuum, where no moral assessment is made of one's emotional states. The training in mindful awareness is part of a Buddhist path with values and goals. Emotional states are evaluated according to whether they increase or decrease the potential for suffering. If an emotion, such as hatred or envy, is judged to be destructive, then it is simply recognized as such. It is neither expressed through violent thoughts, words or deeds, nor is it suppressed or denied as incompatible with a "spiritual" life. In seeing it for what it is—a transient emotional state—one mindfully observes it follow its own nature: to arise, abide for a while, and then pass away.

The Buddha described his teaching as "going against the stream." The unflinching light of mindful awareness reveals the extent to which we are tossed along in the stream of past conditioning and habit. The moment we decide to stop and look at what is going on (like a swimmer suddenly changing course to swim upstream instead of downstream), we find ourselves battered by powerful currents we had never even suspected—precisely because until that moment we were largely living at their command.

The practice of mindful awareness is a first step in the direction of inner freedom. Disciplining oneself to focus attention single-mindedly on the breath (for example) enables one to become progressively more quiet and concentrated. Such stillness, though, is not an end in itself. It serves as a platform from which to observe more clearly what is taking place within us. It allows the steady depth of awareness needed to understand the very origins of conditioning: namely, how delusion and craving are at the top of human suffering. Such meditative understanding is experiential rather than intellectual, therapeutic rather than dogmatic, liberating rather than merely convincing.

The aim of mindful awareness is the understanding that frees one from delusion and craving. In Pali, such understanding is called *vipassana* ("penetrative seeing"), and it is under this name that the traditional practice of mindful awareness is frequently presented in the West today. *Vipassana* is often translated as "insight" and courses are offered on "insight meditation."

This usage has given rise to some confusion. It has led to the impression that some Buddhists practice *vipassana,* while others (such as practitioners of Zen or Tibetan Buddhism) do not. In fact, *vipassana* is central to all forms of Buddhist meditation practice. The distinctive goal of any Buddhist contemplative tradition is a state in which inner calm (*samatha*) is unified with insight (*vipassana*). Over the centuries, each tradition has developed its own methods for actualizing this state. And it is in these methods that the traditions differ, *not* in their end objective of unified calm and insight.

BHIKKHU NANAMOLI AND BHIKKHU BODHI, TRANS.

The Greater Discourse of Advice to Rahula

1. Thus have I heard. On one occasion the Blessed One was living at Savatthi in Jeta's Grove, Anathapindika's Park.

2. Then, when it was morning, the Blessed One dressed, and taking his bowl and outer robe, went into Savatthi for alms. The venerable Rahula [his son] also dressed, and taking his bowl and outer robe, followed close behind the Blessed One.

3. Then the Blessed One looked back and addressed the venerable Rahula thus: "Rahula, any kind of material form whatever, whether past, future, or present, internal or external, gross or subtle, inferior or superior, far or near, all material form should be seen as it actually is with proper wisdom thus: 'This is not mine, this I am not, this is not my self.' "

"Only material form, Blessed One? Only material form, Sublime One?"

"Material form, Rahula, and feeling, perception, formations, and consciousness."

4. Then the venerable Rahula considered thus: "Who would go into the town for alms today when personally admonished by the Blessed One?" Thus he turned back and sat down at the root of a tree, folding his legs crosswise, setting his body erect, and establishing mindfulness in front of him.

5. The venerable Sariputta saw him sitting there and addressed him thus: "Rahula, develop mindfulness of breathing. When mindfulness of breathing is developed and cultivated, it is of great fruit and great benefit."

6. Then, when it was evening, the venerable Rahula rose from meditation and went to the Blessed One. After paying homage to him, he sat down at one side and asked the Blessed One: "Venerable sir, how is mindfulness of breathing developed and cultivated, so that it is of great fruit and great benefit?"

(THE FOUR GREAT ELEMENTS)

8. "Rahula, whatever internally, belonging to oneself, is solid, solidified, and clung-to, that is, head-hairs, body-hairs, nails, teeth, skin, flesh, sinews, bones, bone-marrow, kidneys, heart, liver, diaphragm, spleen, lungs, large intestines, small intestines, contents of the stomach, feces, or whatever else internally, belonging to oneself, is solid, solidified, and clung-to: this is called the internal earth element. Now both the internal earth element and the external earth element are simply earth element. And that should be seen as it actually is with proper wisdom thus: 'This is not mine, this I am not, this is not my self.' When one sees it thus as it actually is with proper wisdom, one becomes disenchanted with the earth element and makes the mind dispassionate towards the earth element.

9. "What, Rahula, is the water element? The water element may be either internal or external. What is the internal water element? Whatever internally, belonging to oneself, is water, watery, and clung-to, that is, bile, phlegm, pus, blood, sweat, fat, tears, grease, spittle, snot, oil-of-the-joints, urine, or whatever else internally, belonging to oneself, is water, watery, and clung-to: this is called the internal water element. Now both the internal water element and the external water element are simply water element. And that should be seen as it actually is with proper wisdom thus: 'This is not mine, this I am not, this is not my self.' When one sees it thus as it actually is with proper wisdom, one becomes disenchanted with the water element and makes the mind dispassionate towards the water element.

10. "What, Rahula, is the fire element? The fire element may be either internal or external. What is the internal fire element? Whatever internally, belonging to oneself, is fire, fiery, and clung-to, that is, that

by which one is warmed, . . . and is consumed, and that by which what is eaten, drunk, consumed, and tasted gets completely digested, or whatever else internally, belonging to oneself, is fire, fiery, and clung-to: this is called the internal fire element. Now both the internal fire element and the external fire element are simply fire element. And that should be seen as it actually is with proper wisdom thus: 'This is not mine, this I am not, this is not my self.' When one sees it thus as it actually is with proper wisdom, one becomes disenchanted with the fire element and makes the mind dispassionate towards the fire element.

11. "What, Rahula, is the air element? The air element may be either internal or external. What is the internal air element? Whatever internally, belonging to oneself, is air, airy, and clung-to, that is, up-going winds, down-going winds, winds in the belly, winds in the bowels, winds that course through the limbs, in-breath and out-breath, or whatever else internally, belonging to oneself, is air, airy, and clung-to: this is called the internal air element. Now both the internal air element and the external air element are simply air element. And that should be seen as it actually is with proper wisdom thus: 'This is not mine, this I am not, this is not my self.' When one sees it thus as it actually is with proper wisdom, one becomes disenchanted with the air element and makes the mind dispassionate towards the air element.

12. "What, Rahula, is the space element? The space element may be either internal or external. What is the internal space element? Whatever internally, belonging to oneself, is space, spatial, and clung-to, that is, the holes of the ears, the nostrils, the door of the mouth, and that [aperture] whereby what is eaten, drunk, consumed, and tasted gets swallowed, and where it collects, and whereby it is excreted from below, or whatever else internally, belonging to oneself, is space, spatial, and clung-to: this is called the internal space element. Now both the

internal space element and the external space element are simply space element. And that should be seen as it actually is with proper wisdom thus: 'This is not mine, this I am not, this is not my self.' When one sees it thus as it actually is with proper wisdom, one becomes disenchanted with the space element and makes the mind dispassionate towards the space element.

13. "Rahula, develop meditation that is like the earth; for when you develop meditation that is like the earth, arisen agreeable and disagreeable contacts will not invade your mind and remain. Just as people throw clean things and dirty things, excrement, urine, spittle, pus, and blood on the earth, and the earth is not horrified, humiliated, and disgusted because of that, so too, Rahula, develop meditation that is like the earth; for when you develop meditation that is like the earth, arisen agreeable and disagreeable contacts will not invade your mind and remain.

14. "Rahula, develop meditation that is like water; for when you develop meditation that is like water, arisen agreeable and disagreeable contacts will not invade your mind and remain. Just as people wash clean things and dirty things, excrement, urine, spittle, pus, and blood in water, and the water is not horrified, humiliated, and disgusted because of that, so too, Rahula, develop meditation that is like water; for when you develop meditation that is like water, arisen agreeable and disagreeable contacts will not invade your mind and remain.

15. "Rahula, develop meditation that is like fire; for when you develop meditation that is like fire, arisen agreeable and disagreeable contacts will not invade your mind and remain. Just as people burn clean things and dirty things, excrement, urine, spittle, pus, and blood in fire, and the fire is not horrified, humiliated, and disgusted because

of that, so too, Rahula, develop meditation that is like fire; for when you develop meditation that is like fire, arisen agreeable and disagreeable contacts will not invade your mind and remain.

16. "Rahula, develop meditation that is like air; for when you develop meditation that is like air, arisen agreeable and disagreeable contacts will not invade your mind and remain. Just as the air blows on clean things and dirty things, on excrement, urine, spittle, pus, and blood, and the air is not horrified, humiliated, and disgusted because of that, so too, Rahula, develop meditation that is like air; for when you develop meditation that is like air, arisen agreeable and disagreeable contacts will not invade your mind and remain.

17. "Rahula, develop meditation that is like space; for when you develop meditation that is like space, arisen agreeable and disagreeable contacts will not invade your mind and remain. Just as space is not established anywhere, so too, Rahula, develop meditation that is like space; for when you develop meditation that is like space, arisen agreeable and disagreeable contacts will not invade your mind and remain.

18. "Rahula, develop meditation on loving-kindness; for when you develop meditation on loving-kindness, any ill will will be abandoned.

19. "Rahula, develop meditation on compassion; for when you develop meditation on compassion, any cruelty will be abandoned.

20. "Rahula, develop meditation on appreciative joy; for when you develop meditation on appreciative joy, any discontent will be abandoned.

21. "Rahula, develop meditation on equanimity; for when you develop meditation on equanimity, any aversion will be abandoned.

22. "Rahula, develop meditation on foulness; for when you develop meditation on foulness, any lust will be abandoned.

23. "Rahula, develop meditation on the perception of impermanence; for when you develop meditation on the perception of impermanence, the conceit 'I am' will be abandoned.

24. "Rahula, develop meditation on mindfulness of breathing. When mindfulness of breathing is developed and cultivated, it is of great fruit and great benefit. And how is mindfulness of breathing developed and cultivated, so that it is of great fruit and great benefit?

25. "Here, Rahula, a bhikkhu, gone to the forest or to the root of a tree or to an empty hut, sits down; having folded his legs crosswise, set his body erect, and established mindfulness in front of him, ever mindful he breathes in, mindful he breathes out.

26. "Breathing in long, he understands: 'I breathe in long'; or breathing out long, he understands: 'I breathe out long.' Breathing in short, he understands: 'I breathe in short'; or breathing out short, he understands: 'I breathe out short.' He trains thus: 'I shall breathe in experiencing the whole body [of breath]'; he trains thus: 'I shall breathe out experiencing the whole body [of breath].' He trains thus: 'I shall breathe in tranquilizing the bodily formation'; he trains thus: 'I shall breathe out tranquilizing the bodily formation.'

27. "He trains thus: 'I shall breathe in experiencing rapture'; he trains thus: 'I shall breathe out experiencing rapture.' He trains thus: 'I shall breathe in experiencing pleasure'; he trains thus: 'I shall breathe out experiencing pleasure.' He trains thus: 'I shall breathe in experiencing the mental formation'; he trains thus: 'I shall breathe out expe-

riencing the mental formation.' He trains thus: 'I shall breathe in tranquilizing the mental formation'; he trains thus: 'I shall breathe out tranquilizing the mental formation.'

28. "He trains thus: 'I shall breathe in experiencing the mind'; he trains thus: 'I shall breathe out experiencing the mind.' He trains thus: 'I shall breathe in gladdening the mind'; he trains thus: 'I shall breathe out gladdening the mind.' He trains thus: 'I shall breathe in concentrating the mind'; he trains thus: 'I shall breathe out concentrating the mind.' He trains thus: 'I shall breathe in liberating the mind'; he trains thus: 'I shall breathe out liberating the mind.'

29. "He trains thus: 'I shall breathe in contemplating impermanence'; he trains thus: 'I shall breathe out contemplating impermanence.' He trains thus: 'I shall breathe in contemplating fading away'; he trains thus: 'I shall breathe out contemplating fading away.' He trains thus: 'I shall breathe in contemplating cessation'; he trains thus: 'I shall breathe out contemplating cessation.' He trains thus: 'I shall breathe in contemplating relinquishment'; he trains thus: 'I shall breathe out contemplating relinquishment.'

30. "Rahula, that is how mindfulness of breathing is developed and cultivated, so that it is of great fruit and great benefit. When mindfulness of breathing is developed and cultivated in this way, even the final in-breaths and out-breaths are known as they cease, not unknown."

That is what the Blessed One said. The venerable Rahula was satisfied and delighted in the Blessed One's words.

THICH NHAT HANH

Necessary Awareness

I REMEMBER A short conversation between the Buddha and a philosopher of his time.

"I have heard that Buddhism is a doctrine of enlightenment. What is your method? What do you practice every day?"

"We walk, we eat, we wash ourselves, we sit down."

"What is so special about that? Everyone walks, eats, washes, sits down . . ."

"Sir, when we walk, we are aware that we are walking; when we eat, we are aware that we are eating. . . . When others walk, eat, wash, or sit down, they are generally not aware of what they are doing."

In Buddhism, mindfulness is the key. Mindfulness is the energy that sheds light on all things and all activities, producing the power of concentration, bringing forth deep insight and awakening. Mindfulness is at the base of all Buddhist practice.

To shed light on all things? This is the point of departure. If I live without mindfulness, in forgetfulness, I am, as Albert Camus says in his novel *The Stranger,* living "like a dead person." The ancient Zen masters used to say, "If we live in forgetfulness, we die in a dream." How many among us live "like a dead person"! The first thing we have to do is to return to life, to wake up and be mindful of each thing we do. Are we aware when we are eating, drinking, sitting in meditation? Or are we wasting our time, living in forgetfulness?

To produce the power of concentration? Mindfulness helps us focus our attention on and know what we are doing. Usually we are a prisoner of society. Our energies are dispersed here and there. Our body and our mind are not in harmony. To begin to be aware of what we are doing, saying, and thinking is to begin to resist the invasion by our surroundings and by all of our wrong perceptions. When the lamp of awareness is lit, our whole being lights up, and each passing thought and emotion is also lit up. Self-confidence is reestablished, the shadows of illusion no longer overwhelm us, and our concentration develops to its fullest. We wash our hands, dress, perform everyday actions as before, but now we are *aware* of our actions, words, and thoughts.

The practice of mindfulness is not only for novices. It is a lifelong practice for everyone, even the Buddha himself. The power of mindfulness and concentration is the spiritual force behind all of the great men and women of human history.

To bring forth deep insight and awakening? The aim of Zen Buddhism is a clear vision of reality, seeing things as they are, and that is acquired by the power of concentration. This clear vision is enlightenment. Enlightenment is always enlightenment about something. It is not abstract.

EIHEI DOGEN

(THIRTEENTH CENTURY)

The Principles of Zazen

THE WAY IS basically perfect and all-pervading. How could it be contingent upon practice and realization? The Dharma-vehicle is free and untrammeled. What need is there for man's concentrated effort? Indeed, the Whole Body is far beyond the world's dust. Who could believe in a means to brush it clean? It is never apart from one right where one is. What is the use of going off here and there to practice?

And yet, if there is the slightest discrepancy, the Way is as distant as heaven from earth. If the least like or dislike arises, the Mind is lost in confusion. Suppose one gains pride of understanding and inflates one's own enlightenment, glimpsing the wisdom that runs through all things, attaining the Way and clarifying the Mind, raising an aspiration to escalade the very sky. One is making the initial, partial excursions about the frontiers but is still somewhat deficient in the vital Way of total emancipation.

Need I mention the Buddha, who was possessed of inborn knowledge?—the influence of his six years of upright sitting is noticeable still. Or Bodhidharma's transmission of the mind-seal?—the fame of his nine years of wall-sitting is celebrated to this day. Since this was the case with the saints of old, how can men of today dispense with negotiation of the Way?

You should therefore cease from practice based on intellectual understanding, pursuing words and following after speech, and learn the backward step that turns your light inwardly to illuminate your self. Body and mind of themselves will drop away, and your original face will be manifest. If you want to attain suchness, you should practice suchness without delay.

For *sanzen* [zazen], a quiet room is suitable. Eat and drink moderately. Cast aside all involvements and cease all affairs. Do not think good or bad. Do not administer pros and cons. Cease all the movements of the conscious mind, the gauging of all thoughts and views. Have no designs on becoming a buddha. Zazen has nothing whatever to do with sitting or lying down.

At the site of your regular sitting, spread out thick matting and place a cushion above it. Sit either in the Full Lotus or Half Lotus position. In the Full Lotus position, you first place your right foot on your left thigh and your left foot on your right thigh. In the Half Lotus, you simply press your left foot against your right thigh. You should have your robes and belt loosely bound and arranged in order. Then place your right hand on your left leg and your left palm [facing upward] on your right palm, thumb-tips touching. Thus sit upright in correct bodily posture, neither inclining to the left nor to the right, neither leaning forward nor backward. Be sure your ears are on a plane with your shoulders and your nose in line with your navel. Place your tongue against the front roof of your mouth, with teeth and lips both shut. Your eyes should always remain open, and you should breathe gently through your nose.

Once you have adjusted your posture, take a deep breath, inhale and exhale, rock your body right and left, and settle into a steady, immobile sitting position. Think of not-thinking. How do you think of not-thinking? Non-thinking. This in itself is the essential art of zazen.

The zazen I speak of is not learning meditation. It is simply the dharma-gate of repose and bliss, the practice-realization of totally culminated enlightenment. It is the manifestation of ultimate reality. Traps and snares can never reach it. Once its heart is grasped, you are like the dragon when he gains the water, like the tiger when he enters the mountain. For you must know that just there [in zazen] the right dharma is manifesting itself and that from the first dullness and distraction are struck aside.

When you arise from sitting, move slowly and quietly, calmly and deliberately. Do not rise suddenly or abruptly. In surveying the past we find that transcendence of both unenlightenment and enlightenment, and dying while either sitting or standing, have all depended entirely on the strength [of zazen].

In addition, the bringing about of enlightenment by the opportunity provided by a finger, a banner, a needle, or a mallet, and the effecting of realization with the aid of a *hossu* [a whisk used by monks to sweep small animals off their path], a fist, a staff, or a shout, cannot be fully understood by man's discriminative thinking. Indeed, it cannot be fully known by the practicing or realizing of supernatural powers either. It must be deportment beyond man's hearing and seeing—is it not a principle that is prior to his knowledge and perceptions?

This being the case, intelligence or lack of it does not matter; between the dull and the sharp-witted there is no distinction. If you concentrate your effort single-mindedly, that in itself is negotiating the Way. Practice-realization is naturally undefiled. Going forward is a matter of everydayness.

SHUNRYU SUZUKI

Practicing Zazen

WHEN WE PRACTICE zazen our mind always follows our breathing. When we inhale, the air comes into the inner world. When we exhale, the air goes out to the outer world. The inner world is limitless, and the outer world is also limitless. We say "inner world" or "outer world," but actually there is just one whole world. In this limitless world, our throat is like a swinging door. The air comes in and goes out like someone passing through a swinging door. If you think, "I breathe," the "I" is extra. There is no you to say "I." What we call "I" is just a swinging door which moves when we inhale and when we exhale. It just moves; that is all. When your mind is pure and calm enough to follow this movement, there is nothing: no "I," no world, no mind nor body; just a swinging door.

So when we practice zazen, all that exists is the movement of the breathing, but we are aware of this movement. You should not be absentminded. But to be aware of the movement does not mean to be aware of your small self, but rather of your universal nature, or Buddha nature. This kind of awareness is very important, because we are usually so one-sided. Our usual understanding of life is dualistic: you and I, this and that, good and bad. But actually these discriminations are themselves the awareness of the universal existence. "You" means to be aware of the universe in the form of you, and "I" means to be aware of it in the form of I. You and I are just swinging doors. This kind of understanding is necessary. This should not even be called understanding; it is actually the true experience of life through Zen practice.

So when you practice zazen, there is no idea of time or space. You may say, "We started sitting at a quarter to six in this room." Thus you have some idea of time (a quarter to six), and some idea of space (in this room). Actually what you are doing, however, is just sitting and being aware of the universal activity. That is all. This moment the swinging door is opening in one direction, and the next moment the swinging door will be opening in the opposite direction. Moment after moment each one of us repeats this activity. Here there is no idea of time or space. Time and space are one. You may say, "I must do something this afternoon," but actually there is no "this afternoon." We do things one after the other. That is all. There is no such time as "this afternoon" or "one o'clock" or "two o'clock." At one o'clock you will eat your lunch. To eat lunch is itself one o'clock. You will be somewhere, but that place cannot be separated from one o'clock. For someone who actually appreciates our life, they are the same. But when we become tired of our life we may say, "I shouldn't have come to this place. It may have been much better to have gone to some other place for lunch. This place is not so good." In your mind you create an idea of place separate from an actual time.

Or you may say, "This is bad, so I should not do this." Actually, when you say, "I should not do this," you are doing not-doing in that moment. So there is no choice for you. When you separate the idea of time and space, you feel as if you have some choice, but actually, you have to do something, or you have to do not-doing. Not-to-do something is doing something. Good and bad are only in your mind. So we should not say, "This is good," or "This is bad." Instead of saying bad, you should say, "not-to-do"! If you think, "This is bad," it will create some confusion for you. So in the realm of pure religion there is no confusion of time and space, or good or bad. All that we should do is just do something as it comes. Do something! Whatever it is, we should do it, even if it is not-doing something. We should live in this moment. So when we sit we concentrate on our breathing, and we become a swinging door, and we do something we should do, something we must do. This is Zen practice. In this practice there is no confusion. If you establish this kind of life you have no confusion whatsoever.

Tozan, a famous Zen master, said, "The blue mountain is the father of the white cloud. The white cloud is the son of the blue mountain. All day long they depend on each other, without being dependent on each other. The white cloud is always the white cloud. The blue mountain is always the blue mountain." This is a pure, clear interpretation of life. There may be many things like the white cloud and blue mountain: man and woman, teacher and disciple. They depend on each other. But the white cloud should not be bothered by the blue mountain. The blue mountain should not be bothered by the white cloud. They are quite independent, but yet dependent. This is how we live, and how we practice zazen.

When we become truly ourselves, we just become a swinging door, and we are purely independent of, and at the same time, dependent upon everything. Without air, we cannot breathe. Each one of us is in the midst of myriads of worlds. We are in the center of the world always, moment after moment. So we are completely dependent and independent. If you have this kind of experience, this kind of existence, you have absolute independence; you will not be bothered by anything. So when you practice zazen, your mind should be concentrated on your breathing. This kind of activity is the fundamental activity of the universal being. Without this experience, this practice, it is impossible to attain absolute freedom.

HENEPOLA GUNARATANA

Vipassana Meditation

THE DISTINCTION BETWEEN Vipassana meditation and other styles of meditation is crucial and needs to be fully understood. Buddhism addresses two major types of meditation. They are different mental skills, modes of functioning or qualities of consciousness. In Pali, the original language of Theravada literature, they are called *Vipassana* and *Samatha*.

Vipassana can be translated as "Insight," a clear awareness of exactly what is happening as it happens. *Samatha* can be translated as "concentration" or "tranquillity." It is a state in which the mind is brought to rest, focused only on one item and not allowed to wander. When this is done, a deep calm pervades body and mind, a state of tranquillity which must be experienced to be understood. Most systems of meditation emphasize the *Samatha* component. The meditator focuses his mind upon some items, such as prayer, a certain type of box, a chant, a candle flame, a religious image or whatever, and excludes all other thoughts and perceptions from his consciousness. The result is a state of rapture which lasts until the meditator ends the session of sitting. It is beautiful, delightful, meaningful and alluring, but only *temporary*. Vipassana meditation addresses the other component, insight.

The Vipassana meditator uses his concentration as a tool by which his awareness can chip away at the wall of illusion that cuts him off from the living light of reality. It is a gradual process of ever-increasing awareness into the inner workings of reality itself. It takes years, but one day the meditator chisels through that wall and tumbles into the presence of light. The transformation is complete. It's called Liberation, and it's permanent. Liberation is the goal of all Buddhist systems of practice. But the routes to the attainment of that end are quite diverse.

VIPASSANA IS THE oldest of Buddhist meditation practices. The method comes directly from the *Satipatthana Sutta* [Foundations of Mindfulness, pages 121–133], a discourse attributed to the Buddha himself. Vipassana is a direct and gradual cultivation of mindfulness or awareness. It proceeds piece by piece over a period of years. The student's attention is carefully directed to an intense examination of certain aspects of his own existence. The meditator is trained to notice more and more of his own flowing life experience. Vipassana is a gentle technique. But it also is very, very thorough. It is an ancient and codified system of training your mind, a set of exercises dedicated to becoming more and more aware of your own life experience. It is attentive listening, mindful seeing and careful testing. We learn to smell acutely, to touch fully, and [to] really pay attention to the changes taking place in all these experiences. We learn to listen to our own thoughts without being caught up in them. The object of Vipassana practice is to learn to see the truth of impermanence, unsatisfactoriness, and selflessness of phenomena. We think we are doing this already, but that is an illusion. It comes from the fact that we are paying so little attention to the ongoing surge of our own life experience that we might just as well be asleep. We are simply not paying enough attention to notice that we are not paying attention. It is another Catch-22.

Through the process of mindfulness, we slowly become aware of what we really are down below the ego image. We wake up to what life really is. It is not just a parade of ups and downs, lollipops and smacks on the wrist. That is an illusion. Life has a much deeper texture than that if we bother to look, and if we look in the right way.

Vipassana is a form of mental training that will teach you to experience the world in an entirely new way. You will learn for the first time what is truly happening to you, around you and within you. It is a process of self-discovery, a participatory investigation in which you observe your own experiences while participating in them as they occur. The practice must be approached with this attitude: "Never mind what I have been taught. Forget about theories and prejudices and stereotypes. I want to understand the true nature of life. I want to know what this experience of being alive really is. I want to apprehend the true and deepest qualities of life, and I don't want to just accept somebody else's explanation. I want to see it for myself."

If you pursue your meditation practice with this attitude, you will succeed. You'll find yourself observing things objectively, exactly as they are—flowing and changing from moment to moment. Life then takes on an unbelievable richness which cannot be described. It has to be experienced.

The Pali term for Insight meditation is *Vipassana Bhavana*. *Bhavana* comes from the root *bh*, which means to grow or to become. Therefore *Bhavana* means to cultivate, and the word is always used in reference to the mind. *Bhavana* means mental cultivation. *Vipassana* is derived from two roots. *Passana* means seeing or perceiving. *Vi* is a prefix with a complex set of connotations. The basic meaning is "in a special way." But there also is the connotation of both "into" and "through." The whole meaning of the word is looking into something with clarity and precision, seeing each component as distinct, and piercing all the way through so as to perceive the most fundamental reality of that thing. This process leads to insight into the basic reality of whatever is being inspected. Put it all together and *Vipassana Bhavana* means the cultivation of the mind, aimed at seeing in the special way that leads to insight and to full understanding. . . .

THE METHOD WE are explaining here . . . is probably what Gotama Buddha taught his students. The *Satipatthana Sutta,* the Buddha's original discourse on mindfulness, specifically says that one must begin by focusing the attention on the breathing and then go on to note all other physical and mental phenomena which arise.

We sit, watching the air going in and out of our noses. At first glance, this seems an exceedingly odd and useless procedure. Before going on to specific instructions, let us examine the reason behind it. The first question we might have is why use any focus of attention at all? We are, after all, trying to develop awareness. Why not just sit down and be aware of whatever happens to be present in the mind? In fact, there are meditations of that nature. They are sometimes referred to as unstructured meditation and they are quite difficult. The mind is tricky. Thought is an inherently complicated procedure. By that we mean that we become trapped, wrapped up, and stuck in the thought chain. One thought leads to another which leads to another, and another, and another, and so on. Fifteen minutes later we suddenly wake up and realize we spent that whole time stuck in a daydream or sexual fantasy or a set of worries about our bills or whatever . . .

We use breath as our focus. It serves as that vital reference point from which the mind wanders and is drawn back. Distraction cannot be seen as distraction unless there is some central focus to be distracted from. That is the frame of reference against which we can view the incessant changes and interruptions that go on all the time as a part of normal thinking.

Ancient Pali texts liken meditation to the process of taming a wild elephant. The procedure in those days was to tie a newly captured animal to a post with a good strong rope. When you do this, the elephant is not happy. He screams and tramples, and pulls against the rope for days. Finally it sinks through his skull that he can't get away, and he settles down. At this point you can begin to feed him and to handle him with some measure of safety. Eventually you can dispense with the rope and post altogether, and train your elephant for various tasks. Now you have got a tamed elephant that can be put to useful work. In this analogy the wild elephant is your wildly active mind, the rope is mindfulness, and the post is our object of meditation, our breathing. The tamed elephant who emerges from this process is a well-trained, concentrated mind that can then be used for the exceedingly tough job of piercing the layers of illusion that obscure reality. Meditation tames the mind.

The next question we need to address is: Why choose breathing as the primary object of meditation? Why not something a bit more interesting? Answers to this are numerous. A useful object of meditation should be one that promotes mindfulness. It should be portable, easily available, and cheap. It should also be something that will not embroil us in those states of mind from which we are trying to free ourselves, such as greed, anger, and delusion. Breathing satisfies all these criteria and more. Breathing is something common to every human being. We all carry it with us wherever we go. It is always there, constantly available, never ceasing from birth till death, and it costs nothing.

Breathing is a non-conceptual process, a thing that can be experienced directly without a need for thought. Furthermore, it is a very living process, an aspect of life that is in constant change. The breath moves in cycles—inhalation, exhalation, breathing in, and breathing out. Thus, it is a miniature model of life itself. . . .

Breath is a phenomenon common to all living things. A true experiential understanding of the process moves you closer to other living beings. It shows you your inherent connectedness with all of life. Finally, breathing is a present-time process. . . .

The first step in using the breath as an object of meditation is to find it. What you are looking for is the physical, tactile sensation of the air that passes in and out of the nostrils. This is usually just inside the tip of the nose. But the exact spot varies from one person to another, depending on the shape of the nose. To find your own point, take a quick deep breath and notice and point just inside the nose or on the upper tip where you have the most distinct sensation of passing air. Now exhale and notice the sensation at the same point. It is from this point that you will follow the whole passage of breath. . . .

When you first begin this procedure, expect to face some difficulties. Your mind will wander off constantly darting, around like a bumble bee and zooming off on wild tangents. Try not to worry. The monkey mind phenomenon is well known. It is something that every advanced meditator has had to deal with. They have pushed through it one way or another, and so can you. When it happens, just note the fact that you have been thinking, day-dreaming, worrying, or whatever. Gently, but firmly, without getting upset or judging yourself for straying, simply return to the simple physical sensation of the breath. Then do it again the next time, and again, and again, and again. . . .

This meditation is a process of retraining the mind. The state you are aiming for is one in which you are totally aware of everything that is happening in your own perceptual universe, exactly the way it happens, exactly when it is happening; total, unbroken awareness in present time. This is an incredibly high goal, and not to be reached all at once. It takes practice, so we start small. We start by becoming totally aware of one small unit of time, just one single inhalation. And, when you succeed, you are on your way to a whole new experience of life.

KATHLEEN MCDONALD

Tibetan Buddhist Meditation

SUBDUING THE MIND and bringing it to the right understanding of reality is no easy task. It requires a slow and gradual process of *listening* to and reading explanations on the mind and the nature of things; *thinking* about and carefully analyzing this information; and finally transforming the mind through *meditation*.

The mind can be divided into *sense consciousness*—sight, hearing, smell, taste and touch—and *mental consciousness*. Mental consciousness ranges from our grossest experiences of anger or desire, for example, to the subtlest level of complete stillness and clarity. It includes our intellectual processes, our feelings and emotions, our memory and our dreams.

Meditation is an activity of the mental consciousness. It involves one part of the mind observing, analyzing and dealing with the rest of the mind. Meditation can take many forms: concentrating single-pointedly on an (internal) object, trying to understand some personal problem, generating a joyful love for all humanity, praying to an object of devotion, or communicating with our own inner wisdom. Its ultimate aim is to awaken a very subtle level of consciousness and to use it to discover reality, directly and intuitively.

This direct, intuitive awareness of how things are is known as enlightenment and is the end result of Mahayana Buddhist practice. The purpose of reaching it—and the driving force behind all practice—is to help others reach it too.

The Tibetan term for meditation (*sgom*) means, literally, "to become familiar." There are many different meditation techniques and many things in the mind to become familiar with. Each technique has specific functions and benefits and each is a part of the framework for bringing our mind to a realistic view of the world.

It might be best to start by saying what meditation is *not*, because there are many misunderstandings about it. For one thing, meditation is not simply a matter of sitting in a particular posture or breathing a particular way; it is a state of mind. Although the best results usually come when we meditate in a quiet place, we can also meditate while working, walking, riding on a bus or cooking dinner. One Tibetan meditator realized emptiness while chopping wood and another attained single-pointed concentration while cleaning his teacher's room.

First, we learn to develop the meditative state of mind in formal, sitting practice, but once we are good at it we can be more freestyle and creative and can generate this mental state at any time, in any situation. By then, meditation has become a way of life.

Meditation is not something foreign or unsuitable for the Western mind. There are different methods practiced in different cultures, but they all share the common principle of the mind simply becoming familiar with various aspects of itself. And the mind of every person, Eastern or Western, has the same basic elements and experiences, the same basic problem—and the same potential.

Meditation is not spacing-out or running away. In fact, it is being totally honest with ourselves: taking a good look at what we are and working with that in order to become more positive and useful, to ourselves and others. There are both positive and negative aspects of the mind. The negative aspects—our mental disorders or, quite literally, delusions—include jealousy, anger, desire, pride and the like. These arise from our misunderstanding of reality and habitual clinging to the way we see things. Through meditation we can recognize our mistakes and adjust our mind to think and react more realistically, more honestly.

The final goal, enlightenment, is a long-term one. But meditations done with this goal in mind can and do have enormous short-term benefits. As our concrete picture of reality softens we develop a more positive and realistic self-image and are thus more relaxed and less anxious. We learn to have fewer unrealistic expectations of the people and things around us and therefore meet with less disappointment; relationships improve and life becomes more stable and satisfying.

But remember, lifelong habits die hard. It is difficult enough simply to recognize our anger and jealousy, much less make an effort to hold back the old familiar tide of feeling or analyze its causes and results. Transforming the mind is a slow and gradual process. It is a matter of ridding ourselves, bit by bit, of instinctive, harmful habit patterns and "becoming familiar" with habits that necessarily bring positive results— to ourselves and others.

There are many meditation techniques but all can be included under two headings: *stabilizing* and *analytical*.

Stabilizing meditation

In general, this type of meditation is used to develop what is known as single-pointed concentration—a prerequisite for any lasting insight. The aim is to concentrate upon one object—the breath, the nature of one's own mind, a concept, a visualized image—without interruption.

Concentration without interruption is the exact opposite of our usual state of mind. If you turn inwards for a few moments you will notice your mind jumping from one thing to another—a thought of something you will do later, a sound outside, a friend, something that happened earlier, a physical sensation, a cup of coffee. We never need to say to the mind, "Think!" or "Feel!" It is always busy doing something, speeding along, all energy of its own.

With such a scattered and uncontrolled mind there is little chance of success in anything we do, whether it is remembering a telephone number, cooking a meal or running a business. And certainly, without concentration successful meditation is impossible.

Stabilizing meditation is not easy, but it is essential for bringing the mind under control. Although the development of actual single-pointed concentration is the work of full-time meditators, we don't need to retreat to the mountains to experience the benefits of this kind of meditation: even in our day-to-day city life we can develop good concentration by regularly doing ten or fifteen minutes a day of stabilizing meditation—keeping the mind focused on a single object and letting go of all other thoughts. It brings an immediate sense of spaciousness and allows us to see the workings of our mind more clearly, both during the meditation and throughout the rest of the day.

Analytical meditation

This type of meditation brings into play creative, intellectual thought and is crucial to our development: the first step in gaining any real insight is to understand *conceptually* how things are. This conceptual clarity develops into firm conviction which, when combined with stabilizing meditation, brings direct and intuitive knowing.

However, even before we can "know how things are" we must first identify our *wrong* conceptions. Using clear, penetrative, analytical thought we unravel the complexities of our attitudes and behavior patterns. Gradually, we can eliminate those thoughts, feelings and ideas that cause ourselves and others unhappiness, and in their place cultivate thoughts, feelings and ideas that bring happiness.

In this way we become familiar with the reality of, for example, cause and effect—that our present experiences are the result of our past actions and the cause of our future experiences—or with the fact that all things lack an inherent nature. We can meditate point by point on the benefits of patience and the disadvantages of anger; on the value of developing compassion; on the kindness of others.

In one sense, an analytical meditation session is an intensive study session. However, the level of conceptual thought that we can reach during these meditations is more subtle and therefore more potent than our thoughts during day-to-day life. Because our senses are not being bombarded by the usual frantic input we are able to concentrate more strongly and develop a finely-tuned sensitivity to the workings of our mind.

Stabilizing and analytical meditations are complementary and are often used together in one session. When doing a meditation on emptiness, for example, we analyze the object (emptiness) using information we have heard or read, as well as our own thoughts, feelings and memories. At some point an intuitive experience of or conviction about the object arises. We should then stop thinking and focus our attention single-pointedly on the feeling for as long as possible. We should soak our mind in the experience. When the feeling fades we can either continue analyzing or conclude the session.

This method of combining the two kinds of meditation causes the mind literally to become one with the object of meditation. The stronger our concentration, the deeper our insight will be. We need to repeat this process again and again with anything we want to understand in order to transform our insight into actual experience.

Stabilizing meditations such as the breathing meditations will also go better if some skillful analysis is used. When we sit down to meditate we should start by examining our state of mind and clarifying our motivation for doing the practice, and this involves analytical thought. During the meditation itself we might find concentration especially difficult; at such times it is good to analyze the problem for a few moments, then to replace the mind on the breath. And sometimes it is useful to check on the mind during the meditation to make sure it is not daydreaming but [is doing] what it is supposed to be doing. . . .

B. ALAN WALLACE

Tibetan Buddhist Meditation

WE CAN BEGIN to stabilize our minds from the beginning of our spiritual practice, while placing our chief emphasis on ethical discipline. By taking out some time each day for the practice of meditative quiescence, we become increasingly aware of how our minds function; and in the process we begin to discover how scattered our minds have been all along. Recognizing this, we may yearn to explore the potentials of the human mind that become apparent only when the awareness is still and lucid. . . .

In Buddhist practice we can choose among a wide variety of objects for stabilizing the mind. One common method in the Tibetan Buddhist tradition is to focus on an image of the Buddha. First we take a physical object, either a statue or painting of the Buddha, and gaze at it until we are very familiar with its appearance. Then we close our eyes and create a simulation of that image with our imagination.

The actual practice is not the visual one—this is only a preparation—for the point is to stabilize the mind, not the eyes. When we first try to visualize the Buddha, the mental image is bound to be vague and extremely unstable. We may not even be able to get an image at all. . . .

While the above method has many benefits, it is not ideal for everyone. For it to be effective, one must have a fairly peaceful mind, and it is helpful to have deep faith and reverence for the Buddha. For people of a devotional nature, this practice can be very inspiring, and effective at stabilizing the mind. One's heart is stirred by bringing the Buddha to mind with devotion, and consequently one's enthusiasm for the meditation grows. On the other hand, if one has a very agitated mind and little faith, this and other visualization techniques may very well lead to tension and unhappiness. And these problems may increase the more one practices.

With an agitated, conceptually congested mind, the sheer effort of imagining a visualized object may be too taxing. So if one is engaging in visualization practices, especially during several sessions a day, it is important to be aware of one's level of stress. It is important not to let it get out of hand; for if it does, instead of stabilizing the mind the practice will damage one's nervous system.

Another method that is practiced widely, especially in the Buddhist countries of East and Southeast Asia, is focusing one's awareness on the breath. A key attribute of this practice, as opposed to visualization of the Buddha, is that in breath awareness the object of meditation, the breath, is present without our having to imagine it.

Awareness of the breath is practiced in many different ways. Some people focus on the rise and fall of the abdomen during the in- and out-breath. Another technique is to focus on the tactile sensations, from the nostrils down to the abdomen, that are associated with the respiration. In yet another method one focuses on the sensations of the breath passing through the apertures of the nostrils and above the upper lip. All of these are valuable methods, and they can be especially useful for people with highly discursive, imaginative minds. They offer a soothing way to calm the conceptually disturbed mind.

A third method of stabilizing the mind involves directing one's awareness to the mind itself. This is the most subtle of all the techniques mentioned here, and its rewards are great. I shall elaborate on this practice in a moment, but first I would like to discuss some of the themes common to all methods of stabilizing the mind.

Two facets of awareness are instrumental in all the above forms of meditative training. These are mindfulness and vigilance. Mindfulness is a mental factor that allows us to focus upon an object with continuity, without forgetting that object. So, if we are focusing on the sensations of our breath at our nostrils, mindfulness enables us to fasten our attention there continuously. When mindfulness vanishes, the mind slips off its object like a seal off a slick rock. Vigilance is another mental factor, whose function is to check up on the quality of awareness itself. It checks to see if the meditating mind is becoming agitated and scattered, or dull and drowsy. It is the task of vigilance to guard against these extremes.

There are many inner hindrances to stabilizing the mind, but they boil down to the two extremes of excitement and laxity. Excitement is a mental factor that draws our attention away from our intended object. This hindrance is a derivative of desire. If we are meditating and suddenly find ourselves thinking about going to the refrigerator and getting a snack, we can identify this impulse as excitement born from desire. Excitement draws the mind outward. It can easily be stimulated by sound such as that of a car driving by. It compulsively latches onto the sound— a kind of mental hitchhiking—and elaborates on it with a series of images and thoughts.

When the mind is not agitated, it is prone to slipping off to the other extreme of laxity. This mental factor does not distract the attention outward, but brings on a sinking sensation. The mind becomes absorbed in its object without clarity, and drowsiness is bound to follow. At that point the object of the meditation is submerged under waves of lethargy or obliviousness.

The chief antidotes to excitement and laxity are mindfulness and vigilance, and the results of overcoming those hindrances are mental stability and clarity. These are the fruits of the practice.

Meditative stability necessarily implies an underlying ground of relaxation and serenity. The mind is peaceful, and the attention remains where we direct it for as long as we wish. Clarity refers more to the vividness of subjective awareness than to the clarity of the object. When it is present we can detect even the subtle and most fleeting qualities of our object. For example, if we are visualizing the Buddha with clarity, he will appear in our mind's eye in three dimensions and very lifelike. We will be able to see the color of his eyes, the individual folds in his robe. He will appear almost as clearly as if we were seeing him directly with our eyes. Such subjective clarity is instrumental in focusing on the breath as well as on the mind.

All of us have experienced moments when our attention is extremely vivid. This may occur, for example, while driving a car or motorcycle at high speed on a winding road, or when rock-climbing. But when such mental clarity is experienced it is usually combined with a high degree of tension, and the mind is neither serene nor stable. On the other hand, mental stability is a common experience when we are pleasantly tired and we lie down to sleep. But in such cases there is rarely much clarity of awareness.

The challenge of meditative quiescence practice is to cultivate stability integrated with clarity, generating an extraordinarily useful quality of awareness. To bring this about, experienced meditators have found that there must be a sequence of emphases in the practice. First seek a relaxed, wholesome, and cheerful state of mind. On this basis, emphasize stability, and then finally let clarity take priority. The importance of this sequence cannot be overemphasized.

Focusing Awareness on the Mind . . .

To engage in meditation on the mind, one first finds a suitable posture. . . . It is important to sit in an erect posture, with the spine straight. It is important not to become slouched forward or to tilt to the side or backward. Throughout the meditation session one should keep the body still and relaxed.

At the outset of this or any other Buddhist practice, it is helpful to take refuge [see pages 215–228]. It is also vital to cultivate a good motivation, for this will profoundly influence the nature of the practice. Finally, it is helpful to be cheerful, cherishing this wonderful opportunity to explore the nature of consciousness.

Although the main practice here is awareness of the mind, it is useful to begin with a more tangible object to calm and refine one's awareness. Breath awareness can be perfect for this. We should cultivate a general awareness of the breath coming in and going out. During inhalation, we should simply be aware that this is taking place. During exhalation, we note that the breath is going out. Awareness is allowed to rest calmly in the present, while we breathe in a natural, unforced way.

As we now move on to the main practice, we may follow the counsel of Tilopa, the great Indian Buddhist contemplative: "Do not indulge in thought, but watch the natural awareness." "Natural" aware-ness has no shape or color, and it has no location. So how can we focus on it? What does it mean "to watch" it?

First of all, our task is to focus our attention on the mind, as opposed to the physical sense fields. One way to do this is to focus our awareness initially on a mental event, such as a thought. This thought could be anything—a word or a phrase—but it is helpful if it is one that does not stimulate either desire or aversion.

One possibility is the phrase: "What is the mind?" The point here is not to speculate on this question, or to try to answer it. Rather, use that thought itself as the object of awareness. Very shortly after having brought that phrase to mind, it is bound to fade out of our consciousness. At that point we keep our awareness right where it is. We have now directed our attention on the mind, and what remains between the vanishing of one thought, and the arising of another, is simply awareness, empty and without obstruction, like space.

An analogy may be helpful. Imagine yourself as a child lying on your back, gazing up into a cloudless sky, and blowing soap bubbles through a plastic ring. As a bubble drifts up into the sky, you watch it rise, and this brings your attention into the sky. While you are looking at the bubble it pops, and you keep your attention right where the bubble had been. Your awareness now lies in empty space.

In the actual meditation practice one focuses initially on the bubble of a thought. When this thought vanishes one does not replace it with some other mental construct. Rather, one stabilizes one's attention in natural awareness, uncontrived, without conceptual elaboration.

This practice is so subtle we may find we become tense in our efforts to do it right. Some people even find the intensity of their concentration impedes their normal respiration—they restrict their breathing for fear it will disturb the delicate equilibrium of their minds. Such tension and constricted respiration can only impair the practice and our health in general. So it is crucial that we engage in the meditation with a sense of physical and mental relaxation.

Starting from relaxation one cultivates meditative stability, resting in natural awareness without being carried away by the turbulence of thoughts or emotions. Finally, it is important to recognize that this practice is not based upon a vague sort of trance or dull absorption; rather, it calls for vivid, clear awareness.

To cultivate these three qualities of relaxation, stability, and clarity, it is usually helpful to keep the meditation sessions relatively short. The chief criterion for determining the length of one's meditation sessions is the quality of one's awareness during the practice. Five minutes of finely conducted meditation is worth more than an hour of low-grade conceptual chatter. Another useful criterion is one's state of mind following meditation. The mind should be refreshed, stable, and clear. If one feels exhausted and dull, one's session was probably too long or of low quality.

Phases of the Practice

Once we have entered into this discipline, it may not be long before we experience short periods—perhaps up to ten seconds or longer—during which we are able to abide in a natural state of awareness, without grasping onto the thoughts and other events that arise in our consciousness. We may well find this delightfully exhilarating, and our minds may then leap upon the experience with glee. But as soon as our minds grasp in this way, the experience will fade. This can be frustrating.

The remedy is to enter into this state of awareness repeatedly. As we become familiar with it, we can then take it in stride, without expectation or anxiety. We learn to just let it be.

As the mind settles in this practice, our awareness of thoughts and other mental events is also bound to change. At times we may no longer sense ourselves thinking, yet a multitude of thoughts and images may arise as simple events. . . .

Do not cling to these thoughts, identify with them, or try to sustain them. But also do not try to suppress them. Simply view them as spontaneous outflows of natural awareness, while centering your attention on the pure, unelaborated awareness from which they arise.

On many occasions we are bound to find ourselves carried away by trains of thought. When we recognize this has happened, we may react with frustration, disappointment, or restlessness.

All such responses are a waste of time. If we find our minds have become agitated, the antidote is to relax more deeply. Relax away the effort that is going into sustaining our conceptual or emotional turbulence. It is best not to silence the mind with a crushing blow of our will. Instead, we may release the effort of grasping onto those mental events. Grasping arises from attachment, and the antidote is simply to let go of this attachment.

On other occasions we may experience mental laxity. Although the mind is not agitated, it may rest in a nebulous blankness. The antidote for this hindrance is to revitalize our awareness by paying closer attention to the practice. The "middle path" here is to invigorate our awareness without agitating it.

The great Indian Buddhist contemplative Saraha says of this practice: "By releasing the tension that binds the mind, one undoubtedly brings about inner freedom."

Tilopa speaks of three phases of the meditation. In the initial stages the onslaught of compulsive ideation is like a stream rushing through a narrow gorge. At this point it may seem that our mind is more out of control, more conceptually turbulent, than it was before we began meditating. But in fact, we are only now realizing how much the mind normally gushes with semiconscious thoughts.

As the mind becomes more quiescent, more stable, the stream of mental activity will become like the Ganges—a broad, quietly flowing river. In the third phase of the practice, the continuum of awareness is like the river flowing into the sea. It is at this point that one recognizes the mind's natural serenity, vividness, transparency, and freshness.

During early stages of practice, we may experience moments of mental quiescence relatively free of conceptualization, and we may wonder whether we are now ascertaining natural awareness. Most likely we are not. Our mind at this point is probably still too gross and unclear for such a realization. Patience is needed to persist in the practice, without expectation or fear, until gradually the essential qualities of awareness become apparent. When we ascertain the simple clarity and knowing qualities of the awareness, we are well established in the practice. We can then proceed to the attainment of meditative quiescence focused on the mind.

The Attainment of Meditative Quiescence

In Buddhist practice the achievement of meditative quiescence is clearly defined. As a result of the practice outlined above, one eventually experiences natural awareness, and the duration of this experience gradually increases. Eventually we no longer become distracted or agitated. At this point the emphasis of the practice should be on cultivating clarity. For the mind, even after it has become well stabilized, can still easily slip into laxity.

When we finally attain meditative quiescence, we are free of even the subtle forms of excitement and laxity. During the early phases of practice, considerable degrees of effort are required, but as we progress, more and more subtle effort suffices. Gradually the meditation becomes effortless, and we can sustain each session for hours on end.

SHARON SALZBERG, TRANS.

The Metta Sutta

This is what should be done
By those who are skilled in goodness,
And who know the path of peace:
Let them be able and upright,
Straightforward and gentle in speech.
Humble and not conceited,
Contented and easily satisfied.
Unburdened with duties and frugal in their ways.

Peaceful and calm, and wise and skillful,
Not proud and demanding in nature.
Let them not do the slightest thing
That the wise would later reprove.
Wishing: in gladness and in safety,
May all beings be at ease.
Whatever living beings there may be;
Whether they are weak or strong, omitting none,
The great or the mighty, medium, short or small,
The seen and the unseen,
Those living near and far away,
Those born and to-be-born—
May all beings be at ease!
Let none deceive another,
Or despise any being in any state.
Let none through anger or ill-will
Wish harm upon another.
Even as a mother protects with her life
Her child, her only child,
So with a boundless heart
Should one cherish all living beings;
Radiating kindness over the entire world:
Spreading upward to the skies,
And downward to the depths;
Outward and unbounded,
Freed from hatred and ill-will.
Whether standing or walking, seated or lying down,
Free from drowsiness,
One should sustain this recollection.
This is said to be the sublime abiding.

By not holding to fixed views,
The pure-hearted one, having clarity of vision,
Being freed from all sense desires,
Is not born again into this world.

SHARON SALZBERG

Metta Practice

IN VIPASSANA PRACTICE, we become aware of our ever-changing experiences, without adding to what is going on through our reactions and projections. In metta practice, we direct lovingkindness toward ourselves and then, in a sequence of expansion, towards somebody we love already, somebody we are neutral towards, somebody we have difficulty with, and ultimately toward all beings everywhere without distinction.

The main difference between metta and vipassana is that metta is a concentration practice, while vipassana is an insight practice. This is a functional difference. If you're doing mindfulness practice, there is no such thing as a distraction. You pay attention to whatever arises in your awareness and make that an object of meditation. There is no sense of preferring one experience over another, since each experience is seen as having the same ultimate nature. Each is characterized by impermanence (*anicca*), unsatisfactoriness (*dukkha*) and having no separate existence (*anatta*). You can see these characteristics by looking at either pleasure or pain.

In contrast to vipassana, in metta practice you are not focusing on the ultimate nature of phenomena. Furthermore, you are choosing a particular object of meditation, which is the metta phrase, such as "May I be happy" or "May I be peaceful." You hold the phrase in your heart just the way you'd hold something fragile and precious in your hand. As you cherish each phrase, distractions inevitably arise. Your head starts itching or your knee starts hurting or you start thinking about the phone call you didn't make. When you get distracted, you drop the distractions as quickly as possible and come back to the phrase, the chosen object of meditation. Choosing a particular object to stay focused on makes metta a concentration practice. When some other experience arises you don't explore it, note it, or try to see its changing nature.

Nonetheless, I still call metta "a sneaky wisdom practice," because people often have enormous insight doing metta. Since it is a concentration practice and you have a chosen object of meditation, you keep shepherding your attention back to that object, which means that you are letting go again and again of everything else that comes up in your awareness. That moment of letting go is very instructive, because it shows you where you are holding on. The only way you can let go with grace and ease is when you begin to understand that the distraction, whatever it may be, has the characteristics of *anicca, dukkha* and *anatta*. You then don't have to fight or fear it. In the moment of letting go— without any intended development of wisdom—you find wisdom. Ultimately, of course, the most powerful insight that comes from metta practice is the sense of nonseparateness, and that insight comes through opening one's heart, from being inclusive rather than exclusive. . . .

In metta practice people are amazed to find out that they have a capacity for lovingkindness, both for themselves and for others. Due to our past conditioning, many of us do not trust our capacity to love. Metta involves a tremendous opening and purifying of our fields of intention, which can then infuse our vipassana practice as well as our entire life. We discover that we can indeed love and that everything comes back to love.

AYYA KHEMA

The Heart Essence

METTA IS A quality of our own heart. It has nothing to do with being loved back, or with one or more specific persons, or with any ideal or activity or any particular direction. It is simply the training of our heart. Just as meditation is training of the mind and does not depend on any input into the mind, the same goes for *metta* in the heart.

In Pali, heart and mind are one word (*citta*), but in English we have to differentiate between the two to make the meaning clear. When we attend to the mind, we are concerned with the thinking process and the intellectual understanding that derives from knowledge, and with our ability to retain knowledge and make use of it. When we speak of "heart" we think of feelings and emotions, our ability to respond with our fundamental being. Although we may believe that we are leading our lives according to our thinking process, that is not the case. If we examine this more closely, we will find that we are leading our lives according to our feelings and that our thinking is dependent upon our feelings. The emotional aspect of ourselves is of such great importance that its purification is the basis for a harmonious and peaceful life, and also for good meditation.

Wisdom

Wisdom is the third of the essential elements of Buddhist practice embodied in the Noble Eightfold Path. Among the discourses dealing with wisdom, at about the beginning of the Common Era some forty Mahayana sutras on the perfection of wisdom, or prajnaparamita, *were composed. Of these, the best known are the* Diamond Sutra *and the* Heart Sutra, *which today are still an integral part of daily practice for many Mahayana Buddhists.*

ZEN COMMUNITY OF NEW YORK, TRANS.

The Great Prajna Paramita Heart Sutra

Avalokitesvara Bodhisattva doing deep Prajna Paramita
Perceived the emptiness of all five conditions, and was freed of pain.
O Sariputra, form is no other than emptiness, emptiness no other than form;
Form is precisely emptiness, emptiness precisely form;
Sensation, perception, reaction, and consciousness are also like this.
O Sariputra, all things are expressions of emptiness, not born, not destroyed,
Not stained, not pure; neither waxing nor waning.
Thus emptiness is not form; not sensation nor perception, reaction nor consciousness;

No eye, ear, nose, tongue, body, mind;
No color, sound, smell, taste, touch, thing;
No realm of sight, no realm of consciousness;
No ignorance, no end to ignorance;
No old age and death, no cessation of old age and death;
No suffering, no cause or end to suffering, no path;
No wisdom and no gain. No gain——thus;
Bodhisattvas live this Prajna Paramita
With no hindrance of mind——no hindrance therefore no fear
Far beyond all such delusion, Nirvana is already here.
All past, present, and future Buddhas live this Prajna Paramita
And attain supreme, perfect enlightenment.
Therefore know that Prajna Paramita is
The holy mantra, the luminous mantra
The supreme mantra, the incomparable mantra
By which all suffering is cleared. This is no other than truth.
Therefore set forth the Prajna Paramita mantra,
Set forth this mantra and proclaim:
Gate Gate Paragate Parasamgate Bodhi Svaha!

EDITORS OF *TRICYCLE*

The Heart Sutra

PERHAPS BECAUSE OF both its profundity and its brevity, the
Heart Sutra is the most familiar of all the original teachings of the

Buddha. (The Sino-Japanese version comprises a mere 262 characters.) Recited daily by Buddhists in China, Korea, Vietnam, Japan, Tibet, Mongolia, Bhutan, and Nepal, the Heart Sutra is now also recited by many Buddhists in North America. The Sino-Japanese and monosyllabic Korean versions lend themselves well to chanting, and there are now several English translations. The basic text of the Zen tradition, it must also be the only sutra to be found (in Japan) printed on a man's tie.

According to Buddhist lore, the Heart Sutra was first preached on Vulture Peak, which lies near the ancient Indian city of Rajagraha, and is said to have been the Buddha's favorite site.

In this sutra, the Buddha inspires one of his closest disciples, Sariputra, to request Avalokitesvara, the Bodhisattva of compassion, to instruct him in the practice of *prajnaparamita,* the perfection of wisdom. Avalokitesvara's response contains one of the most celebrated of all Buddhist paradoxes—"form is emptiness; emptiness is form." And the sutra ends with one of the most popular Buddhist mantras—*gate gate paragate parasamgate bodhi svaha*: gone, gone, gone beyond, gone completely beyond . . . (When chanted, *gate* has two short vowels with the accent on the first syllable.)

The tradition of composing commentaries on the Heart Sutra goes back to at least the eighth century, and includes many of the great Buddhist philosophers and meditation masters.

THICH NHAT HANH

The Heart of Understanding

PERFECT UNDERSTANDING IS prajnaparamita. The word "wisdom" is usually used to translate *prajna,* but I think that wisdom is somehow not able to convey the meaning. Understanding is like water flowing in a stream. Wisdom and knowledge are solid and can block our understanding. In Buddhism, knowledge is regarded as an obstacle for understanding. If we take something to be the truth, we may cling to it so much that even if the truth comes and knocks at our door, we won't want to let it in. We have to be able to transcend our previous knowledge the way we climb up a ladder. If we are on the fifth rung and think that we are very high, there is no hope for us to step up to the sixth. We must learn to transcend our own views. Understanding, like water, can flow, can penetrate. Views, knowledge, and even wisdom are solid, and can block the way of understanding.

Avalokita found the five skandhas empty. But, empty of what? The key word is empty. To be empty is to be empty of something.

If I am holding a cup of water and I ask you, "Is this cup empty?" you will say, "No, it is full of water." But if I pour out the water and ask you again, you may say, "Yes, it is empty." But, empty of what? Empty means empty of something. The cup cannot be empty of nothing. "Empty" doesn't mean anything unless you know empty of what. My cup is empty of water, but it is not empty of air. To be empty is to be empty of something. This is quite a discovery. When Avalokita says that the five skandhas are equally empty, to help him be precise we must ask, "Mr. Avalokita, empty of what?"

The five skandhas, which may be translated into English as five heaps, or five aggregates, are the five elements that comprise a human being. These five elements flow like a river in every one of us. In fact, these are really five rivers flowing together in us: the river of form, which means our body, the river of feelings, the river of perceptions, the river of mental formations, and the river of consciousness. They are always flowing in us. So according to Avalokita, when he looked deeply into the nature of these five rivers, he suddenly saw that all five are empty.

And if we ask, "Empty of what?" he has to answer. And this is what he said: "They are empty of a separate self." That means none of these five rivers can exist by itself alone. Each of the five rivers has to be made by the other four. They have to co-exist; they have to inter-be with all the others.

Avalokita looked deeply into the five skandhas of form, feelings, perceptions, mental formations, and consciousness, and he discovered that none of them can be by itself alone. Each can only inter-be with all the others. So he tells us that form is empty. Form is empty of a separate self, but it is full of everything in the cosmos. The same is true with feelings, perceptions, mental formations, and consciousness.

Geshe Rabten

The Heart Sutra

THE TIBETAN TEXT starts by giving the title of the sutra, first in transliterated Sanskrit, *Bhagavatiprajnaparamitahrdya,* and then in Tibetan, which, when translated, means: *The Essence of the Sacred Mother: The Perfection of Wisdom.*

The perfection of wisdom refers specifically to the wisdom that directly and intuitively understands the voidness of all phenomena. This wisdom is said to be the sacred mother because it is the mother of, i.e., that which gives rise to, the sacred ones, namely the buddhas. It is through developing an understanding of voidness in one's own mind that one is enabled finally to realize the state of buddhahood. Just as a child cannot be born without a mother, likewise a buddha cannot be born without relying upon the "mother" of the perfection of wisdom. . . .

The sutra itself starts with an introductory passage that mentions who gave the teaching, where it was given, to whom and so forth. . . . I would think it most likely that Ananda is the one who is heard introducing this sutra. . . .

After the description of those who were assembled, attention is now turned to the Buddha himself. As the *Heart of Wisdom* was about to be delivered we find him absorbed in meditation upon what is called the profound appearance. In general "profound appearance" refers simply to voidness. In other words, the Buddha was dwelling in single-pointed concentration upon voidness, i.e. the true nature of all phenomena. More specifically, however, profound appearance has a twofold connotation: it indicates the two truths—ultimate and conventional—and the relation between them. "Profound" refers to the ultimate truth of voidness, which, as we shall see later, is defined as the mere absence of inherent existence. "Appearance" refers to the conventional truths that appear to us and perform functions although their ultimate nature is one of voidness of any inherent existence. . . .

Two of the principal members of the audience at this time were the arhat Shariputra and the bodhisattva Avalokiteshvara. Shariputra is commonly regarded as . . . the most learned and wise of the Buddha's disciples. Avalokiteshvara is usually presented as a bodhisattva renowned for his compassion. . . . Through the power of the Buddha's concentration these two disciples became involved in a dialogue. This took place quite spontaneously and without any intention on their behalf. The content of their entire conversation was determined solely by the power of the Buddha's concentration. Furthermore, because they themselves had already achieved a complete understanding of voidness, they were not speaking for their own benefit. The purpose of their dialogue was to clarify the meaning of voidness to those disciples who did not yet understand it and to improve the understanding of those who had only partially understood it. . . . Avalokiteshvara starts to set forth the way in which any son or daughter of the noble lineage should meditate on voidness. It should be noted that he says, "*Whatever* son or daughter. . . ." This emphasizes the fact that the perfection of wisdom is something that can be attained by all people, whether they are men or women, rich or poor, monks or laymen.

We often think of buddhahood, or enlightenment, as something very far away from us and practically unattainable. But we should remember that enlightenment is a result that arises in dependence upon its own particular causes. If we possess the cause, the result will inevitably occur. This means that if we earnestly study, contemplate and meditate, the result of buddhahood will definitely come about. But if we fail to make sufficient effort, then no matter how much we may wish for enlightenment, it will never come. . . .

Voidness is neither holy nor precious; it has no particular value in itself. However, the *understanding* of voidness is something very precious, meaningful and holy. This understanding is equivalent to the perfection of wisdom: a state of consciousness that is worthy of much devotion and respect. Furthermore, voidness is not something that exists separately, in a realm of its own, apart from the phenomena of the empirical world. It is a quality present in every existent phenomenon, without exception. As soon as an entity comes into existence, so does its voidness—the very moment that an entity ceases to exist, its quality of voidness also disappears. Voidness is an essential quality of everything that exists. All phenomena have two distinct modes of being: the ultimate and conventional. Voidness is the ultimate mode of being of every phenomenon; it is the way in which phenomena actually exist.

No single phenomenon lacks the quality of being a dependently arising event. Thus every phenomenon is said to be a "dependent arising." Nevertheless, all things instinctively appear to us as though they did exist independently, as though they were endowed with their own autonomous self-existence. . . . The same is true for all material phenomena, however large or small they may be. Imagine that one is holding a grape in one's hand. If one considers just this small, relatively insignificant object, one will start to notice the vast number of diverse conditions that were responsible for its present existence. Just think of the field in which it was grown, the vine from which it came, the efforts of the farmer, the sun and the rain that helped it grow. In this way we can understand how every phenomenon is dependent for its existence upon a whole multitude of conditioning factors. There is nothing to be found that lacks such a dependent existence. Even the tiny atomic particles that are the basic constituents of matter are dependent events. They depend upon their directional parts, as well as the causes that produced them and the effects that they in turn produce. . . .

The mind too has no independent existence. Any one state of mind depends upon numerous moments of consciousness and various mental factors. A mind that has been meditating for an hour appears to have an independent self-identity. But upon analysis it is found to be utterly dependent upon the various individual thoughts, perceptions and feelings that occurred during the hour, as well as upon the objects the mind was contemplating. The individual mental factors—for example, feelings of pleasure and pain—are also dependent upon a variety of conditions that, once assembled, cause a particular feeling to occur. The beginningless and endless stream of consciousness that passes from one life to another and finally reaches buddhahood is not independently existent either. It is in a constant state of momentary change and thus depends upon the infinite number of moments that constitute its continuity.

The person is also dependent. We can talk of a person as *having* a body and a mind, but we cannot identify the person with either body or mind. We cannot think of someone as being his bones or his flesh, nor can we consider him to be one of his states of perception or consciousness. In reality, the person exists merely in dependence upon the physical and mental components of which he is constituted. Thus he has no inherent independent existence apart from these things, but neither is he identical with them.

Even permanent, unconditioned phenomena such as abstract-space are dependent entities. The abstract-space, i.e. the mere lack of obstructive contact, in this room is dependent upon its directional parts, i.e. the lack of obstructive contact in the different parts of the room.

In addition to being dependent upon causes and parts, phenomena are also dependent upon their being imputed by the mind. This is a much subtler mode of dependence and is more difficult to understand than dependence on causes and parts. However, it is very important to grasp what this means. It is often said that all phenomena are merely imputed by the mind and that nothing whatsoever can exist independently of such imputation. But what does it mean to impute something with the mind? Actually, to impute (*btags.pa*) means nothing more than to apprehend (*dzin.pa*). We may think of a lamp in our room at home. In thinking of it we apprehend it, and in apprehending it we are "imputing" it. Thus imputation is the mind's fundamental quality of apprehending objects.

We can apprehend, or impute, both existent and non-existent entities. If what we apprehend is existent, the mind that apprehends it is a valid mind, whereas if we apprehend something that does not exist, the mind that apprehends it is mistaken. For example, we may walk into the garden and notice a longish, slightly coiled object partially concealed in the high grass. We immediately recognize it as a snake and stand back in fear. However, as we cautiously approach the snake for a closer look, we suddenly realize that it is not a snake at all, but the garden hose. Thus the initial perception imputed a snake, but since its object was not in reality a snake, the perception was mistaken. Nevertheless, on other occasions we may see an object and correctly apprehend it as a snake. In this case the imputation of a snake is in accordance with reality and the mind that apprehends a snake is thereby a valid mind. Therefore, when it is said that all existent phenomena are imputations of the mind, we must understand that "mind" in this sense means a *valid* mind. It does not mean that an existent phenomenon is something that can just be imagined by any particular state of mind.

All phenomena exist in dependence upon causes and conditions (if they are conditioned phenomena), component parts and mental imputation. This being the case we can conclude that nothing has any autonomous existence independent of causes, parts and imputation. Whatever appears to us as existing inherently and not dependently is called "that which is negated in voidness." Now, that which is negated here, i.e. inherent, independent existence, is utterly non-existent; but the voidness of it is existent. *Voidness is the mere absence of what is negated.* If what was to be negated—inherent existence—were existent, voidness would then be nonexistent. However, as soon as something comes into existence, it is, in its very nature, something merely imputed by the mind and thereby void of any independent existence. Therefore, what we mean by voidness is the sheer lack or absence of any inherent, independent existence within phenomena. . . . This sutra contains many negative expressions: "there are no forms, no feelings, no minds" and so forth. However, we should always remember exactly what is negated when speaking of voidness. It is not phenomena themselves that are being negated but inherently existent phenomena that seem to be independent of mental imputation. . . .

Avalokiteshvara begins by emphasizing that anyone who wants to develop the perfection of wisdom must understand that none of the five aggregates exists inherently, independently of mental imputation. The five aggregates are one way of classifying all conditioned phenomena. They are (1) the aggregate of forms, (2) the aggregate of feelings, (3) the aggregate of discernments, (4) the aggregate of formative elements and (5) the aggregate of consciousness. . . .

Avalokiteshvara begins by considering the aggregate of forms. He points out that forms, such as the material elements of the body for example, are void of any inherent, autonomous existence. But he immediately goes on to affirm the essential identity of form with its voidness of inherent existence. He states that voidness is form, meaning that the voidness of the inherent existence of form is essentially identical with form. The same point is made even clearer in the following sentence. There he asserts that the voidness of form is not essentially distinct from form and neither is form essentially distinct from its voidness. The two modes of being of form—its ultimate truth of being void of inherent existence and its conventional truth of being merely a mental imputation—are shown in these lines to be essentially identical although conceptually distinct. For someone who has gained genuine insight into this point, when perceiving form he likewise understands it to be void of inherent existence, and when he contemplates the voidness of form he is fully aware of the fact that conventionally form validly appears and functions.

Such insight into form automatically counteracts the disturbing conceptions such as attachment and aversion that we habitually have with regard to form. This happens because such an understanding is the direct opponent of the ignorant grasping at the inherent existence of form which acts as the basis for all other disturbing conceptions of it. Of the five aggregates, form is mentioned first because it is that which usually gives rise to the greatest amount of attachment and other disturbing conceptions. Once we have understood the nature of form as described here, the following explanation of the remaining aggregates will be relatively straightforward.

Similarly, feelings, discernments, formative elements and consciousness are also void.

Feelings too are void of any inherent existence, yet that voidness of inherent existence is essentially identical with the feelings. Thus exactly the same considerations we made with regard to forms should also be applied here to feelings.

The aggregate of feeling is composed primarily of the experiences of pleasure and pain. These are mental factors. When we have a pain in the knee, the pain is not identifiable with the bones and muscles, but is a mental experience that arises upon the basis of a particular configuration of physical elements. These feelings of pleasure and pain play a very great role in our lives. When we say that all beings in samsara [day-to-day life] are basically striving to find happiness and avoid suffering, this means that they are seeking the *feeling* of happiness and trying to dispel the *feeling* of suffering. However, the fulfillment of this goal forever seems to elude them. Happiness always declines into sorrow and the absence of suffering is invariably replaced by some conflict or frustration. But by contemplating that these feelings are void of any inherent existence, we can resolve these feeling-associated problems.

Discernment is the mind's quality of distinguishing and identifying its objects. It is possible to discern things in both a positive and a negative way. If we discern something in a positive, realistic manner, we find all ensuing communication with others to be fruitful and free from conflict. But if our discernment is negative and unrealistic, there is a great danger that problems such as one-sidedness and fanaticism will follow, serving only to create disharmony. In order to counteract these negative discernments it is very helpful to meditate upon their voidness of inherent existence.

The aggregate of formative elements is composed of numerous wholesome and unwholesome mental factors. On the one hand it includes faith, compassion and wisdom—on the other, attachment, hatred and confusion. Considering the voidness of the unwholesome factors is a powerful means for overcoming them. The problem associated with the fifth aggregate, consciousness, is to regard it as a permanent essence of the person and equate it with the self. Reflection on the voidness of inherent existence of consciousness serves to dispel such misconceptions. . . .

To emphasize that the path of meditation is a process of further acquaintance with what has been seen, the passage repeats that when meditating on voidness one should recognize the five aggregates of form, feeling and so forth as having no inherent existence. And to indicate the extensiveness and greater profundity of this stage of meditation, further classifications of phenomena are also listed. First it is said that one should contemplate that the six sense bases—the eyes, ears and so forth are void of any inherent self-existence. Likewise, the corresponding six objects of the six senses—visual-forms, sounds and so forth—should also be seen repeatedly as void. . . .

Finally . . . there follows a contemplation of the noninherent existence of the states of samsara and liberation and of the path to enlightenment. . . . Likewise, the four noble truths—suffering, the origin of suffering, cessation and the path—should also be seen to be void of independent, autonomous existence. Even the wisdom of the Buddha must be realized to be in its very nature void. Similarly all the attainments that one may gain along the path, as well as the state of having no attainments prior to engaging in the path, are also without any inherent existence. When reading or reciting this passage one must be clear that Avalokiteshvara does not intend to deny that all these things exist. Conventionally they do exist in dependence upon mental imputation and other conditions. All that is being denied is that they exist inherently and independently of such conditions. . . .

All the buddhas of the past, present and future have depended, do and will depend upon the perfection of wisdom. Thereby they became, are becoming and will become unsurpassably, perfectly and completely awakened buddhas.

This passage is a summary of all that has been said so far. It emphasizes the extreme importance and power of meditation upon voidness; for it is only through gaining and developing this insight that buddhahood is possible. All the beings in the past who have attained buddhahood, all those who are presently attaining it and all those in the future who will attain it must invariably depend upon an understanding of the voidness of inherent existence of all phenomena. . . .

Thus the purpose of meditating on voidness and reciting the perfection of wisdom texts is to enable us to develop further along the path to enlightenment. But how, specifically, is this to be done? The answer is given in condensed form in the following line of the text:

I proclaim the mantra of the perfection of wisdom:
tayatha gate gate paragate parasamgate bodhi svaha.

Tayatha means "it is like this"; in other words, one should develop the perfection of wisdom in the following way: The first *gate* is interpreted here as meaning that one should firmly apply oneself to the practices of the path of accumulation [of mindfulness]. The next three words—*gate, paragate* and *parasamgate*—have the same meaning with respect to the paths of preparation, seeing and meditation, respectively. Finally, *bodhi svaha* means that one should strive to realize the fifth path, the path of no-more-learning: the state of buddhahood itself. Therefore, the perfection of wisdom is developed by means of progressively cultivating the five paths that culminate in buddhahood. . . .

MU SOENG SUNIM

The Heart Sutra

GATE, GATE MEANS gone, gone; *paragate* means gone over; *parasamgate* means gone beyond (to the other shore of suffering or the bondage of samsara); *bodhi* means the Awakened Mind; *svaha* is the Sanskrit word for homage or proclamation. So, the mantra means "Homage to the Awakened Mind which has gone over to the other shore (of suffering)."

Whatever perspective one may take on the inclusion of the mantra at the end of the sutra, it does not put a blemish on what the sutra has tried to convey earlier: the richness of intuitive wisdom coming out of the pure experience of complete stillness, of complete cessation, away from all concepts and categories.

Zen masters, in echoing the theme of emptiness, like to agree with existentialist thinkers that "life" has no meaning or reason. The Heart Sutra uses the methodology of negation as a way of pointing to this lack of any inherent meaning or reason in the phenomenal world, including the world of the mind. It takes each of the existents, holds it up under an unflinching gaze and declares it to have no sustaining self-nature. This is the wisdom teaching of sunyata [empty of permanent, independent existence] of the Mahayana tradition. But, at the same time, compassion is the other and equally important teaching of Mahayana. How do we then bridge the gap between sunyata as ultimate reality and the conventionality of human existence? The existentialist thinkers agonized over this problem and were led to despair and anarchy. In Mahayana, compassion, which is a natural, unenforced by-product of a deep state of meditation, supports the wisdom of emptiness, yet allows the individual to have empathy with the conventional appearance of the world without getting lost in it. It may be that compassion works best as a post-enlightenment existential crisis, but nonetheless without compassion as a guiding paradigm, the unrelenting precision of sunyata can make life bearable.

SHUNRYU SUZUKI
The Prajna Paramita Sutra

IN THE PRAJNA Paramita Sutra the most important point, of course, is the idea of emptiness. Before we understand the idea of emptiness, everything seems to exist substantially. But after we realize the emptiness of things, everything becomes real-not substantial. When we realize that everything we see is a part of emptiness, we can have no attachment to any existence; we realize that everything is just a tentative form and color. Thus we realize the true meaning of each tentative existence. When we first hear that everything is a tentative existence, most of us are disappointed; but this disappointment comes from a wrong view of man and nature. It is because our way of observing things is deeply rooted in our self-centered ideas that we are disappointed when we find everything has only a tentative existence. But when we actually realize this truth, we will have no suffering.

This sutra says, "Bodhisattva Avalokitesvara observes that everything is emptiness, thus he forsakes all suffering." It was not *after* he realized this truth that he overcame suffering—to realize this fact is itself to be relieved from suffering. So realization of the truth is salvation itself. We say, "to realize," but the realization of the truth is always near at hand. It is not after we practice zazen that we realize the truth; even before we practice zazen, realization is there. It is not after we understand the truth that we attain enlightenment. To realize the truth is to live—to exist here and now. So it is not a matter of understanding or of practice. It is an ultimate fact. In this sutra Buddha is referring to the ultimate fact that we always face moment after moment. This point is very important. This is Bodhidharma's zazen. Even before we practice it, enlightenment is there. But usually we understand the practice of zazen and enlightenment as two different things: here is practice, like a pair of glasses, and when we use the practice, like putting the glasses on, we see enlightenment. This is the wrong understanding. The glasses themselves are enlightenment, and to put them on is also enlightenment. So whatever you do, or even though you do not do anything, enlightenment is there, always. This is Bodhidharma's understanding of enlightenment.

You cannot practice true zazen, because you practice it; if you do not, then there is enlightenment, and there is true practice. When you do it, you create some concrete idea of "you" or "I," and you create some particular idea of practice or zazen. So here you are on the right side, and here is zazen on the left. So zazen and you become two different things. If the combination of practice and you is zazen, it is the zazen of a frog. For a frog, his sitting position is zazen. When a frog is hopping, that is not zazen. This kind of misunderstanding will vanish if you really understand emptiness means everything is always here. One whole being is not an accumulation of everything. It is impossible to divide one whole existence into parts. It is always here and always working. This is enlightenment. So there actually is no particular practice. In the sutra it says, "There are no eyes, no ears, no nose, no tongue, no body or mind. . . ." This "no mind" is Zen mind, which includes everything.

The important thing in our understanding is to have a smooth, free-thinking way of observation. We have to think and to observe things without stagnation. We should accept things as they are without difficulty. Our mind should be soft and open enough to understand things as they are. When our thinking is soft, it is called imperturbable thinking. This kind of thinking is always stable. It is called mindfulness. Thinking which is divided in many ways is not true thinking. Concentration should be present in our thinking. This is mindfulness. Whether you have an object or not, your mind should be stable and your mind should not be divided. This is zazen.

It is not necessary to make an effort to think in a particular way. Your thinking should not be one-sided. We just think with our whole mind, and see things as they are without any effort. Just to see, and to be ready to see things with our whole mind, is zazen practice. If we are prepared for thinking, there is no need to make an effort to think. This is called mindfulness. Mindfulness is, at the same time, wisdom. By wisdom we do not mean some particular faculty or philosophy. It is the readiness of the mind that is wisdom. So wisdom could be various philosophies and teachings, and various kinds of research and studies. But we should not become attached to some particular wisdom, such as that which was taught by Buddha. Wisdom is not something to learn. Wisdom is something which will come out of your mindfulness. So the point is to be ready for observing things, and to be ready for thinking. This is called emptiness of your mind. Emptiness is nothing but the practice of zazen.

KOSHO UCHIYAMA

Interdependence and the Middle Way

IF WE ARE going to look more deeply into the Buddhist notion of life, we shall have to take up the teaching of interdependence and the Middle Way. When I speak of the Self settling on Itself . . . I necessarily have to question what this Self is; for what is called "self" in Buddhism is quite distinct from that which we ordinarily speak of as "I." It is not just in regard to the term "self," but also in regard to the world we see that the Buddhist way of looking at things is totally different from the commonsense way of thinking. The Buddhist teachings explain self as life, and the living world in which self lives, as interdependence or the Middle Way. Therefore, in order that readers may correctly digest the zazen of self settling on itself as Buddhism, I have to talk about interdependence and the Middle Way, though it may seem somewhat indirect.

The early scriptures known as the *Agamas,* or the *Nikayas,* refer directly to these teachings: "Truly seeing the aggregation of the world, the view of nonexistence does not arise. Truly seeing the annihilation of the world, the view of existence does not arise. The view that all things exist is one extreme; the view that nothing exists is the other extreme. Being apart from these two extremes, the Tathagata teaches the dharma of the Middle Way: because this exists, that exists, because this arises, that arises."

The entire teaching of interdependence and the Middle Way is explained in this one quotation from ancient scripture. Moreover, what is expressed here is the very essence of the spirit that developed as Mahayana Buddhism. Although the language of this passage is too simple to be easily understood, we can try to get a sense of it in terms of our everyday life.

The scripture says of interdependence: "Because this exists, that exists, because this arises, that arises." But what does this mean? It means that all concrete entities occur in accordance with various conditions, that they always happen based on conditions and never apart from or separate from such factors, and that all abstract entities have meaning because of their mutual relations. Accordingly, what is being said here is that there are no independent substantial entities—that is, no things existing by themselves.

Let me take myself as an example. Usually we think of our "self" as an individual independent substance, as an enduring existence. But if we think about it carefully, this is by no means the case. I have an album of photographs taken of me every few years from infancy to the present. When I look at it these days I'm filled with an utterly strange feeling.

It so clearly shows the changes I have gone through while gradually advancing in age. How my face and figure have changed with the years! I can only wonder at the marvel of creation. Within this constant change, what endures? The birthmark under my eye, the peculiar slope of my head—only these meaningless facts remain. And if it is true that I am only what endures through time, then this birthmark and thin, oddly shaped head are what I truly am. Consequently, I cannot help but wonder whether these pictures are all of the same I or not.

Not only the appearance of the body, but the inside as well, is gradually being regenerated and transformed; so what does not appear in photographs is also undergoing change.

Moreover, the content of my thoughts, which I refer to as *I*, has also been radically changing, from infancy to childhood, adolescence, maturity, and now in old age. Not just that, even this present I is an unceasing stream of consciousness. Yet, taken momentarily at a given time, we grasp the stream of consciousness as I.

In this respect, we are as selves quite like the flame of a candle. As wax melts near a lit wick and burns, it emits light near the tip of the candle. For the most part, this place from which light is emitted remains the same and appears as a fixed shape; it is this seemingly unchanging shape that we refer to as flame. That which is called I is similar to the flame. Although both body and mind are an unceasing flow, since they preserve what seems to be a constant form, we refer to them as I. Therefore, actually there is no I existing as some substantial thing; there is only the ceaseless flow. This is true not only of this sentient being I, it is true of all things. In Buddhism, this truth is expressed as *shogyo mujo,* the First Undeniable Reality, that all things are flowing and changing, and *shoho muga,* the Third Undeniable Reality, that all things are insubstantial.

Impermanence is ungraspable, but this never implies nonexistence.

We live within the flow of impermanence, maintaining a temporary form similar to an eddy in the flow of a river. Though the water is always flowing, the eddy, like the flame of the candle, arises out of various conditions as a form that seems to be fixed. That there is this seemingly fixed form based on various conditions is interdependence. In the case of the flame, it is the interdependence of such things as the wax, the temperature, and the air; in the case of the eddy, it is the volume and speed of the current, the topography, and so forth, that form the conditions of its existence.

Not only such things as eddies and flames, but indeed everything in the universe can be considered in a similar way. For example, we who live in the age of natural science can easily appreciate that no matter how solid a thing may appear, it is not really different from the flame or the eddy—its apparent solidity is merely a question of degree.

Now, let us return to the problem of *self*. Of course, I, too, am an interdependent existence that is impermanent and at the same time takes a particular form. Buddhism teaches that our attachment to our self as though it were a substantial being is the source of our greed, anger, suffering, and strife. It is crucial that we reflect thoroughly on the fact that our self does not have a substantial existence, but merely an interdependent one.

What is it that we think of as our *self* [see also pages 275–288]? Physically, this self originates in the union of sperm and egg and is brought to its present form through the combination of such factors as temperature, moisture, nutrition, and the like. And what is it that makes up our mental life or personality? Here again, I have not chosen this self, but have simply received life in my mother's womb unconsciously (in Buddhism, this is called *mumyo,* or ignorance). I received the foundation of my personality plus certain hereditary elements from my parents, and the circumstances of my birth also determined the age I was born in, my nationality, and my family environment. Without realizing it, I was educated according to my particular society and internalized my experiences within the context of this environment. In this way, through the combination of an accidental set of factors, the views I now hold have been formed.

So our *self* is a random collection of elements and circumstances and not some sort of lump, as it is usually understood. This self may become deluded, but as it is not a fixed entity, this delusion also breaks apart. The true reality of life is expressed in the Buddha's twelve-fold chain of interdependence, insight into which is said to have been the source of his enlightenment.

For the time being, let us put aside the important problem of delusion, the view of myself as an independent substantial entity, and concentrate further on this question of self, that is, this interdependent being. While the self as an interdependent being remains merely a collection, insofar as it possesses some form as a random collection of elements it is not nonexistent. This is the point of the scriptural passage from the *Samyutta Nikaya* quoted earlier: "Truly seeing the aggregation of the world, the view of nonexistence does not arise."

But, if this present *self* is not nonexistent, can we say that it is a constant entity? No; rather, it is continually breaking apart and changing moment by moment into a new form. This is the meaning of "Truly seeing the annihilation of the world, the view of existence does not arise."

Consequently, the Buddha said: "Being apart from these two extremes [the views based on existence or nonexistence], the Tathagata—the Enlightened One—teaches the dharma of the Middle Way." This means that our very own life cannot be grasped as a lump (existence), nor as nonexistence. In other words, without being caught up in our thoughts, the Middle Way is nothing other than seeing interdependence as it is, moment by moment, seeing our life as it is.

Therefore, the middle way in Buddhism does not mean taking some in-between position that has been conjured up in our heads, nor acting in a compromising way. Rather, despite the fact that we latch on to our ideas of being or nonbeing, taking the Middle Way means to demolish all concepts set up in our minds and, without fixing on reality as any particular thing, to open the hand of thought, allowing life to be life.

THICH NHAT HANH, TRANS. AND COMMENTARY

From The Diamond Sutra

3. The First Flash of Lightning

The Buddha said to Subhuti, "This is how the bodhisattva mahasattvas master their thinking. 'However many species of living beings there are—whether born from eggs, from the womb, from moisture, or spontaneously; whether they have form or do not have form; whether they have perceptions or do not have perceptions; or whether it cannot be said of them that they have perceptions or that they do not have perceptions, we must lead all these beings to the ultimate nirvana so that they can be liberated.' "

THE WORD *MAHA* means "great," so *mahasattva* means "a great being." Liberation here means arriving at *nirvana*, "extinction," a joyful, peaceful state in which all causes of afflictions have been uprooted and we are totally free. The mahasattvas take the great vow to relieve the suffering of all living beings, to bring all to absolute nirvana where they can realize ultimate peace and joy. Absolute nirvana is also called nirvana without residue of affliction, as compared to nirvana with some residue of afflictions. Some commentators explain that nirvana with some residue of afflictions is a state in which the body of the five aggregates (form, feelings, perceptions, mental formations, and consciousness) still exists. They regard the body as a residue of the afflictions of our previous lives. After we die, they say, the body of the five aggregates disintegrates completely, and we enter "nirvana without residue of affliction," leaving no trace behind.

I do not fully agree. It is true that once we put an end to the causes of suffering and transform them, we will not bring about new consequences of suffering in the future. But what has existed for a long time, even after it is cut off, still has momentum and will continue for a while before stopping completely. When an electric fan is switched off, although the current has been cut, the blades keep moving for a while longer. Even after the cause has been cut off, the consequence of this past cause continues for a while. The residue of afflictions is the same. What comes to a stop is the creation of new causes of suffering, not the body of the five aggregates. One day, Devadatta threw a rock at the Buddha, and his foot was wounded. The Buddha was no longer creating new karma, but he experienced this karmic consequence as the result of a past action that had some energy left over before it could stop. This does not mean that the Buddha had not realized complete extinction after he passed away.

The Mahayana sutras say that bodhisattvas ride on the waves of birth and death. Riding on the waves of birth and death means that although birth and death are there, they are not drowned by them. While traveling in the ocean of birth and death, the bodhisattvas are in perfect nirvana, that is, nirvana without any residue of afflictions—not in the imperfect nirvana that has some residue of afflictions. Although their bodies are there and they are riding on birth and death, they do not suffer. Therefore the residues of afflictions in the imperfect nirvana are not the five aggregates themselves, but rather the afflictions that remain as the karmic consequence of past actions.

> However many species of living beings there are—whether born from eggs, from the womb, from moisture, or spontaneously; whether they have form or do not have form; whether they have perceptions or do not have perceptions; or whether it cannot be said of them that they have perceptions or that they do not have perceptions, we must lead all these beings to the ultimate nirvana so that they can be liberated.

This sentence exemplifies the bodhisattva's Great Vow. It is the prerequisite of becoming a bodhisattva, an awakened person, a person for whom the work for enlightenment is his or her life work, a person who is called a great being, a person to whom the Buddha gives special support and attention. This vow is not only the basic condition of being a bodhisattva, it is also the primary condition. It is the foundation of the highest, most fulfilling wish of a bodhisattva.

When we read this passage, we must look at ourselves and ask, "Is this vow at all related to my life and the life of my community? Are we practicing for ourselves or for others? Do we only want to uproot our own afflictions, or is our determination to study and practice to bring happiness to other living beings?" If we look at ourselves, we will see if we are among the bodhisattvas the Buddha is addressing, supporting, and investing in. If we study and practice with a heart like this, we won't have to wait several years for others to notice. They will see it right away by the way we treat the cat, the caterpillar, or the snail. When we wash the dishes, do we put the leftover food aside to feed the birds? These kinds of small acts show our love for all living beings. The great heart of a bodhisattva mahasattva can be seen throughout his or her daily life. While studying the bodhisattva's actions in the Mahayana sutras, we should also practice looking at ourselves—the way we drink tea, eat our food, wash the dishes, or tend our garden. If we observe ourselves in this way, we will see whether we have the understanding of a bodhisattva, and our friends will also know.

The living beings mentioned in this sutra are not only remote strangers. They are the brothers and sisters with whom we study and practice the Dharma. They too have joy and pain, and we must see them and be open to them. If we are only an independent island, living in a community but not seeing or smiling with the community, we are not practicing as a bodhisattva. Besides just our Dharma brothers and sisters, there are also other species of animals, as well as the plants in the garden and the stars in the sky. This sutra is addressing all of them, and explaining how all are related to our daily life and practice. If we are mindful, we will see.

And when this innumerable, immeasurable, infinite number of beings has become liberated, we do not, in truth, think that a single being has been liberated.

This is the first flash of lightning. The Buddha goes directly to the heart of the prajnaparamita, presenting the principle of formlessness. He tells us that a true practitioner helps all living beings in a natural and spontaneous way, without distinguishing between the one who is helping and the one who is being helped. When our left hand is injured, our right hand takes care of it right away. It doesn't stop to say, "I am taking care of you. You are benefiting from my compassion." The right hand knows very well that the left hand is also the right hand. There is no distinction between them. This is the principle of interbeing—co-existence, or mutual interdependence. "This is because that is." With this understanding—the right hand helping the left hand in a formless way—there is no need to distinguish between the right hand and the left hand.

For a bodhisattva, the work of helping is natural, like breathing. When her brother suffers, she offers care and support. She does not think that she has to help him in order to practice the Dharma or because her teacher says she should. It isn't necessary to have an idea of helping. We feel the need to do it, and we do it. This is easy to understand. If we act in this spirit of formlessness, we will not say, later on, "When my brother was sick, I took care of him every day. I made him soup and did many other things for him, and now he is not at all grateful." If we speak like that, our actions were done in the spirit of form. That is not what is called a good deed according to the teaching of prajna-paramita. Formlessness is something concrete that we can put into practice here and now.

If someone in your community is lazy and does not work hard when everyone else does, you may think, "She is awful. She stays in her room and listens to music while I have to work hard." The more you think about her, the more uncomfortable you become. In that state, your work does not bring happiness to you or anyone else. You should be able to enjoy what you are doing. Why should the absence of one person affect your work so? If, when you are working, you do not distinguish between the person who is doing the work and the one who is not, that is truly the spirit of formlessness. We can apply the practice of prajna-paramita into every aspect of our lives. We can wash the dishes or clean the bathroom in exactly the way our right hand puts a Band-Aid on our left hand, without discrimination.

When the Buddha says, "When innumerable, immeasurable, infinite beings become liberated, we do not think that a single being has been liberated," these are not empty words. The Buddha is encouraging us to support and love all living beings. It would be wonderful if those who study Buddhism understood this one sentence. The teaching here is so complete and profound.

Why is this so? If, Subhuti, a bodhisattva holds on to the idea that a self, a person, a living being, or a life span exists, that person is not an authentic bodhisattva.

Our right hand is an authentic bodhisattva, because it does not discriminate between itself and our left hand. There is just "taking care."

The words "self," "person," "living being," and "life span" are important for us to understand. "Self" refers to a permanent, changeless identity, but since, according to Buddhism, nothing is permanent and what we normally call a self is made entirely of non-self elements, there is really no such entity as a self [see also pages 275–288]. Our concept of self arises when we have concepts about things that are not-self. Using the sword of conceptualization to cut reality into pieces, we call one part "I" and the rest "not I."

The concept of "person," like the concept of self, is made only of non-person elements—sun, clouds, wheat, space, and so on. Thanks to these elements, there is something we call a person. But erecting a barrier between the idea of person and the idea of non-person is erroneous. If we say, for example, that the cosmos has given birth to humankind and that other animals, plants, the moon, the stars, and so forth, exist to serve us, we are caught up in the idea of person. These kinds of concepts are used to separate self from non-self and person from non-person, and they are erroneous.

We put a lot of energy into advancing technology in order to serve our lives better, and we exploit the non-human elements, such as the forests, rivers, and oceans, in order to do so. But as we pollute and destroy nature, we pollute and destroy ourselves as well. The results of discriminating between human and non-human are global warming, pollution, and the emergence of many strange diseases. In order to protect ourselves, we must protect the non-human elements. This fundamental understanding is needed if we want to protect our planet and ourselves.

The concept of "living being," *sattva* in Sanskrit, arises the moment we separate living from non-living beings. The poet Lamartine once asked, "Inanimate objects, do you have a soul?" to challenge our popular understanding. But what we call non-living makes what we call living beings possible. If we destroy the non-living, we also destroy the living. In Buddhist monasteries, during the Ceremony of Beginning Anew, each monk and nun recites, "I vow to practice wholeheartedly so that all beings, living and non-living, will be liberated." In many ceremonies, we bow deeply to show our gratitude to our parents, teachers, friends, and numerous beings in the animal, vegetal, and mineral worlds. Doing this helps us realize that there is no separation between the living and the so-called non-living. Vietnamese composer Trinh Cong Con wrote, "How do we know the stones are not suffering? Tomorrow the pebbles will need one another." When we really understand love, our love will include all beings, living and so-called non-living. . . .

7. Entering the Ocean of Reality

"What do you think, Subhuti, has the Tathagata ["the thus-come one," one of the ten titles of the Buddha] *arrived at the highest, most fulfilled, awakened mind? Does the Tathagata give any teaching?"*

The Venerable Subhuti replied, "As far as I have understood the Lord Buddha's teachings, there is no independently existing object of mind called the highest, most fulfilled, awakened mind, nor is there any independently existing teaching that the Tathagata gives. Why? The teachings that the Tathagata has realized and spoken of cannot be conceived of as separate, independent existences and therefore cannot be described. The Tathagata's teaching is not self-existent nor is it non-self-existent. Why? Because the noble teachers are only distinguished from others in terms of the unconditioned."

THE BUDDHA IS testing Subhuti to see if he understands what he has said concerning the dialectics of prajnaparamita. In answering the question whether the Tathagata has arrived at the highest, most fulfilled awakened mind and if there is any teaching that the Tathagata gives, Subhuti demonstrates his understanding by using the language of prajna-paramita. He goes on to explain that the teachings of the Tathagata can neither be grasped nor described. This is a very wise reply.

The Buddha has already explained these points, and now Subhuti repeats them in his own way by saying, "There is no independently existing object of mind called the highest, most fulfilled, awakened mind." If we say that there is a dharma called the highest, most fulfilled awakened mind, we are using the sword of conceptualization to slice out a piece of reality and call it the highest, most fulfilled, awakened mind. We should also be able to see the non-highest, non-most fulfilled, non-awakened mind just as we saw the non-rose elements while looking at a rose.

When Subhuti says that there is no independently existing object of mind called "the highest, most fulfilled, awakened mind" he means that what is called "the highest, most fulfilled, awakened mind" has no separate existence. Just as the rose cannot be separated from clouds, sun, soil, and rain, the teaching of the Buddha cannot be found outside of daily life. No dharma—not "the highest, most fulfilled, awakened mind," suchness, nirvana, Tathagata, a rose, eating a meal, washing the dishes, Subhuti, a friend, a house, a horse, or the teachings the Tathagata has realized—can be grasped or described.

The notion that things can exist independently of one another comes from the perception that they have a beginning and an end. But it is impossible to find the beginning or end of anything. When you look at your close friend, you may think that you understand her completely, but that is difficult because she is a river of reality. In every moment, dharmas that are not her enter and leave her. You cannot take hold of her. By observing her form, feelings, perceptions, mental formations, and consciousness, you can see that she is here sitting next to you, and she is elsewhere at the same time. She is in the present, the past, and the future. Your friend, the Tathagata, Subhuti, and the rose cannot be grasped because they have no beginning and no end. Their presence is deeply connected to all dharmas, all objects of mind in the universe.

When we practice Zen, we may be assigned the *kung-an* [koan] "What was your face before your parents were born?" We cannot grasp or describe this because it transcends forms. We have only our concepts, and we cannot grasp these dharmas through our perceptions. It is like trying to hold on to the air with our hand. The air slips out. This is why Subhuti said, "The teachings that the Tathagata has realized and spoken of cannot be conceived of as separate, independent existences and therefore cannot be described. The Tathagata's teaching is not self-existent nor is it non-self-existent." It is not correct to call the Tathagata's teaching a dharma, since by doing so we put it into a box, a pattern, and isolate it from other things. But saying it is not a dharma is also not correct, because it really is a dharma—not one that can be isolated but one that transcends all perceptions.

Then Subhuti says that the noble teachers can be distinguished from others only in terms of the unconditioned. "Noble teachers" is a translation of the Sanskrit term *arya pudgala*. *Arya* means "honor." *Pudgala* means "person." Aryapudgala are those who have attained the status of "Stream-Enterer" (*sotapatti-phala*), "Once-Returner" (*sakadagami-phala*), "Never-Returner" (*anagami-phala*), or "the one who is free from craving and rebirth" (*arhat*). *Asamskrita dharmas* are unconditioned. They transcend all concepts. The noble teachers are liberated. They are distinguished from others because they are in touch with and realize the unconditioned dharmas. They are no longer imprisoned by forms and concepts.

This section of the sutra shows that all dharmas are without form and transcend conceptual knowledge. When we realize the suchness of all dharmas, we are freed from our conceptual prisons. In daily life, we usually use our conceptual knowledge to grasp reality. But this is impossible. Meditation aims at breaking through all conceptual limitations and barriers so that we can move freely in the boundless ocean of reality. . . .

10. Creating a Formless Pure Land

The Buddha asked Subhuti, "In ancient times when the Tathagata practiced under Buddha Dipankara [considered the first of the twenty-four buddhas who preceded the historic Buddha], did he attain anything?"

Subhuti answered, "No, World-Honored One. In ancient times when the Tathagata was practicing under Buddha Dipankara, he did not attain anything."

"What do you think, Subhuti? Does a bodhisattva create a serene and beautiful Buddha field?"

"No, World-Honored One. Why? To create a serene and beautiful Buddha field is not in fact creating a serene and beautiful Buddha field. That is why it is called creating a serene and beautiful Buddha field."

UPON ATTAINING ENLIGHTENMENT, all Buddhas and bodhisattvas open a new world for people on the path of realization who want to study and practice with them. Every Buddha creates a pure land as a practice center. A pure land is a fresh, beautiful place where people are happy and peaceful. Creating a pure land is called "setting up a serene and beautiful Buddha field." Teachers and students work together to make such a place beautiful, pleasant, and fresh, so that many people can go there to live and practice. The greater their power of awakening and peace, the more pleasant is their pure land.

Amitabha Buddha has a Pure Land in the Western Paradise. Aksobhya Buddha has a place called Wondrous Joy. After a period of practice, if you have some attainment and peace, you may wish to share them with others and establish small practice community. But this should always be done in the spirit of formlessness. Do not be bound by the practice center you establish. "To create a serene and beautiful Buddha field is not in fact creating a serene and beautiful Buddha field" means to do so in the spirit of formlessness. Do not let yourself be devoured by your Buddha field or you will suffer. Do not allow yourself to be burnt out in the process of setting up a practice center.

The Buddha said, "So, Subhuti, all the bodhisattva mahasattvas should give rise to a pure and clear intention in this spirit. When they give rise to this intention, they should not rely on forms, sounds, smells, tastes, tactile objects, or objects of mind. They should give rise to an intention with their minds not dwelling anywhere."

Not dwelling anywhere means not relying on anything. Giving rise to an intention means having the wish to attain the highest awakening. Relying on forms, sounds, smells, tastes, tactile objects, and objects of minds means being caught by perceptions, ideas, and concepts. In Section Two of this sutra, the first question Subhuti asked the Buddha was, "If sons and daughters of good families want to give rise to the highest, most fulfilled, awakened mind, what should they rely on and what should they do to master their thinking?" This passage is the Buddha's answer.

"Subhuti, if there were someone with a body as big as Mount Sumeru, would you say that his was a large body?"

Subhuti answered, "Yes, World-Honored One, very large. Why? What the Tathagata says is not a large body, that is known as a large body."

The word "body" is a translation of the Sanskrit word *atmabhava*, not the word *kaya*. Mount Sumeru is the king of all mountains. In this paragraph, the teacher and his student are still using the language of dialectics of prajnaparamita. When the Buddha asks, "Would you say that his was a large body?" Subhuti answers, "Very large," because he understands clearly the Buddha's language. He is aware that the Buddha says "large" because he is free of the concepts of large and small. If we are aware of the way the Buddha uses words, we will not be caught by any of his words. The teacher is important, the director of the practice center is important, but if the idea of being important becomes an obstacle for the teaching and the practice, then the meaning will be lost. . . .

13. The Diamond That Cuts Through Illusion

After that, Subhuti asked the Buddha, "What should this sutra be called and how should we act regarding its teachings?"

The Buddha replied, "This sutra should be called The Diamond That Cuts Through Illusion because it has the capacity to cut through all illusions and afflictions and bring us to the shore of liberation. Please use this title and practice according to its deepest meaning. Why? What the Tathagata has called the highest, transcendent understanding is not, in fact, the highest, transcendent understanding. That is why it is truly the highest, transcendent understanding."

The Buddha asked, "What do you think, Subhuti? Is there any dharma that the Tathagata teaches?"

Subhuti replied, "The Tathagata has nothing to teach, World-Honored One."

"What do you think, Subhuti? Are there many particles of dust in the 3,000 chiliocosms ["thousand universes"; innumerable number of universes]?"

"Very many, World-Honored One."

"Subhuti, the Tathagata says that these particles of dust are not particles of dust. That is why they are truly particles of dust. And what the Tathagata calls chiliocosms are not in fact chiliocosms. That is why they are called chiliocosms.

"What do you think, Subhuti? Can the Tathagata be recognized by the possession of the thirty-two marks [of perfection distinguishing a buddha]?"

The Venerable Subhuti replied, "No, World-Honored One. Why? Because what the Tathagata calls the thirty-two marks are not essentially marks and that is why the Tathagata calls them the thirty-two marks."

"Subhuti, if as many times as there are grains of sand in the Ganges a son or daughter of a good family gives up his or her life as an act of generosity and if another daughter or son of a good family knows how to accept, practice, and

explain this sutra to others, even if only a gatha [verse] of four lines, the
happiness resulting from explaining this sutra is far greater.''

SUBHUTI ASKS WHAT this sutra should be called and how we
should practice its teachings, and the Buddha answers that it should be
called *The Diamond That Cuts Through Illusion*. A diamond has the capacity
to cut through all ignorance and afflictions. He also says that we should
practice in an intelligent way, that we should learn to look deeply so
that we will realize that even transcendent understanding is not an independently existing dharma and that his teaching has no separate nature.
That is why Subhuti says, "The Tathagata has nothing to teach."

If someone were to grind the 3,000 chiliocosms into dust, these
particles of dust would be very, very many. We should look deeply into
the concepts of "many" and "chiliocosms" with the eye of transcendent
understanding if we want to avoid being caught by these concepts. The
same is true of the concepts of "dust" and "thirty-two marks." Although such words are used, we should not be caught by them. If
someone were to accept, practice, and explain these teachings, even if
only one verse of four lines, the happiness resulting from this would be
far greater than the happiness that would result from any other virtuous
act. Because the practice of non-attachment as it is taught in the sutra
can liberate us completely from wrong views, the happiness that results
from this practice is far greater than any kind of happiness. Virtuous
acts still based on the ground of self, person, living being, and life span
may bring some happiness, but compared to the happiness of true liberation, it is still quite small. When a person is absolutely free from
wrong views, his or her actions will greatly benefit the world. The
practice of *The Diamond That Cuts Through Illusion* is thus the basis for all
meaningful action.

The Three Refuges/The Triple Treasure

In the Buddha's day, followers who wished to formally become his disciples did so by publicly repeating the Three Refuges (or taking refuge in the Three Jewels or Triple Treasure) three times, a practice that still continues. Taking the Refuges in daily practice is a way of renewing the commitment to follow the Buddhist path, and contemplating the Three Jewels—the Buddha (the Awakened One), the Dharma (his Truth), and the Sangha (the followers of his Truth)—is perceiving the expression of Buddha-nature and the universe itself.

EDWARD CONZE, TRANS.

The Triple Refuge

To the Buddha for refuge I go; to the Dharma for refuge I go; to the Sangha for refuge I go.

For the second time to the Buddha for refuge I go; for the second time to the Dharma for refuge I go; for the second time to the Sangha for refuge I go.

For the third time to the Buddha for refuge I go; for the third time to the Dharma for refuge I go; for the third time to the Sangha for refuge I go.

The Buddha

This Lord is truly the Arhat, fully enlightened, perfect in his knowledge and conduct, well-gone, world-knower, unsurpassed, leader of men to be tamed, teacher of gods and men, the Buddha, the Lord.

What had to be fully known, that I have fully known;
What had to be developed, that I have developed;
What was to be forsaken, that I have forsaken.
Therefore, O Brahmin, I am the Buddha.

The Dharma

Well taught has the Lord the Dharma, it is verifiable, not a matter of time, inviting all to come and see, leading to Nirvana, to be known by the wise, each one for himself. . . . Who sees Dharma, he sees me. Who sees me, he sees Dharma. Because it is by seeing Dharma that he sees me, it is by seeing me that he sees Dharma.

The Dharma, incomparably profound and exquisite,
Is rarely met with, even in hundreds of thousands of millions of kalpas [eons].
We are now permitted to see it, to listen to it, to accept and to hold it.
May we truly understand the meaning of the Tathagata's words!

The Sangha

Well-behaved is the Community of the Lord's disciples, straight in their behaviour, upright and correct. . . . Worthy they are of offerings, worthy of hospitality, worthy of gifts, worthy of respectful salutation, they, the world's peerless field of merit.

And for a disciple, rightly delivered, whose thought is calm, there is nothing to be added to what has been done, and naught more remains for him to do. Just as a rock of one solid mass remains unshaken by the wind, even so, neither forms, nor sounds, nor smells, nor tastes, nor contacts of any kind, neither desired nor undesired dharmas, can agitate such a one. . . .

B. ALAN WALLACE

Taking Refuge

THE GATEWAY TO the Buddhist path of liberation is taking refuge in the Buddha, the Dharma, and the spiritual community, known as the Sangha. Taking refuge involves wholehearted commitment to this spiritual path and to the one who revealed it—the Buddha. This does not mean that one cannot engage in certain Buddhist practices without making such a commitment. A wide range of Buddhist methods can be practiced by people of other faiths and ideologies. But in terms of progressing along the Buddhist path, trust and commitment are essential.

The notion of taking refuge may appear strange until we recognize the many ways in which we have already taken refuge by placing our trust, faith, or confidence in other people, institutions, and so on. Most of us take refuge in banks by entrusting them with our savings. For physical ailments we take refuge in doctors; we take refuge in the government to protect our homeland, to educate our children, and to give us a stipend in our old age. . . .

What is it that makes the Buddha, Dharma, and Sangha worthy

objects of refuge? A Buddha, first of all, is free not only of all mental distortions, as are arhats, but of even subtler cognitive obscurations. Buddhas are forever free of all fear and danger and are skillful in leading others to freedom. They feel great compassion toward all living creatures, and offer Dharma to everyone without discrimination. Regardless of what we have or have not done to the Buddhas, they show no favoritism but treat all with equal loving concern.

The historical Buddha is the source of the Dharma to which Buddhists entrust themselves. The Dharma can be understood in two ways: as spiritual realization and as the teachings that lead to such realization. The Sangha originates from the practice of Dharma. Strictly speaking, the Sangha refers only to [those] who have gained a nonconceptual realization of ultimate truth. More loosely, it refers to the community of spiritual practitioners. Fellow practitioners can be a vital aid to us as we progress along the path, for many of them are far more advanced than we, and even those at our own level may have special insights to share with us. They offer us experiential guidance and act as living examples of the practice of Dharma. Finally, they can be a great source of inspiration, for in them we can see the tangible benefits of spiritual practice.

The refuges of the Buddha, Dharma, and Sangha can be understood using a common analogy in Tibetan Buddhism. We go for refuge out of need, like a person afflicted with countless diseases. The Buddha can then be likened to a physician, the Dharma to the medical treatment and therapy, and the Sangha to the nurses who care for us. The Buddha's chief task is to reveal the Dharma, and the Sangha's is to assist us in our practice. The most direct refuge is the Dharma.

How do we go about taking refuge in the Three Jewels? If we recognize our personal need for refuge and entrust ourselves to the Buddha, Dharma, and Sangha, we have taken refuge. We are now Buddhist. We may celebrate this step by participating in a ritual of taking refuge with a spiritual mentor, but the ritual is not essential. And if we have not inwardly taken refuge, the external ritual is meaningless.

THICH NHAT HANH
The Three Gems

WHEN WE SAY, "I take refuge in the Buddha," we should also understand that "The Buddha takes refuge in me," because without the second part the first part is not complete. The Buddha needs us for awakening, understanding, and love to be real things and not just concepts. They must be real things that have real effects on life. Whenever I say, "I take refuge in the Buddha," I hear "Buddha takes refuge in me."

We are all Buddhas, because only through us can understanding and love become tangible and effective. Thich Thanh Van was killed during his effort to help other people. He was a good Buddhist, he was a good Buddha, because he was able to help tens of thousands of people, victims of the war. Because of him, awakening, understanding, and love were real things. So we can call him a Buddha body, in Sanskrit *Buddhakaya*. For Buddhism to be real, there must be a Buddhakaya, an embodiment of awakened activity. Otherwise Buddhism is just a word. Thich Thanh Van was a Buddhakaya. Shakyamuni was a Buddhakaya. When we realize awakening, when we are understanding and loving, each of us is a Buddhakaya.

The second gem is the Dharma. Dharma is what the Buddha taught.

It is the way of understanding and love—how to understand, how to love, how to make understanding and love into real things. Before the Buddha passed away, he said to his students, "Dear people, my physical body will not be here tomorrow, but my teaching body will always be here to help. You can consider it as your own teacher, a teacher who never leaves you." That is the birth of *Dharmakaya*. The Dharma has a body also, the body of the teaching, or the body of the way. As you can see, the meaning of Dharmakaya is quite simple, although people in Mahayana have made it very complicated. Dharmakaya just means the teaching of the Buddha, the way to realize understanding and love. Later it became something like the ontological ground of being.

Anything that can help you wake up has Buddha nature. When I am alone and a bird calls me, I return to myself, I breathe, and I smile, and sometimes it calls me once more. I smile and I say to the bird, "I hear already." Not only sounds, but sights can remind you to return to your true self. In the morning when you open your window and see the light streaming in, you can recognize it as the voice of the Dharma, and it becomes part of the Dharmakaya. That is why people who are awake see the manifestation of the Dharma in everything. A pebble, a bamboo tree, the cry of a baby, anything can be the voice of the Dharma calling. We should be able to practice like that. . . .

Dharmakaya is not just expressed in words, in sounds. It can express itself in just being. Sometimes if we don't do anything, we help more than if we do a lot. We call that non-action. It is like the calm person on a small boat in a storm. That person does not have to do much, just be himself, and the situation can change. That is also an aspect of Dharmakaya: not talking, not teaching, just being. . . .

The Sangha is the community that lives in harmony and awareness. *Sanghakaya* is a new Sanskrit term.

The Sangha needs a body also. When you are with your family and you practice smiling, breathing, recognizing the Buddha body in yourself and your children, then your family becomes a Sangha. If you have a bell in your home, the bell becomes part of your Sanghakaya, because the bell helps you to practice. If you have a cushion, then the cushion also becomes part of the Sanghakaya. Many things help us practice. The air, for breathing. If you have a park or a riverbank near your home, you are very fortunate because you can enjoy practicing walking meditation. You have to discover your Sanghakaya—invite a friend to come and practice with you, have tea meditation, sit with you, join you for walking meditation. All those efforts are to establish your Sanghakaya at home. Practice is easier if you have a Sanghakaya. . . .

Practicing Buddhism, practicing meditation is for us to be serene and happy, understanding and loving. In that way we work for the peace and happiness of our family and our society. If we look closely, the Three Gems are actually one. In each of them, the other two are already there. In Buddha, there is Buddhahood, there is the Buddha body. In Buddha there is the Dharma body because without the Dharma body, he could not have become a Buddha. In the Buddha there is the Sangha body because he had breakfast with the bodhi tree, with the other trees, and birds and environment. In a meditation center, we have a Sangha body, Sanghakaya, because the way of understanding and compassion is practiced there. Therefore the Dharma body is present, the way, the teaching is present. But the teaching cannot become real without the life and body of each of us. So the Buddhakaya is also present. If Buddha and Dharma are not present, it is not a Sangha. Without you, the Buddha is not real, it is just an idea.

Without you, the Dharma cannot be practiced. It has to be practiced by someone. Without each of you, the Sangha cannot be. That is why when we say, "I take refuge in the Buddha," we also hear, "The Buddha takes refuge in me." "I take refuge in the Dharma. The Dharma takes refuge in me. I take refuge in the Sangha. The Sangha takes refuge in me."

DAININ KATAGIRI

The Triple Treasure

BUDDHA IS THE universe and Dharma is the teaching from the universe, and Sangha is the group of people who make the universe and its teaching alive in their lives. In our everyday life we must be mindful of Buddha, Dharma and Sangha whether we understand this or not. We have to be mindful from day to night, through countless lives, over an immense span of time. Then our life will be very stable.

To "take refuge" does not mean to escape from the human world or from one another. In Japanese, to "take refuge" is *namu* or *namu kie;* in Sanskrit it is *namo. Namo* means full devotion or throwing away the body and mind. Full devotion is just like the relationship between your mind and your body. The body seems to be different from the mind, but actually the relationship between them is very close. For instance, if your thoughts make you nervous, your stomach becomes upset. They are separate, but they are not separate; they work together without leaving any trace of the stomach or of the thought. This is the meaning of full devotion. In English we also say to "take refuge in" or sometimes to "go to Buddha for guidance."

We take refuge in the Buddha because Buddha is our great teacher. "Great" in this sense is completely beyond the human evaluation of good or bad. The spirit, the essence of the universe, the merit of the universe, and the functioning of the universe are great beyond our speculation. When we realize this, we become the universe and we are called buddha. So Siddhartha Gautama realized the essence of the universe, the merit or virtue of the universe, the attributes and functioning of the universe. Then Siddhartha Gautama became Buddha. We take refuge in the Buddha because he is our great teacher.

We take refuge in the law, in the Dharma, because it is good medicine. Dharma is teaching; this teaching is completely beyond human evaluation, beyond moral sense or ethical sense. Dharma is the Truth, something coming from the Truth. It really benefits everyone, all beings, just as rain nurtures grass, trees, pebbles, human beings, air, everything. Dharma is good medicine.

We take refuge in Buddha's community, or Sangha, because it is composed of excellent friends. Sangha is a community, but it's not the usual sense of community, because this community has many people who try to follow the Buddha's way, so they are excellent friends for you. . . .

Only by taking refuge in the Triple Treasure can we become disciples of the Buddha. In other words, we can become a child of the Buddha. Being a child of the Buddha means that we have to accept completely the universe where all sentient beings exist. There is no excuse for ignoring anything in this world. If we accept ourselves, we have to accept all sentient beings, not as something separate from our life, but as the contents of our life. . . .

Let's look at the three treasures in terms of spiritual or functional worth, ethical or virtuous worth, emotional worth, and intellectual or philosophical worth. If we ignore intellectual worth our effort directed toward the three treasures becomes very emotional. And if we depend on intellectual worth alone, we ignore the emotional aspect of human life. But we cannot do this; it is not the right way of faith. So we have to accept faith or the three treasures in terms of the whole situation of our lives—emotional, intellectual, spiritual and ethical.

First let us look at the three treasures in terms of philosophical or intellectual worth. Buddha means exactly Truth itself, the whole universe itself. The essence of the universe, the essence of being itself, we call the Truth, we call the universal life, common to all sentient beings—trees, birds, human beings, pebbles, rivers, mountains. This is Dharma. Dharma refers to cleanness and purity, which allow all beings to be free from worldly dust. For example, look at winter. According to our individual emotional pattern of life, some accept winter, some don't; some hate it, some love it. So various styles of life appear. But according to the Dharma, in terms of philosophical worth, I think winter is a constant manifestation of beauty itself. When you see winter, you are impressed by it, because winter is Dharma, which shows us the cleanness and purity that allow all beings to be free from worldly affairs, free from our thoughts and evaluations or judgments. The Dharma allows everything to be free from any dust. This is why, at the very moment of meeting winter, we are really moved. The next moment we don't know why we are moved, but we are moved. This means we are connected, we have had real communion with the universe. So, from this point of view we say winter, bare trees, snow, sky, all are Dharma. All sentient beings are really peaceful and harmonious, perfectly clear and pure. This is the state of all sentient beings in terms of philosophical worth, completely beyond our judgment or evaluation. Sangha means, in this case, peace and harmony that allow all beings to be free from confusion, perverted views and misunderstanding. Originally, all sentient beings are very peaceful, exactly peaceful and harmonious. This is called Sangha. In terms of philosophical or intellectual worth, Buddha is truth itself, Dharma is the form of all sentient beings regarded as purity and cleanness, and Sangha means all sentient beings are originally peaceful and harmonious. This is why, if we open our hearts, we communicate, naturally. We can have spiritual communion between us and the universe. This is the philosophical worth of the three treasures.

Second, let us look at the three treasures in terms of virtue or ethical worth. From this point of view, Buddha means actualized realization of the supreme way. Buddha means that the universe, existence, is nothing but the total manifestation of the truth. Temporarily, we use the term "existence," but existence is something more than a philosophical concept. Very naturally, we have to see something more than the philosophical sense of existence, so we say "nonexistent." Intellectually, we have to negate the usual concept of existence in order to see something more than the philosophical concept of existence. So we should forget this term, and then open ourselves and see, practically, what is is, if we want to see existence as a whole. The truth is already actualized before we poke our heads into existence. This is why I say "actualized realization." Realization means to accept and to digest. Realization means we should accept subject and object, and then we have to digest both of them totally until they disappear, leaving no trace of subject and object, concept or idea. They completely turn into life energy. The world and all sentient beings are exactly the actualized realization of the truth. This is why we can live in the world.

In terms of the virtue of the three treasures, Dharma means that which the Buddha has realized. What he has realized is, "I have attained enlightenment simultaneously with all sentient beings." This is the Dharma. In other words, all beings are nothing but realized beings, enlightened beings, because Buddha realized this. So we have to see or hear with our whole body and mind and deal with all sentient beings in terms of enlightened beings. Then, very naturally, we can share compassion or kindness with everyone, with all beings in which the Buddha is amply present, or, in other words, in which the Truth is amply present. So everyone is the Truth. The form of everyone is the manifestation of Buddha, or truth, because this is the content that Buddha realized twenty-five hundred years ago. Even though we don't understand it, it is really true. Buddhas from generation to generation have transmitted this essence, this essential teaching, to the next generation.

In terms of virtue, Sangha is to learn, to study, to practice this Buddha, this Dharma. Very naturally, we can feel appreciation because the world, existence, is that in which Buddha or the Truth is constantly manifested. All beings are nothing but that which Buddha has realized. So all sentient beings are enlightened beings; there is no waste. We have to deal with all sentient beings with compassion, with kindness, with appreciation. Whether we understand or not, it *doesn't* matter. We have to continually study and learn and practice this Buddha, this Dharma in everyday life. This is the Sangha. These are the three treasures in terms of virtue or ethical worth.

Third, let us consider the three treasures in terms of functioning or spiritual worth. In this case, the Buddha constantly edifies all beings wherever they may be. In Buddhist psychology there are ten categories of existence in the world: hell, hungry ghosts, fighting spirits, animal spirits, human beings, celestial beings, *pratyeka* buddhas ["solitary enlightened ones"], *shravaka* buddhas [arhats], bodhisattvas, and buddhas. And each of the ten categories of existence contains all the rest. This means that hell is not only hell; within hell are hungry ghosts, fighting spirits, animal spirits, human beings, celestial beings, pratyeka buddhas, shravaka buddhas, bodhisattvas and also Buddha's world. So within hell there is buddha. Even in the hell world, still there are all the rest of the worlds, always. Wherever you may go, you have great opportunities to be saved. Whatever you do, wherever you may be, you are doing it in the Buddha's world. Buddha's world means the universe. The universe is nothing but the total manifestation of the truth by which all sentient beings are supported, upheld, naturally, if we open our hearts. If we don't open our hearts, it's a little bit difficult. Difficult means it takes a long time. But, basically, the universe and truth are very compassionate and kind toward all sentient beings. Constantly the compassionate universe is helping, just like the rain. Rain is accepted by many kinds of beings; some of the plants that are rained on grow, but some of them do not. If we don't open our hearts it's pretty hard to grow; it really takes time. But still, the rain is just the rain. Rain continues to fall to support all sentient beings. So in terms of functioning or spiritual worth, Buddha refers to a person who consistently edifies all beings, wherever they may be.

Dharma means to edify animate and inanimate beings by virtue of appearing as, for example, Buddha statues and as Buddha paintings. Truth manifests itself constantly by virtue of appearing as statues, paintings and as Buddhist scriptures written in words, because it's very difficult for human beings to have communion with the Truth itself. Human beings naturally have deep feelings and sensations and we try to make things through which we can experience a deep, compassionate communion with the universe. This is art, Buddhist art, religious art. This is a Buddha statue. The statue is not an idol. This beautiful art is the manifestation of perfect beauty coming from the human heart. This is the Dharma. From the point of view of functioning, not only paintings and statues, but also the form of the trees, the color of the mountains, the sounds of the valley streams, all are teaching us the truth. The Chinese poet Su Tung p'o (So Toba) says, "The sounds of the valley streams are his lord's broad tongue. The colors of the mountains are his pure body. At night I heard the eighty-four thousand verses uttered. How can I show others what they say?"

Sangha, in terms of the functioning of the Triple Treasure, means saving all beings from their suffering and freeing them from worldly affairs. This refers to the profound aspiration for letting all beings be free from suffering, all beings including subject and object, because generally, Sangha means peace and harmony. There must be something actualized by you. This is refined human action and it must last for a long time, not only in your lifetime, but life after life. In order to carry on this refined human behavior for a long time, we need profound aspiration, or what we call the vow to help all sentient beings be free from suffering. Then, simultaneously, this profound aspiration based on the vow to let all beings be free from suffering naturally turns into human action to establish a world where all beings can live in peace and harmony. There are many ways we can help. This is Sangha.

We have to understand the Triple Treasure in terms of philosophical or intellectual worth, virtue or ethical worth, and functioning or spiritual worth. Then we can see a dim image of the lofty ideal of human life toward which our effort should be directed. Very naturally, we can establish our life as a whole personality that is profound, and that helps all sentient beings emotionally, philosophically, ethically, in many ways. This is called Buddhist faith.

Buddha Nature

Within Mahayana Buddhism, a commonly held belief is that all sentient beings are endowed with Buddha nature, which is sometimes described as the eternal, unchangeable Original Mind. It is this mind that has the potential both for achieving enlightenment and for causing suffering. The relationship of Buddha nature to human nature has concerned Mahayana thinkers from ninth-century Ch'an master Huang-Po to the contemporary Zen teacher Charlotte Joko Beck and was explored in the early Vajrayana Uttaratantra text.

HUANG PO (NINTH CENTURY)

The One Mind

ALL THE BUDDHAS and all sentient beings are nothing but the One Mind, beside which nothing exists. This Mind, which is without beginning, is unborn and indestructible. It is not green nor yellow, and has neither form nor appearance. It does not belong to the categories of things which exist or do not exist, nor can it be thought of in terms of new or old. It is neither long nor short, big nor small, for it transcends all limits, measures, names, traces and comparisons. It is that which you see before you—begin to reason about it and you at once fall into error. It is like the boundless void that cannot be fathomed or measured. The One Mind alone is the Buddha, and there is no distinction between the

Buddha and sentient things, but that sentient beings are attached to forms and so seek externally for Buddhahood. By their very seeking they lose it, for that is using the Buddha to seek for the Buddha and using mind to grasp Mind. Even though they do their utmost for a full eon, they will not be able to attain to it. They do not know that, if they put a stop to conceptual thought and forget their anxiety, the Buddha will appear before them, for this Mind is the Buddha and the Buddha is all living beings. It is not the less for being manifested in ordinary beings, nor is it greater for being manifested in the Buddhas.

The building up of good and evil both involve attachment to form. Those who, being attached to form, do evil have to undergo various incarnations unnecessarily; while those who, being attached to form, do good, subject themselves to toil and privation equally to no purpose. In either case it is better to achieve sudden self-realization and to grasp the fundamental Dharma. This Dharma is Mind, beyond which there is no Dharma; and this Mind is the Dharma, beyond which there is no mind. Mind in itself is not mind, yet neither is it no-mind. To say that Mind is no-mind implies something existent. Let there be a silent understanding and no more. Away with all thinking and explaining. Then we may say that the Way of Words has been cut off and movements of the mind eliminated. This Mind is the pure Buddha-Source inherent in all men. All wriggling beings possessed of sentient life and all the Buddhas and bodhisattvas are of this one substance and do not differ. Differences arise from wrong-thinking only and lead to the creation of all kinds of karma.

Our original Buddha-nature is, in highest truth, devoid of any atom of objectivity. It is void, omnipresent, silent, pure; it is glorious and mysterious peaceful joy—and that is all. Enter deeply into it by awaking to it yourself. That which is before you is it, in all its fullness, utterly complete. There is naught beside. Even if you go through all the stages of a bodhisattva's progress towards Buddhahood, one by one; when at last, in a single flash you attain to full realization, you will only be realizing the Buddha-nature, which has been with you all the time; and by all the foregoing stages you will have added to it nothing at all. You will come to look upon those eons of work and achievement as no better than unreal actions performed in a dream. That is why the Tathagata said: "I truly attained nothing from complete, unexcelled Enlightenment. Had there been anything attained, Dipankara Buddha would not have made the prophecy concerning me [see pages 9–10]". He also said: "This Dharma is absolutely without distinctions, neither high nor low, and its name is Bodhi. It is pure Mind, which is the source of everything and which, whether appearing as sentient beings or as Buddhas, as the rivers and mountains of the world which has form, as that which is formless, or as penetrating the whole universe, is absolutely without distinctions, there being no such entities as selfness and otherness.

SHUNRYU SUZUKI

True Nature

WHEN WE EXPRESS our true nature, we are human beings. When we do not, we do not know what we are. We are not an animal, because we walk on two legs. We are something different from an animal, but what are we? We may be a ghost; we do not know what to call ourselves. Such a creature does not actually exist. It is a delusion. We are not a human being anymore, but we do exist. When Zen is not Zen, nothing exists. Intellectually my talk makes no sense, but if you have experienced true practice, you will understand what I mean. If something exists, it has its own true nature, its Buddha nature. In the Pari-nirvana Sutra, Buddha says, "Everything has Buddha nature," but Dogen reads it in this way: "Everything is Buddha nature." There is a difference. If you say, "Everything has Buddha nature," it means Buddha nature is in each existence, so Buddha nature and each existence are different. But when you say, "Everything is Buddha nature," it means everything is Buddha nature itself. When there is no Buddha nature, there is nothing at all. Something apart from Buddha nature is just a delusion. It may exist in your mind, but such things actually do not exist.

So to be a human being is to be a Buddha. Buddha nature is just another name for human nature, our true human nature. Thus even though you do not do anything, you are actually doing something. You are expressing yourself. You are expressing your true nature. Your eyes will express; your voice will express; your demeanor will express. The most important thing is to express your true nature in the simplest, most adequate way and to appreciate it in the smallest existence.

While you are continuing this practice, week after week, year after year, your experience will become deeper and deeper, and your experience will cover everything you do in your everyday life. The most important thing is to forget all gaining ideas, all dualistic ideas. In other words, just practice zazen in a certain posture. Do not think about anything. Just remain on your cushion without expecting anything. Then eventually you will resume your own true nature. That is to say, your own true nature resumes itself.

CHARLOTTE JOKO BECK

Aspiration

ASPIRATION IS A basic element of our practice. We could say that the whole practice of Zen comes out of our aspiration; without it nothing can happen. At the same time we hear that we should practice without any expectation. It sounds contradictory because we quite often confuse aspiration and expectation.

Aspiration, in the context of practice, is nothing but our own true nature seeking to realize and express itself. Intrinsically we are all Buddhas, but our Buddha nature is covered up. Aspiration is the key to practice because, without it, our Buddha nature is like a beautiful car: until someone gets in the driver's seat and turns on the ignition it is useless. When we begin to practice our aspiration may be very small; but as we continue in the practice aspiration grows. After six months of practice one's aspiration is different from what it was when just beginning practice, and after ten years it will be different than after six months. It is always changing in its outward form, yet essentially it is always the same. As long as we live it will continue to grow.

One sure clue as to whether we're being motivated by aspiration or expectation is that aspiration is always satisfying; it may not be pleasant, but it is always satisfying. Expectation, on the other hand, is always unsatisfying, because it comes from our little minds, our egos. . . .

There's a story of three people who are watching a monk standing on top of a hill. After they watch him for a while, one of the three says, "He must be a shepherd looking for a sheep he's lost." The second person says, "No, he's not looking around. I think he must be waiting for a friend." And the third person says, "He's probably a monk. I'll bet he's meditating." They begin arguing over what this monk is doing, and eventually, to settle the squabble, they climb up the hill and approach him. "Are you looking for a sheep?" "No, I don't have any sheep to look for." "Oh, then you must be waiting for a friend." "No, I'm not waiting for anyone." "Well, then you must be meditating." "Well, no. I'm just standing here. I'm not doing anything at all."

It's very difficult for us to conceive of someone just standing and doing nothing because we are always frantically trying to get somewhere to do *something*. It's impossible to move outside of this moment; nevertheless, we habitually try to. We bring this same attitude to Zen practice: "I know Buddha-nature must be out there somewhere. If I look hard enough and sit hard enough, I'll find it eventually!" But seeing Buddha nature requires that we drop all that and completely be each moment, so that whatever activity we are engaged in—whether we're looking for a lost sheep, or waiting for a friend, or meditating—we are standing right here, right now, doing nothing at all.

If we try to make ourselves calm and wise and wonderfully enlightened through Zen practice, we're not going to understand. Each moment, just as it is, *is* the sudden manifestation of absolute truth. And if we practice with the aspiration just to be the present moment, our lives will gradually transform and grow wonderfully. At various times we'll have sudden insights; but what's most important is just to practice moment by moment by moment with deep aspiration.

B. ALAN WALLACE

Buddha-Nature

BUDDHA-NATURE HAS two major aspects: one aspect is discovered, while the other is developed. With regard to the first of these, it is said that each of us has an essential, beginningless nature that never perishes. And this essence, hidden though it seems to be from our normal understanding, is the source of infinite wisdom and compassion.

This point is illustrated by the following analogy. Imagine a very poor man living in a decrepit little shanty, the only thing he owns in the world. What he does not know is that just beneath his shanty, but hidden in the dirt, is an inexhaustible vein of gold. As long as he remains ignorant of his hidden wealth, this pauper remains in poverty; but when he attends more closely to his own dwelling, he is bound to discover his own fathomless wealth. Similarly, all we need to do is unveil our own nature, and we will find an inexhaustible source of wisdom, compassion, and power. It is nothing we need to acquire, from anywhere or anything. It has always been there.

Seen in this light, the Buddha-nature requires no additions. One does not have to memorize sutras, recite prayers, or accumulate virtues to create it. All one needs to do is unveil it.

This aspect of Buddha-nature which unveils itself is the dharmakaya. Dharmakaya is undifferentiated, noncompartmentalized, and omnipresent. When one's own Buddha-nature is completely unveiled, one's own mind is revealed as dharmakaya, and the dharmakaya one experiences when becoming a Buddha is not intrinsically separate from anybody else's dharmakaya. This has been likened to the sea dissolving into a drop of water. The awareness of a realized person merges with dharmakaya, but the person's identity is not lost. Continuity of consciousness is maintained.

The second aspect of Buddha-nature is developed and perfected by means of spiritual practice. Here the analogy of a seed is often used. As a seed has the potential of growing into a great and glorious tree, so also can this Buddha-nature grow into Buddhahood. But unlike a seed, the Buddha-nature cannot be destroyed. It is simply there, always present, ready like a seed to sprout when it is brought into contact with appropriate conditions. Those germinating conditions are such things as beneficial spiritual teachings and practices, a spiritual mentor, that is, those conditions which enable us to practice.

Now we encounter one of the more puzzling questions about all this, which is: How can the Buddha-nature be essentially perfect, yet be in need of being "developed"? The answer may be one of perspective. In other words, whether we see the Buddha-nature as complete and perfect in itself with no need for development, or whether we see it as evolving and ripening toward Buddhahood, may not be a matter of the Buddha-nature itself, but how we perceive it.

If we look at this question from the point of view of Buddha-nature itself, we might conclude that it is not evolving. It has no need to evolve, for it is already taintless from the perspective of the fully awakened quality of a Buddha. But if we regard Buddha-nature from an ordinary human perspective, we recognize that we have obscurations that need to be dispelled through spiritual practice. And as we make progress we see that the obscurations lift, and our minds become purified. From this point of view we might understand the Buddha-nature as evolving.

There may be a parallel here with two perspectives on the Buddha's own enlightenment. From the perspective of the individual vehicle, he was not a Buddha until his very last lifetime, 2,500 years ago, when he attained Buddhahood. There was a point, early in the morning when he was thirty-five years old, when this man achieved spiritual awakening.

From the Mahayana point of view we get a quite different picture, that is, that the Buddha was already a fully awakened being when he was born. In his incarnation as the historical Buddha he appeared to strive diligently, to practice austerities, and to find the middle way; but the whole time he was simply "manifesting" the deeds of a Buddha. From the perspective of sentient beings, he appeared to attain spiritual awakening through diligent effort; but from a transcendent perspective it would appear he was enlightened throughout the course of his practice here in this realm.

We must initially take the existence of Buddha-nature on faith, but it can be aroused, made manifest in our daily lives. How? One crucial element is the cultivation of great compassion, which is grounded in the understanding that all sentient beings are alike in terms of their essential nature. Buddha-nature also can be realized by meditatively penetrating into the most fundamental nature of our own minds. Together with compassion as a crucial formative element, arousal of the Buddha-nature then opens the door to the bodhisattva's way of life, which is directed toward enlightenment for the sake of all sentient beings.

Enlightenment

The inquiry into Buddha nature in the preceding section involves the potential for enlightenment—the fully awakened mind—in all sentient beings. Interpretations of enlightenment range from a sudden change in perception, represented here in three Zen selections, to an intensive developing of a perfected state described in Shantideva's Guide to a Bodhisattva's Way of Life *(from about the seventh–eighth centuries). The* Lotus Sutra *is the record of a discourse given by the Buddha to a multitude of monks, nuns, and laypeople on the subject of emancipating living beings. He elaborated on this subject at the request of all present, who, led by Maitreya, the Bodhisattva of the future, asked the Buddha three times to share with them this discourse.*

EIHEI DOGEN

(THIRTEENTH CENTURY)

Enlightenment

ONE DAY A student asked: "I have spent months and years in earnest study, but I have yet to gain enlightenment. Many of the old Masters say that the Way does not depend on intelligence and cleverness and that there is no need for knowledge and talent. As I understand it, even though my capacity is inferior, I need not feel badly of myself. Are there not any old sayings or cautionary words that I should know about?"

Dogen replied: "Yes, there are. True study of the Way does not rely on knowledge and genius or cleverness and brilliance. But it is a mistake to encourage people to be like blind men, deaf mutes, or imbeciles. Because study has no use for wide learning and high intelligence, even those with inferior capacities can participate. True study of the Way is an easy thing.

"But even in the monasteries of China, only one or two out of several hundred, or even a thousand, disciples under a great Ch'an master actually gained true enlightenment. Therefore, old sayings and cautionary words are needed. As I see it now, it is a matter of gaining the desire to practice. A person who gives rise to a real desire and puts his utmost efforts into study under a teacher will surely gain enlightenment. Essentially, one must devote all attention to this effort and enter into practice with all due speed. More specifically, the following points must be kept in mind:

"In the first place, there must be a keen and sincere desire to seek the Way. For example, someone who wishes to steal a precious jewel, to attack a formidable enemy, or to make the acquaintance of a beautiful woman must, at all times, watch intently for the opportunity, adjusting to changing events and shifting circumstances. Anything sought for with such intensity will surely be gained. If the desire to search for the Way becomes as intense as this, whether you concentrate on doing zazen alone, investigate a koan by an old master, interview a Zen teacher, or practice with sincere devotion, you will succeed no matter how high you must shoot or no matter how deep you must plumb. Without arousing this wholehearted will for the Buddha Way, how can anyone succeed in this most important task of cutting the endless round of birth-and-death? Those who have this drive, even if they have little knowledge or are of inferior capacity, even if they are stupid or evil, will without fail gain enlightenment.

"Next, to arouse such a mind, one must be deeply aware of the impermanence of the world. This realization is not achieved by some temporary method of contemplation. It is not creating something out of nothing and then thinking about it. Impermanence is a fact before our eyes. Do not wait for the teachings from others, the words of the scriptures, and for the principles of enlightenment. We are born in the morning and die in the evening; the man we saw yesterday is no longer with us today. These are facts we see with our own eyes and hear with our own ears. You see and hear impermanence in terms of another person, but try weighing it with your own body. Even though you live to be seventy or eighty, you die in accordance with the inevitability of death. How will you ever come to terms with the worries, joys, intimacies, and conflicts that concern you in this life? With faith in Buddhism, seek the true happiness of nirvana. How can those who are old or who have passed the halfway mark in their lives relax in their studies when there is no way of telling how many years are left?"

D. T. SUZUKI

Satori

THE ESSENCE OF Zen Buddhism consists in acquiring a new viewpoint on life and things generally. By this I mean that if we want to get into the inmost life of Zen, we must forgo all our ordinary habits of thinking which control our everyday life, we must try to see if there is any other way of judging things, or rather if our ordinary way is always sufficient to give us the ultimate satisfaction of our spiritual needs. If we feel dissatisfied somehow with this life, if there is something in our ordinary way of living that deprives us of freedom in its most sanctified sense, we must endeavour to find a way somewhere which gives us a sense of finality and contentment. Zen proposes to do this for us and assures us of the acquirement of a new point of view in which life assumes a fresher, deeper, and more satisfying aspect. This acquirement, however, is really and naturally the greatest mental cataclysm one can go through with in life. It is no easy task, it is a kind of fiery baptism, and one has to go through the storm, the earthquake, the overthrowing of the mountains, and the breaking in pieces of the rocks.

This acquiring of a new point of view in our dealings with life and the world is popularly called by Japanese Zen students "satori" (*wu* in Chinese). It is really another name for Enlightenment (*anuttara-samyak-sambodhi*), which is the word used by the Buddha and his Indian followers ever since his realization under the Bodhi-tree by the River Nairanjana. There are several other phrases in Chinese designating this spiritual experience, each of which has a special connotation, showing tentatively how this phenomenon is interpreted. At all events there is no Zen without satori, which is indeed the Alpha and Omega of Zen Buddhism. Zen devoid of satori is like a sun without its light and heat. Zen may lose all its literature, all its monasteries, and all its paraphernalia; but as long as there is satori in it it will survive to eternity. I want to emphasize this most fundamental fact concerning the very life of Zen; for there are some even among the students of Zen themselves who are blind to this central fact and are apt to think when Zen has been explained away logically or psychologically, or as one of the Buddhist philosophies which can be summed up by using highly technical and conceptual Buddhist phrases, Zen is exhausted, and there remains nothing in it that makes it what it is. But my contention is, the life of Zen begins with the opening of satori. . . .

Satori may be defined as an intuitive looking into the nature of things in contradistinction to the analytical or logical understanding of it. Practically, it means the unfolding of a new world hitherto unperceived in the confusion of a dualistically-trained mind. Or we may say that with satori our entire surroundings are viewed from quite an unexpected angle of perception. Whatever this is, the world for those who have gained satori is no more the old world as it used to be; even with all its flowing streams and burning fires, it is never the same one again. Logically stated, all its opposites and contradictions are united and harmonized into a consistent organic whole. This is a mystery and a miracle, but according to the Zen masters such is being performed every day. Satori can thus be had only through our once personally experiencing it.

Its semblance or analogy in a more or less feeble and fragmentary way is gained when a difficult mathematical problem is solved, or when a great discovery is made, or when a sudden means of escape is realized in the midst of most desperate complications; in short, when one exclaims, "Eureka! Eureka!" But this refers only to the intellectual aspect of satori, which is therefore necessarily partial and incomplete and does not touch the very foundations of life considered one indivisible whole. Satori as the Zen experience must be concerned with the entirety of life. For what Zen proposes to do is the revolution, and the revaluation as well, of oneself as a spiritual unity. The solving of a mathematical problem ends with the solution; it does not affect one's whole life. So with all other particular questions, practical or scientific, they do not enter the basic life-tone of the individual concerned. But the opening of satori is the remaking of life itself. When it is genuine—for there are many simulacra of it—its effects on one's moral and spiritual life are revolutionary, and they are so enhancing, purifying, as well as exacting. When a master was asked what constituted Buddhahood, he answered,

"The bottom of a pail is broken through." From this we can see what a complete revolution is produced by this spiritual experience. The birth of a new man is really cataclysmic.

In the psychology of religion this spiritual enhancement of one's whole life is called "conversion." But as the term is generally used by Christian converts, it cannot be applied in its strict sense to the Buddhist experience, especially to that of the Zen followers; the term has too affective or emotional a shade to take the place of satori, which is above all noetic. The general tendency of Buddhism is, as we know, more intellectual than emotional, and its doctrine of Enlightenment distinguishes it sharply from the Christian view of salvation; Zen as one of the Mahayana schools naturally shares a large amount of what we may call transcendental intellectualism, which does not issue in logical dualism. When poetically or figuratively expressed, satori is "the opening of the mindflower," or "the removing of the bar," or "the brightening up of the mind-works."

PAUL REPS

No Water, No Moon

WHEN THE NUN Chiyono studied Zen under Bukko of Engaku she was unable to attain the fruits of meditation for a long time.

At last one moonlit night she was carrying water in an old pail bound with bamboo. The bamboo broke and the bottom fell out of the pail and at that moment Chiyono was set free!

In commemoration, she wrote a poem:

In this way and that I tried to save the old pail
Since the bamboo strip was weakening and about to break
Until at last the bottom fell out.
No more water in the pail!
No more moon in the water!

KELSANG GYATSO

The Mind of Enlightenment: Commentary on Shantideva's Guide

THE ULTIMATE GOAL of Buddhist spiritual practice is the attainment of the fully awakened state of mind. This completely perfected state—variously known as enlightenment, buddhahood or the highest nirvana—can be achieved by anyone who removes the gross and subtle obstructions clouding his or her mind and develops positive mental qualities to their fullest potential. However, we shall not be able to attain this fully awakened state if we do not first develop bodhichitta, the mind of enlightenment. What is bodhichitta? It is the continual and spontaneous state of mind that constantly strives to attain this perfect enlightenment *solely for the benefit of all living beings. . . .*

If we are to develop bodhichitta we must destroy all obstacles hindering its growth as well as accumulate the necessary prerequisites for its cultivation. The main obstacle to the development of bodhichitta is evil, defined [by Shantideva] as that which has the potential power to produce the fruit, suffering. Because we have a large accumulation of such misery-producing tendencies from the unwholesome actions we have done in the past, we find it extremely difficult to give birth to the precious and virtuous thought of bodhichitta. . . .

However, the purification of evil is not, by itself, sufficient for our purposes. We must also accumulate a great deal of merit, or positive potential energy, and this comes from the practice of virtue. . . .

Once we have taken hold of the precious bodhichitta, we must prevent it from decreasing. This is done by conscientiously attending to the wholesome actions of our body, speech and mind. . . .

Having grasped and then stabilized the bodhichitta by means of conscientiousness, we must strive to bring this mind to its complete fruition: perfect enlightenment. This is done by taking the bodhisattva vows [see pages 264–267] and practising the six perfections. . . . The development of bodhichitta takes place in three stages. The ten chapters of Shantideva's book cover this threefold development, which is outlined concisely in the following often-recited prayer of generation:

> May the supreme and precious bodhichitta
> Take birth where it has not yet done so;
> Where it has been born may it not decrease;
> Where it has not decreased may it abundantly grow.

In the first two lines we pray that those sentient beings, including ourselves, who have not yet given birth to bodhichitta may do so. Next we pray that those who have already given birth to this altruistic mind may be able to maintain it without letting it decrease. In the final line, we pray that those who have cultivated and stabilized bodhichitta may be able to bring it to its full completion. In the same order, the method of giving birth to bodhichitta is explained in the first three chapters of this text, the way to stabilize it is the subject of the fourth chapter, while chapters five to ten describe the methods whereby the stabilized bodhichitta may be continually increased until full enlightenment is achieved.

If we practise in accordance with the instructions set forth in the ten chapters of the *Bodhisattvacharyavatara* [see pages 252–257], it will not be too difficult to attain the exalted state of mind known as enlightenment, pristine fulfilment or full and complete buddhahood. In this state all our human potentialities will be fully developed and we shall be able to benefit others to the greatest possible extent.

Bodhisattvas

Enlightenment has always been the ultimate goal of Buddhism, but with the emergence of Mahayana Buddhism, the goal became the enlightenment of all sentient beings. Beings who seek enlightenment for themselves in order to lead all beings to nirvana are known as bodhisattvas, and the Bodhisattva Vow, taken by both monastics and lay Buddhists, is the expression of that resolution. The Lotus Sutra, *the central discourse of the Chinese Tendai and Japanese Nichirin sects, stresses the role of faith in the liberation of all beings.*

THE DALAI LAMA
Bodhicitta and Enlightenment

WHAT DO WE mean by *bodhisattva? Bodhi* means enlightenment, the state devoid of all defects and endowed with all good qualities. *Sattva* refers to someone who has courage and confidence and who strives to attain enlightenment for the sake of all beings. Those who have this spontaneous, sincere wish to attain enlightenment for the ultimate benefit of all beings are called bodhisattvas. Through wisdom, they direct their minds to enlightenment, and through their compassion, they have concern for beings. This wish for perfect enlightenment for the sake of others is what we call *bodhicitta*, and it is the starting point on the path. By becoming aware of what enlightenment is, one understands not only that there is a goal to accomplish but also that it is possible to do so. Driven by the desire to help beings, one thinks, For their sake, I must attain enlightenment.

KOSHO UCHIYAMA

What Is a Bodhisattva?

A BODHISATTVA IS an ordinary person who takes up a course in his or her life that moves in the direction of buddha. You're a bodhisattva, I'm a bodhisattva; actually, anyone who directs their attention, their life, to practicing the way of life of a buddha is a bodhisattva. We read about Kannon Bosatsu (Avalokiteshvara Bodhisattva) or Monju Bosatsu (Manjushri Bodhisattva), and these are great bodhisattvas, but we, too, have to have confidence or faith that we are also bodhisattvas.

Most people live by their desires or karma. That's what the expression *gossho no bompu* means. *Gossho* are the obstructions to practicing the Way caused by our evil actions in the past. *Bompu* simply means ordinary human being—that is, one who lives by karma. Our actions are dictated by our karma: We are born into this world with our desires and may live our lives just by reacting or responding to them. In contrast is *gansho no bosatsu,* or a bodhisattva who lives by vow.

The life that flows through each of us and through everything around us is actually all connected. To say that, of course, means that who I really am cannot be separated from all the things that surround me. Or, to put it another way, all sentient beings have their existence and live within my life. So needless to say, that includes even the fate of all mankind—that, too, lies within me. Therefore, just how mankind might truly live out its life becomes what I aim at as my direction. This aiming or living while moving in a certain direction is what is meant by vow. In other words, it is the motivation for living that is different for a bodhisattva. Ordinary people live thinking only about their own personal, narrow circumstances connected with their desires. In contrast to that, a bodhisattva, though undeniably still an ordinary human being like everyone else, lives by vow. Because of that, the significance of his or her life is not the same. For us as bodhisattvas, all aspects of life, including the fate of humanity itself, live within us. It is with this in mind that we work to discover and manifest the most vital and alive posture that we can take in living out our life. . . .

[I]t's not enough for a bodhisattva of the Mahayana to just uphold the precepts. There are times when you have to break them, too. It's just that when you do, you have to do so with the resolve of also being willing to accept whatever consequences might follow. That's what *issai shujo to tomo ni* ("together with all sentient beings"—regardless of what hell one might fall into) really means. . . .

It's not enough just to know the definition of bodhisattva. What's much more important is to study the actions of a bodhisattva and then to behave like one yourself.

Regarding the question "What is a bodhisattva?" you could also define a bodhisattva as one who acts as a true adult. That is, most people in the world act like children. The word *dainin* means "true adult" or "bodhisattva." Today most people who are called adults are only pseudoadults. Physically they grow up and become adult but spiritually too many people never mature to adulthood. They don't behave as adults in their daily lives. A bodhisattva is one who sees the world through adult eyes and whose actions are the actions of a true adult. That is really what a bodhisattva is.

SHANTIDEVA

(SEVENTH–EIGHTH CENTURY)

From Guide to the Bodhisattva's Way of Life

Gladly do I rejoice
In the virtue that relieves the misery
Of all those in unfortunate states
And that places those with suffering in happiness.

I rejoice in that gathering of virtue
That is the cause for [the Arhat's] Awakening,
I rejoice in the definite freedom of embodied creatures
From the miseries of cyclic existence.

I rejoice in the Awakening of the Buddhas
And also in the spiritual levels of their Children.

And with gladness I rejoice
In the ocean of virtue from developing an Awakening Mind
That wishes all beings to be happy,
As well as in the deeds that bring them benefit.

With folded hands I beseech
The Buddhas of all directions
To shine the lamp of Dharma
For all bewildered in misery's gloom.

With folded hands I beseech
The Conquerors who wish to pass away,
To please remain for countless aeons
And not to leave the world in darkness.

Thus by the virtue collected
Through all that I have done,
May the pain of every living creature
Be completely cleared away.

May I be the doctor and the medicine
And may I be the nurse
For all sick beings in the world
Until everyone is healed.

May a rain of food and drink descend
To clear away the pain of thirst and hunger
And during the aeon of famine
May I myself change into food and drink.

May I become an inexhaustible treasure
For those who are poor and destitute;
May I turn into all things they could need
And may these be placed close beside them.

Without any sense of loss
I shall give up my body and enjoyments
As well as all my virtues of the three times
For the sake of benefiting all.

By giving up all, sorrow is transcended
And my mind will realize the sorrowless state.
It is best that I [now] give everything to all beings
In the same way as I shall [at death].

Having given this body up
For the pleasure of all living beings,
By killing, abusing, and beating it
May they always do as they please.

Although they may play with my body
And make it a source of jest and blame,
Because I have given it up to them
What is the use of holding it dear?

Therefore I shall let them do anything to it
That does not cause them any harm,
And when anyone encounters me
May it never be meaningless for him.

If in those who encounter me
A faithful or an angry thought arises,
May that eternally become the source
For fulfilling all their wishes.

May all who say bad things to me
Or cause me any other harm,
And those who mock and insult me
Have the fortune to fully awaken.

May I be a protector for those without one,
A guide for all travelers on the way;
May I be a bridge, a boat, and a ship
For all who wish to cross [the water].

May I be an island for those who seek one
And a lamp for those desiring light,
May I be a bed for all who wish to rest
And a slave for all who want a slave.

May I be a wishing jewel, a magic vase,
Powerful mantras and great medicine,
May I become a wish-fulfilling tree
And a cow of plenty for the world.

Just like space
And the great elements such as earth,
May I always support the life
Of all the boundless creatures.

And until they pass away from pain
May I also be the source of life
For all the realms of varied beings
That reach unto the ends of space.

Just as the previous Sugatas
Gave birth to an Awakening Mind,
And just as they successively dwelt
In the Bodhisattva practices;

Likewise for the sake of all that lives
Do I give birth to an Awakening Mind,
And likewise shall I too
Successively follow the practices.

In order to further increase it from now on,
Those with discernment who have lucidly seized
An Awakening Mind in this way,
Should highly praise it in the following manner:

Today my life has [borne] fruit;
[Having] well obtained this human existence,
I've been born in the family of Buddha
And now am one of Buddha's Children.

Thus whatever actions I do from now on
Must be in accord with the family.
Never shall I disgrace or pollute
This noble and unsullied race.

Just like a blind man
Discovering a jewel in a heap of rubbish,
Likewise by some coincidence
An Awakening Mind has been born within me.

It is the supreme ambrosia
That overcomes the sovereignty of death,
It is the inexhaustible treasure
That eliminates all poverty in the world.

It is the supreme medicine
That quells the world's disease.
It is the tree that shelters all beings
Wandering and tired on the path of conditioned existence.

It is the universal bridge
That leads to freedom from unhappy states of birth,
It is the dawning moon of the mind
That dispels the torment of disturbing conceptions.

It is the great sun that finally removes
The misty ignorance of the world,
It is the quintessential butter
From the churning of the milk of Dharma.

For all those guests traveling on the path of conditioned existence
Who wish to experience the bounties of happiness,
This will satisfy them with joy
And actually place them in supreme bliss.

Today in the presence of all the Protectors
I invite the world to be guests
At [a festival of] temporary and ultimate delight.
May gods, anti-gods and all be joyful.

SHARON SALZBERG

The Perfections

THERE IS A common misconception that there is no such thing as the Bodhisattva Vow in the Theravadin tradition. However, there is such a path. In the classical Theravadin tradition, the Bodhisattva Vow is undertaken by those who aspire to full buddhahood, rather than to the liberation of an arhant. While an arhant is said to be entirely free of grasping, aversion, and delusion, and thus enlightened, his or her scope of manifestation is more limited than that of a fully awakened buddha. We are, as an example, all still enjoying the legacy of the Buddha's enlightenment of 2,500 years ago. It is vast compassion which motivates one to endeavor to full buddhahood, and the aeons of fulfilling the *paramis,* or perfections, that are necessary. A Theravadin practitioner who aspires to serve that powerfully takes the Bodhisattva Vow. While most Theravadin practitioners aspire to the condition of an arhant, there are said to be some following the bodhisattva path today.

The paramis are the contributory conditions to enlightenment, or the facets of an enlightened mind. According to the Buddhist teaching there is an accumulated force of purity in the mind that is the ground out of which freedom arises. The bodhisattva will spend lifetime after lifetime creating this ground by cultivating generosity, morality, renunciation, energy, truthfulness, patience, resoluteness, lovingkindness, equanimity, and wisdom. It is only in the particular lifetime during which the bodhisattva becomes a buddha that wisdom itself is brought to perfection. The role of the paramis is often depicted in the legend surrounding the enlightenment of the Buddha.

On the very eve of his enlightenment, the Buddha, then still a bodhisattva, sat under the bodhi tree and was attacked by Mara. Mara is a mythic figure in the Buddhist cosmology who is the "killer of virtue" and the "killer of life." Mara, recognizing that his kingdom of delusion was greatly jeopardized by the Bodhisattva's aspiration to full awakening, came with many different challenges in an attempt to get the Bodhisattva to give up his resolve. He challenged him through lust, anger, and fear. He showered him with hailstorms, mudstorms, and other travails. No matter what happened, the Bodhisattva sat serenely, unmoved by the challenge and unswayed in his determination.

The final challenge of Mara in effect was one of self-doubt. He said to the Bodhisattva, "By what right are you even sitting there with that goal? What makes you think you have the right even to aspire to full enlightenment, to complete awakening?" In response to that challenge, the Bodhisattva reached over his knee and touched the earth. He called upon the earth itself to bear witness to all of the lifetimes in which he had practiced generosity, patience, morality, and other perfections. Lifetime after lifetime he had built a wave of moral force that had given him the right to that aspiration.

Any practitioner of the Buddha's teaching is called upon to practice the perfections, to make heroic effort, and to be able to rest confidently on a base of moral force. The distinction between those determining to realize full buddhahood and those committed to arhanthood is actually one of degree. The Buddha's teaching, whatever one's goal, is never removed from a sense of humanity. He described the motivation principle of his own life as a dedication to the welfare and the happiness of all beings, and also encouraged the same dedication in others: we all can see our lives as vehicles to bring happiness, to bring peace, to bring benefit to all living things, without exception.

PAT ENKYO O'HARA

Seeing Interdependence

SITTING ON MY zafu [meditation sitting cushion], the Bodhisattva Vow seems natural, almost automatic. The heart opens, and then the day follows with *The New York Times*—a picture of people cheering around Baruch Goldstein's grave in Hebron; two Japanese boys killed in an L.A. mall; news that the Mayor proposes to eliminate the Department of AIDS Services, which has enabled several of my friends to die in dignity. My anger rises like a wind. Words float to the surface of my consciousness: racism, homophobia, hatred, greed. How can I open my heart, how can I even want to save all sentient beings?

That is the crux of it: how to see my interdependence with those I instinctively want to shun, to shut out of my world.

Politically, I came of age with so many others in the sixties. We marched, protested, and learned not to blindly accept the way things were—to be arrested, to "put our bodies on the line," to, in today's words, "act up." Many of us also learned to hate, to view the "other"—cop, soldier, politician—not as a brother or sister conditioned by karma, not as self, but as an enemy.

And yet, what such separation breeds is readily apparent: more rage, more violence, more suffering. The answer doesn't lie there. But seeing the other as self is not easy, which is why I sit. Ultimately, it's what makes working with the Bodhisattva Vow possible.

So, as I read my newspaper and catch myself solidifying that sense of separation, I take in a breath, soften and loosen myself a little. I ask myself where my commonality with Baruch Goldstein and his followers, with the Mayor, with the L.A. killers lies? Another breath. What must it have been like to grow up as a Goldstein in Brooklyn? As a gang member in L.A.? What kind of terrible conditions did they face? What kind of suffering did they endure? Can I imagine the pain, smell the fear?

I think of how some babies come screaming into the world, seem bad-tempered from the start, and how hard it is to hold a baby like that. Can I feel myself as the screaming baby—uncomfortable, dissatisfied? As the mother—frightened, irritated?

Can I catch my own irritation and fear and not run from it? Can I tolerate my own helplessness? Can I observe myself as I rush to defend my point of view with the same bullying tactics I condemn in "the other"? To the extent that I can see the soldier, the fundamentalist, the terrorist in me—view my own "stuff" and not separate from it—to that extent can I connect to "the other." It's the same stuff.

So with each breath, I confirm that the skinheads are my sons, the fundamentalists, me. And each time I do this, there's more space inside of me and I can allow more in. Their suffering, my suffering. In breath, out breath.

TETSUO UNNO

Amida Buddha

Pure Land Buddhism, particularly of the Jodoshin tradition, bases itself on the fundamental understanding that it is not the sentient being who strives toward bodhisattvahood; to the contrary, it is the bodhisattva who strives to save and ultimately enlighten the sentient being, transforming it into a bodhisattva.

Sentient beings, in other words, are viewed as being powerless and incapable of bringing about their own salvation, enlightenment, or bodhisattvahood. They are seen as lacking, in an absolute way, the moral and spiritual capacity to transform themselves into bodhisattvas.

Any spiritual transformation is viewed as being wholly and merely superficial and therefore, inauthentic. This is somewhat like the monkey in the parable who was trained to mimic the actions of a human being. To the bemused amazement of many, the trainers succeeded to the point that the monkey was able to perform in Kabuki plays.

For his humanlike performances, the monkey even drew shouts of approval. One day, however, when someone threw peanuts onto the stage, the monkey instantaneously reverted to his original, simian nature, scampering after and shoving the peanuts into his mouth.

The Bodhisattva Dharmakara, in his Wisdom, perceived the absolute inability of the sentient being to transform, in a fundamental way, itself, and thereby save and enlighten itself. Moved by Compassion, He gave rise to a series of vows that promised to create and bring to fruition those conditions that would lead to the salvation of such sentient beings, who, if left to their own devices, would be utterly beyond salvation.

To actualize these vows, Bodhisattva Dharmakara undergoes measureless aeons of spiritual practices, perfecting such religious virtues as selfless giving or charity, morality, patience, energy, meditation, and wisdom. Ultimately He attains Buddhahood and becomes the Buddha of Infinite Wisdom and Compassion; that is, Amida Buddha.

The role or task of the sentient being, then, is to serve only or merely as the recipient of the Amida Buddha's salvific efforts. It does so by simply and absolutely entrusting itself to Amida's vow of unconditional salvation. The seemingly passive act of entrusting oneself and the active act of Amida's saving of the sentient being are, in reality, one and the same.

The following incident illustrates the nature of this oneness. A number of years ago, a sailor aboard a freighter crossing the Pacific Ocean fell overboard. The crew noticed that he was missing eighteen hours later. The captain ordered the ship to turn around to go back in search of the lost sailor. Miraculously, the sailor was found floating in the ocean water.

He later explained that there was nothing at all he could do to save himself, he simply entrusted himself to the buoyant powers of the ocean, which, in turn, floated and thereby saved him. The seemingly contradictory notion of entrustment and salvation being one finds a parallel in myths in which death and birth are viewed as being two aspects of the same experience, or in philosophy where negation and affirmation are seen as being identical, or in Zen where passivity and activity are regarded as being equal.

Beyond this, Shinran Shonin of the Jodoshin Sect teaches that those sentient beings who entrust themselves to Amida Buddha are coequal of Bodhisattva Maitreya, who resides in the penultimate stage of bodhisattvahood and is soon destined for Buddhahood. Unlike other traditions that hold forth the promise of Buddhahood in this life and in "this very body," the Jodoshin Sect affirms that Buddhahood is attained only after shedding one's physical body; that is, after one's death. In other words, the "entruster," despite being made the equal of the Bodhisattva Maitreya, is subject to all the physical limitations of this life. However, with regard to his or her spirtual life, he or she is essentially freed, by virtue of Amida's salvation, of all suffering-causing "blockages."

It must be emphasized at this point that the "entruster" himself or herself regards all spiritual benefits as emanating from the Amida Buddha, the *Other* Power, and therefore, has no consciousness of, not to speak of attachment to, the benefits bestowed on him, such as being made the equal of the Bodhisattva Maitreya.

Rather, having been bestowed this great gift, or more precisely, "benefit," of salvation and by implication bodhisattvahood and eventual Buddhahood, not despite the fact that but *because* sentient beings are absolutely beyond salvation and enlightenment, sentient beings are simply filled with a transcendent sense of absolute gratitude. Ethically, this gratitude, which Cicero, in a different context, once described as being "the greatest of virtues because it is the parent of all others," serves as the foundation, in this life, of the Pure Land Buddhist.

GESHE SONAM RINCHEN

The Bodhisattva Vow

When your mothers, who've loved you since time
without beginning,
Are suffering, what use is your own happiness?
Therefore to free limitless living beings
Develop the altruistic intention—
This is the practice of Bodhisattvas.

Cyclic existence is beginningless and our rebirths, too, are without beginning. Therefore all living beings in the six realms of existence have been our fathers, mothers, sisters, brothers and beloved friends and, as such, have shown us loving care and kindness. What's happening to them? They're tormented by the suffering of cyclic existence in general . . . When we see how much they suffer with our own eyes, what kind of people are we, if we turn our back and are concerned only with our own peace and happiness? It's like a mother leaving her only child, a little baby, lying out on the hot sand, while she enjoys a picnic under a shady tree. We must help and look after these suffering beings.

Buddhas first develop the altruistic intention to attain enlightenment in order to free living beings and bring them happiness. Then, to accomplish this, they train themselves in the six perfections [generosity, discipline, patience, endeavor, meditative concentration, wisdom]. The closer we feel to living beings, the more we wish to help them overcome their suffering, which seems unbearable. This impels us to accept personal responsibility to rid them of it and bring them happiness. We then make the commitment to achieve enlightenment in order to carry out our resolve.

> All suffering comes from the wish for your own
> happiness.
> Perfect Buddhas are born from the thought to help others.
> Therefore exchange your own happiness for the suffering of others—
> This is the practice of Bodhisattvas.

Another approach to developing the altruistic intention is the practice of equalizing and exchanging self and others. All the past, present and future suffering in the three realms of existence comes from our compulsive desire for happiness and our misconception of the self. The thought "I" is ever-present, even in our dreams. We cling to the self and are concerned for its happiness, but happiness doesn't come of its own accord, so we grasp at everything we consider a means of insuring it. We're attached to our bodies and senses through which we hope to experience pleasure. We crave friends, possessions and places which we hope will make us happy. We try to acquire them but face frustration as we fail to get what we want and get much that we don't want. All this entails suffering now and in the future as well, since we perform many negative actions in our pursuit of happiness.

Buddhas, whose exclusive concern is others' well-being, are the source of good rebirths and liberation. As Bodhisattvas they developed the altruistic intention which grew out of their love and compassion. We, too, can do this. When we recognize that living beings are like wish-fulfilling jewels that grant us all temporal and ultimate happiness, we'll try to avoid harming them and help them as much as we can. Once we really understand the faults of selfishness and the great benefits of cherishing others, we'll begin to put others first instead of ourselves and readily undergo whatever hardships are necessary for their sake.

The meditation of giving and taking is done to develop the willingness to alleviate others' suffering and bring them happiness. When practicing this, we begin by taking away the suffering and only then give happiness because normally it's impossible to enjoy anything while one is in pain. Traditionally, we include within our focus all sentient beings . . . , taking away everything unpleasant which afflicts or limits them and harms their environment.

Although the aim is to include all living beings, as beginners, to make the practice more immediate, we may choose to concentrate on one group at a time. We can, for instance, imagine taking on the suffering of those in the area where we live. We may confine ourselves to human beings who are physically or mentally ill or those in a particular country where there is war or famine. To begin with whatever stimulates intense compassion in us is best. The practice may also be directed specifically towards humans and non-humans who harm us. We need to develop enough courage to take on every shred of their suffering and its causes and give away all our happiness.

If we're suffering from a particular disease or problem, we can imagine taking on the suffering of others in a similar situation, while making prayers that our suffering may replace theirs. . . . If at first we find taking on others' suffering too daunting, we should start by accepting our own future suffering—the suffering we may experience later in the day, later in the year or later in this life. . . .

Like the practice of taking, giving too can be performed in *more* specific contexts. We must employ whatever techniques are most effective to combat our narrow self-concern. We shouldn't feel frightened of giving and taking because they cannot harm us in any way. The practice is intended to build up courage and willingness to dedicate ourselves to others' well-being. It helps us to cherish others instead of just cherishing ourselves and to forget about ourselves instead of forgetting about them. At first it's hard to arouse real feeling but without discouragement we should at least repeat words that express our wish to give happiness and take on suffering. When we're familiar with the practice, we take on the suffering as we breathe in and give happiness as we breathe out. One day we may actually become able to do so. This is a very potent practice, and since mind and breath are *closely* connected, doing it will increase our love and compassion.

BURTON WATSON, TRANS.

From The Lotus Sutra

"GOOD MEN, IF there are living beings who come to me, I employ my Buddha eye to observe their faith and to see if their other faculties are keen or dull, and then depending upon how receptive they are to salvation, I appear in different places and preach to them under different names, and describe the length of time during which my teachings will be effective. Sometimes when I make my appearance I say that I am about to enter nirvana, and also employ different expedient means to preach the subtle and wonderful Law, thus causing living beings to awaken joyful minds.

"Good men, the Thus Come One observes how among living beings there are those who delight in a little Law, meager in virtue and heavy with defilement. For such persons I describe how in my youth I left my household and attained *anuttara-samyak-sambodhi* [perfect universal enlightenment]. But in truth the time since I attained Buddhahood is extremely long, as I have told you. It is simply that I use this expedient means to teach and convert living beings and cause them to enter the Buddha way. That is why I speak in this manner.

"Good men, the scriptures expounded by the Thus Come One are all for the purpose of saving and emancipating living beings. Sometimes I speak of myself, sometimes of others; sometimes I present myself, sometimes others; sometimes I show my own actions, sometimes those of others. All that I preach is true and not false.

"Why do I do this? The Thus Come One perceives the true aspect of the threefold world exactly as it is. There is no ebb or flow of birth and death, and there is no existing in this world and later entering extinction. It is neither substantial nor empty, neither consistent nor diverse. Nor is it what those who dwell in the threefold world perceive it to be. All such things the Thus Come One sees clearly and without error.

"Because living beings have different natures, different desires, different actions, and different ways of thinking and making distinctions, and because I want to enable them to put down good roots, I employ a variety of causes and conditions, similes, parables, and phrases, and preach different doctrines. This, the Buddha's work, I have never for a moment neglected.

"Thus, since I attained Buddhahood, an extremely long period of time has passed. My life span is an immeasurable number of *asamkhya kalpas* [an infinite number of aeons], and during that time I have constantly abided here without ever entering extinction. Good men, originally I practiced the bodhisattva way, and the life span that I acquired then has yet to come to an end but will last twice the number of years that have already passed. Now, however, although in fact I do not actually enter extinction, I announce that I am going to adopt the course of extinction. This is an expedient means which the Thus Come One uses to teach and convert living beings.

"Why do I do this? Because if the Buddha remains in the world for a long time, those persons with shallow virtue will fail to plant good roots but, living in poverty and lowliness, will become attached to the five desires and be caught in the net of deluded thoughts and imaginings. If they see that the Thus Come One is constantly in the world and never enters extinction, they will grow arrogant and selfish, or become discouraged and neglectful. They will fail to realize how difficult it is to encounter the Buddha and will not approach him with a respectful and reverent mind.

"Therefore as an expedient means the Thus Come One says:

'Monks, you should know that it is a rare thing to live at a time when one of the Buddhas appears in the world.' Why does he do this? Because persons of shallow virtue may pass immeasurable hundreds, thousands, ten thousands, millions of *kalpas* with some of them chancing to see a Buddha and others never seeing one at all. For this reason I say to them: 'Monks, the Thus Come One is hard to get to see.' When living beings hear these words, they are certain to realize how difficult it is to encounter the Buddha. In their minds they will harbor a longing and will thirst to gaze upon the Buddha, and then they will work to plant good roots. Therefore the Thus Come One, though in truth he does not enter extinction, speaks of passing into extinction.

"Good men, the Buddhas and Thus Come Ones all preach a Law such as this. They act in order to save living beings, so what they do is true and not false.

"Suppose, for example, that there is a skilled physician who is wise and understanding and knows how to compound medicines to effectively cure all kinds of diseases. He has many sons, perhaps ten, twenty, or even a hundred. He goes off to some other land far away to see about a certain affair. After he has gone, the children drink some kind of poison that makes them distraught with pain and they fall writhing to the ground.

"At that time the father returns to his home and finds that his children have drunk poison. Some are completely out of their minds, while others are not. Seeing their father from far off, all are overjoyed and kneel down and entreat him, saying: 'How fine that you have returned safely. We were stupid and by mistake drank some poison. We beg you to cure us and let us live out our lives!'

"The father, seeing his children suffering like this, follows various prescriptions. Gathering fine medicinal herbs that meet all the requirements of color, fragrance, and flavor, he grinds, sifts, and mixes them together. Giving a dose of these to his children, he tells them: 'This is a highly effective medicine, meeting all the requirements of color, fragrance, and flavor. Take it and you will quickly be relieved of your sufferings and will be free of all illness.'

"Those children who have not lost their senses can see that this is good medicine, outstanding in both color and fragrance, so they take it immediately and are completely cured of their sickness. Those who are out of their minds are equally delighted to see their father return and beg him to cure their sickness, but when they are given the medicine, they refuse to take it. Why? Because the poison has penetrated deeply and their minds no longer function as before. So although the medicine is of excellent color and fragrance, they do not perceive it as good.

"The father thinks to himself. My poor children! Because of the poison in them, their minds are completely befuddled. Although they are happy to see me and ask me to cure them, they refuse to take this excellent medicine. I must now resort to some expedient means to induce them to take the medicine. So he says to them: 'You should know that I am now old and worn out, and the time of my death has come. I will leave this good medicine here. You should take it and not worry that it will not cure you.' Having given these instructions, he then goes off to another land, where he sends a messenger home to announce, 'Your father is dead.'

"At that time the children, hearing that their father has deserted them and died, are filled with great grief and consternation and think to themselves: If our father were alive he would have pity on us and see that we are protected. But now he has abandoned us and died in some other country far away. We are shelterless orphans with no one to rely on!

"Constantly harboring such feelings of grief, they at last come to their senses and realize that the medicine is in fact excellent in color and fragrance and flavor, and so they take it and are healed of all the effects of the poison. The father, hearing that his children are all cured, immediately returns home and appears to them all once more.

"Good men, what is your opinion? Can anyone say that this skilled physician is guilty of lying?"

"No, World-Honored One."

The Buddha said: "It is the same with me. It has been immeasurable, boundless hundreds, thousands, ten thousands, millions of *nayuta* [countless aeons] and *asamkhya kalpas* since I attained Buddhahood. But for the sake of living beings I employ the power of expedient means and say that I am about to pass into extinction. In view of the circumstances, however, no one can say that I have been guilty of lies or falsehoods."

STEPHEN BATCHELOR

Nichiren and The Lotus Sutra

THE SUPREMACY OF *The Lotus Sutra* was a central doctrine of the Tendai school, a syncretic tradition founded in sixth-century China that arranged the bewildering array of translated Buddhist texts into a coherent chronology. According to this school, the Buddha spent the last eight years of his life teaching *The Lotus Sutra,* in which he revealed the true purpose of his life. All earlier teachings were considered as only provisionally true.

Nichiren [the thirteenth-century founder of the Nichiren sect of Japan] refined this principle of Tendai Buddhism even further. *"Myoho-renge-kyo"*(*The Lotus Sutra*'s full title in Sino-Japanese), he declared in a letter written two years after arriving in Kamakura, "is the king of sutras, flawless in both letter and principle."

> *Its words are the reality of life, and the reality of life is the Mystic Law (myoho).* It is called the Mystic Law because it explains the mutually inclusive relationship of life and all phenomena. . . . Chanting *Myoho-renge-kyo* will therefore enable you to grasp the mystic truth within you.

He assured his correspondent that "if you have deep faith in this truth and chant *Myoho-renge-kyo,* you are certain to attain Buddhahood in this lifetime."

Nichiren's philosophy taps a current of Chinese Buddhist thought whose source is *The Avatamsaka (Hua-yen) Sutra*'s doctrine of the "mutual interpenetration of all phenomena." Buddhahood, according to this doctrine, is not separate from oneself as the distant culmination of life to which one ultimately aspires, but is immanent within each moment of life. This idea likewise underpinned the philosophy of Zen. But whereas for Dogen [the thirteenth-century master who brought Soto Zen to Japan], the immanent truth of enlightenment could be immediately manifested only through *zazen,* Nichiren insisted that it could only be achieved through chanting *Nam-myoho-renge-kyo.* . . .

In defining the heart of *The Lotus Sutra,* Nichiren declared that only the second half of the fifteenth chapter, the whole of the sixteenth and the first half of the seventeenth were revelatory. Everything else the Buddha taught was "Hinayana in nature and heretical." Here, concealed in the heart of this "one chapter and two halves," he claimed to find the characters of *Nam-myoho-renge-kyo,* which Gautama did not transmit to the disciples of his time, but entrusted to the myriad "Bodhisattvas of the Earth," who were destined to surge forth as soon as the Dharma entered its period of degeneration. The task of these Bodhisattvas was to usher in an era of worldwide Buddhism.

According to *The Lotus Sutra,* the Bodhisattvas of the Earth first appeared during the "Ceremony in Space," when a "treasure tower" magically crystallized in the sky. Inside was the former Buddha Prabhu-taratna, by whose side Gautama sat to announce the transmission of his deepest teaching to the Bodhisattva Visistacaritra Gogyo. According to Nichiren, it was to this Bodhisattva that Gautama (presumably breaking into Sino-Japanese) first revealed *Nam-myoho-renge-kyo.* Since Nichiren saw himself as the sole person to propagate this truth in the Latter Day of the Law, he came to identify himself as a Bodhisattva of the Earth, . . . and the "votary of *The Lotus Sutra.*"

Nichiren emphasizes that even the Buddha realized how difficult it would be for people to believe and understand these teachings of *The Lotus Sutra.* The only reason that people of this degenerate age could believe in them at all was "due to the fact that the world of Buddhahood is present in the human realm." The teaching of Gautama, he declared, "is the Buddhism of the harvest," whereas that of the Bodhisattvas of the Earth is the "Buddhism of the sowing." Whereas Gautama revealed the fruits of Buddhahood, Nichiren revealed its cause: *Nam-myoho-renge-kyo,* the mystic law of life by resonating with which Buddhahood is manifested here and now.

The Self

A basic tenet of Buddhism is that nothing has permanent, independent existence—including us. In the discourse excerpted here, the Buddha responds to inquiries about how the mind creates, reflects, and conditions the sense of self. Confronting the question of identity is an integral aspect of spiritual practice, for the illusion of a permanent self is at the core of the suffering described in the Four Noble Truths.

MAURICE WALSHE, TRANS.

The Buddha on Origination of Self

THUS HAVE I heard. Once the Lord was staying among the Kurus. There is a market town there called Kammasadhamma. And the Venerable Ananda [the Buddha's cousin, a devoted disciple] came to the Lord, saluted him, sat down to one side, and said: "It is wonderful, Lord, it is marvelous how profound this dependent origination [see also pages 80–83] is, and how profound it appears! And yet it appears to me as clear as clear!"

"Do not say that, Ananda, do not say that! This dependent origination is profound and appears profound. It is through not understanding, not penetrating this doctrine that this generation has become like a tangled ball of string, covered as with a blight, tangled like coarse grass, unable to pass beyond states of woe, the ill destiny, ruin, and the round of birth-and-death.

"If, Ananda, you are asked: 'Has aging-and-death a condition for its existence?' you should answer: 'Yes.' If asked: 'What conditions aging-and-death?' you should answer 'Aging-and-death is conditioned by birth. What conditions birth?' . . . 'Becoming conditions birth. Clinging conditions becoming.' . . . 'Craving conditions clinging.' . . . 'Feeling conditions craving.' . . . 'Contact conditions feeling.' . . . 'Mind-and-body conditions contact.' . . . 'Consciousness conditions mind-and-body.' . . . If asked: 'Has consciousness a condition for its existence?' you should answer: 'Yes.' If asked, 'What conditions consciousness?' you should answer: 'Mind-and-body conditions consciousness.'

"Thus, Ananda, mind-and-body conditions consciousness and consciousness conditions mind-and-body, mind-and-body conditions contact, contact conditions feeling, feeling conditions craving, craving conditions clinging, clinging conditions becoming, becoming conditions birth, birth conditions aging-and-death, sorrow, lamentation, pain, grief and distress. Thus this whole mass of suffering comes into existence.

"I have said: 'Birth conditions aging-and-death,' and this is the way that should be understood. If, Ananda, there were no birth at all, anywhere, of anybody or anything: of devas to the devastate, of gandhabbas . . . of yakkhas . . . of ghosts . . . of humans . . . of quadrupeds . . . of birds . . . of reptiles to the reptile state, if there were absolutely no birth at all of all these beings, then, with the absence of all birth, the cessation of birth, could aging-and-death appear?" "No, Lord." "Therefore, Ananda, just this is the root, the cause, the origin, the condition for aging-and-death—namely birth.

"I have said: 'Becoming conditions birth.' . . . If there were absolutely no becoming: in the World of Sense-Desires, of Form or the Formless World . . . could birth appear?

"No, Lord." "Therefore just this is the condition of birth—namely becoming.

" 'Clinging conditions becoming.' . . . If there were absolutely no clinging: sensuous clinging, clinging to views, to rite-and-ritual, to personality-belief . . . could becoming appear?

" 'Craving conditions clinging.' If there were absolutely no craving: for sights, sounds, smells, tastes, tangibles, mind-objects . . . could clinging appear?

" 'Feeling conditions craving, . . . If there were absolutely no feeling: feeling born of eye-contact, ear-contact, nose-contact, tongue-contact, body-contact, mind-contact—in the absence of all feeling, with the cessation of feeling, could craving appear?

"No, Lord." "Therefore, Ananda, just this is the root, the cause, the origin, the condition for craving—namely feeling.

"And so, Ananda, feeling conditions craving, craving conditions seeking, seeking conditions acquisition, acquisition conditions decision-making, decision-making conditions lustful desire, lustful desire conditions attachment, attachment conditions appropriation, appropriation conditions avarice, avarice conditions guarding of possessions, and because of the guarding of possessions there arise the taking up of stick and sword, quarrels, disputes, arguments, strife, abuse, lying and other evil unskilled states.

"I have said: 'All these evil unskilled states arise because of the guarding of possessions.' For if there were absolutely no guarding of possessions . . . would there be the taking up of stick or sword . . . ?" "No, Lord." "Therefore, Ananda, the guarding of possessions is the root, the cause, the origin, the condition for all these evil unskilled states.

"I have said: 'Avarice conditions the guarding of possessions. . . .'

" 'Appropriation conditions avarice, . . . attachment conditions appropriation, . . . lustful desire conditions attachment, . . . decision-making conditions lustful desire, . . . acquisition conditions decision-making, . . . seeking conditions acquisition . . .'

"I have said: 'Craving conditions seeking.' If there were no craving, . . . would there be any seeking?" "No, Lord." "Therefore, Ananda, craving is the root, the cause, the origin, the condition for all seeking. Thus these two things become united in one by feeling.

"I have said: 'Contact conditions feeling.' Therefore contact is the root, the cause, the origin, the condition for feeling.

" 'Mind-and-body conditions contact.' By whatever properties, features, signs or indications the mind-factor is conceived of, would there, in the absence of such properties . . . pertaining to the mind-factor, be manifest any grasping at the idea of the body-factor?" "No, Lord."

"Or in the absence of any such properties pertaining to the body-factor, would there be any grasping at sensory reaction on the part of the mind-factor?" "No, Lord."

"By whatever properties the mind-factor and the body-factor are designated—in their absence is there manifested any grasping at the idea, or at sensory reaction?" "No, Lord."

"By whatever properties, features, signs or indications the mind-factor is conceived of, in the absence of these is there any contact to be found?" "No, Lord."

"Then, Ananda, just this, namely mind-and-body, is the root, the cause, the origin, the condition for all contact.

"I have said: 'Consciousness conditions mind-and-body.' . . . If consciousness were not to come into the mother's womb, would mind-and-body develop there?" "No, Lord."

"Or if consciousness, having entered the mother's womb, were to be deflected, would mind-and-body come to birth in this life?" "No, Lord." "And if the consciousness of such a tender young being, boy or girl, were thus cut off, would mind-and-body grow, develop and mature?" "No, Lord." "Therefore, Ananda, just this, namely consciousness, is the root, the cause, the origin, the condition of mind-and-body.

"I have said: 'Mind-and-body conditions consciousness.' . . . If consciousness did not find a resting-place in mind-and-body, would there subsequently be an arising and coming-to-be of birth, aging, death and suffering?" "No, Lord." "Therefore, Ananda, just this, namely mind-and-body, is the root, the cause, the origin, the condition of consciousness. Thus far then, Ananda, we can trace birth and decay, death and falling into other states and being reborn, thus far extends the way of designation, of concepts, thus far is the sphere of understanding, thus far the round goes as far as can be discerned in this life, namely to mind-and-body together with consciousness.

"In what ways, Ananda, do people explain the nature of the self? Some declare the self to be material and limited, saying: 'My self is material and limited'; some declare it to be material and unlimited . . . ; some declare it to be immaterial and limited . . . ; some declare it to be immaterial and unlimited, saying: 'My self is immaterial and unlimited.'

"Whoever declares the self to be material and limited, considers it to be so either now, or in the next world, thinking: 'Though it is not so now, I shall acquire it there.' That being so, that is all we need say about the view that the self is material and limited, and the same applies to the other theories. So much, Ananda, for those who proffer an explanation of the self.

"How is it with those who do not explain the nature of the self? . . .

"In what ways, Ananda, do people regard the self? They equate the self with feeling: 'Feeling is my self,' or: 'Feeling is not my self, my self is impercipient,' or: 'Feeling is not my self, but my self is not impercipient, it is of a nature to feel.'

"Now, Ananda, one who says: 'Feeling is my self' should be told:

'There are three kinds of feeling, friend: pleasant, painful, and neutral. Which of the three do you consider to be your self?' When a pleasant feeling is felt, no painful or neutral feeling is felt, but only pleasant feeling. When a painful feeling is felt, no pleasant or neutral feeling is felt, but only painful feeling. And when a neutral feeling is felt, no pleasant or painful feeling is felt, but only neutral feeling.

"Pleasant feeling is impermanent, conditioned, dependently-arisen, bound to decay, to vanish, to fade away, to cease—and so too are painful feeling and neutral feeling. So anyone who, on experiencing a pleasant feeling, thinks: 'This is my self,' must, at the cessation of that pleasant feeling, think: 'My self has gone!' and the same with painful and neutral feelings. Thus whoever thinks: 'Feeling is my self' is contemplating something in this present life that is impermanent, a mixture of happiness and unhappiness, subject to arising and passing away. Therefore it is not fitting to maintain: 'Feeling is my self.'

"But anyone who says: 'Feeling is not my self, my self is impercipient' should be asked: 'If, friend, no feelings at all were to be experienced, would there be the thought: "I am"?' [to which he would have to reply:] 'No, Lord.' Therefore it is not fitting to maintain: 'Feeling is not my self, my self is impercipient.'

"And anyone who says: 'Feeling is not my self, but my self is not impercipient, my self is of a nature to feel' should be asked: 'Well, friend, if all feelings absolutely and totally ceased, could there be the thought: "I am this"?' [to which he would have to reply:] 'No, Lord.' "Therefore it is not fitting to maintain: 'Feeling is not my self, but my self is not impercipient, my self is of a nature to feel.'

"From the time, Ananda, when a monk no longer regards feeling as the self, or the self as being impercipient, or as being percipient and of a nature to feel, by not so regarding, he clings to nothing in the world; not clinging, he is not excited by anything, and not being excited he gains personal liberation, and he knows: 'Birth is finished, the holy life has been led, done was what had to be done, there is nothing more here.' ''

JACK KORNFIELD
No Self or True Self?

SPIRITUAL PRACTICE INEVITABLY brings us face to face with the profound mystery of our own identity. We have taken birth in a human body. What is this force that gives us life, that brings us and the world into form? The world's great spiritual teachings tell us over and over we are not who we think we are.

Persian mystics say we are sparks of the divine, and Christian mystics say we are filled with God. We are one with all things, say others. The world is all illusion, say others. Some teachings explain how consciousness creates life to express all possibilities, to be able to love, to know oneself. Others point out how consciousness gets lost in its patterns, loses its way, incarnates out of ignorance. Hindu yogas call the world a *lila*, or a dance of the divine, much like Dante's phrase, "the divine comedy."

Buddhist texts describe how consciousness itself creates the world like a dream or a mirage. Modern accounts of near-death experiences are filled with reports of wonderful ease after leaving the body, of golden light and luminous beings. Perhaps these, too, confirm how we are unaware of our true identity most of the time.

When we look into the question of self and identity in spiritual practice, we find it requires us to understand two distinct dimensions of self—selflessness and true self. . . .

When the Buddha confronted the question of identity on the night of his enlightenment, he came to the radical discovery that we do not exist as separate beings. He saw into the human tendency to identify with a limited sense of existence and discovered that this belief in an individual small self is a root illusion that causes suffering and removes us from the freedom and mystery of life. He described this as *interdependent arising* [see pages 275–281], the cyclical process of consciousness creating identity by entering form, responding to contact of the senses, then attaching to certain forms, feelings, desires, images, and actions to create a sense of self.

In teaching, the Buddha never spoke of humans as persons existing in some fixed or static way. Instead, he described us as a collection of five changing processes: the processes of the physical body, of feelings, of perceptions, of responses, and of the flow of consciousness that experiences them all. Our sense of self arises whenever we grasp at or identify with these patterns. The process of identification, of selecting patterns to call "I," "me," "myself," is subtle and usually hidden from our awareness. We can identify with our body, feelings, or thoughts; we can identify with images, patterns, roles, and archetypes. Thus, in our culture, we might fix and identify with the role of being a woman or a man, a parent or a child. We might take our family history, our genetics, and our heredity to be who we are. Sometimes we identify with our desires: sexual, aesthetic, or spiritual. In the same way we can focus on our intellect or take our astrological sign as an identity. We can choose the archetype of hero, lover, mother, ne'er-do-well, adventurer, clown, or thief as our identity and live a year or a whole lifetime based on that. To the extent that we grasp these false identities, we continually have to protect and defend ourselves, strive to fulfill what is limited or deficient in them, to fear their loss.

Yet, these are not our true identity. One master with whom I studied used to laugh at how easily and commonly we would grasp at new identities. As for himself, he would say, "I am none of that. I am not this body, so I was never born and will never die. I am nothing and I am everything. Your identities make all your problems. Discover what is beyond them, the delight of the timeless, the deathless."

Because the question of identity and selflessness is subject to confusion and misunderstanding, let us go into it more carefully. When Christian texts speak of losing the self in God, when Taoists and Hindus speak of merging with a *True Self* beyond all identity, when Buddhists speak of emptiness and of no *self*, what do they mean? Emptiness does not mean that things don't exist, nor does "no self" mean that we don't exist. Emptiness refers to the underlying nonseparation of life and the fertile ground of energy that gives rise to all forms of life. Our world and sense of self is a play of patterns. Any identity we can grasp is transient, tentative. This is difficult to understand from words such as *selflessness* or *emptiness of self*. In fact, my own teacher Achaan Chah said, "If you try to understand it intellectually, your head will probably explode." However, the experience of selflessness in practice can bring us to great freedom.

. . . [D]eep meditation [see pages 121–133] can untangle the sense of identity. There are, in fact, many ways in which we can realize the emptiness of self. When we are silent and attentive, we can sense directly how nothing in the world can be truly possessed by us. Clearly we do not possess outer things; we are in some relationship with our cars, our home, our family, our jobs, but whatever that relationship is, it is "ours" only for a short time. In the end, things, people, or tasks die or change or we lose them. Nothing is exempt.

When we bring attention to any moment of experience, we discover that we do not possess it either. As we look, we find that we neither invite our thoughts nor own them. We might even wish them to stop, but our thoughts seem to think themselves, arising and passing according to their nature.

The same is true of our feelings. How many of us believe we control our feelings? As we pay attention, we see that they are more like the weather—moods and feelings change according to certain conditions, and are neither possessed nor directed by our consciousness or desires. Do we order happiness, sadness, irritation, excitement, or restlessness to come? Feelings arise by themselves, as the breath breathes itself, as sounds sound themselves.

Our body, too, follows its own laws. The body which we carry is a bag of bones and fluid that cannot be possessed. It ages, gets sick, or changes in ways we might not wish it to, all according to its own nature. The more we look, in fact, the more deeply we see that we possess nothing within or without.

We encounter another aspect of the emptiness of self when we notice how everything arises out of nothing, comes out of the void, returns to the void, goes back to nothing. All our words of the past day have disappeared. Similarly, where has the past week or the past month or our childhood gone? They arose, did a little dance, and now they've vanished, along with the 1980s, the nineteenth and eighteenth centuries, the ancient Romans and Greeks, the Pharaohs, and so forth. All experience arises in the present, does its dance, and disappears. Experience comes into being only tentatively, for a little time in a certain form; then that form ends and a new form replaces it moment by moment. . . .

In meditation . . . precise and deep attention shows us emptiness everywhere. Whatever sensation, thought, whatever aspect of body or mind we focus on carefully, the more space and the less solidity we experience there. Experience becomes like the particle waves described in modern physics, a pattern not quite solid, ever-changing. Even the sense of the one who is observing changes in the same way, our perspectives shifting from moment to moment as much as our sense of ourselves shifts from childhood to adolescence to old age. Wherever we focus carefully, we find a veneer of solidity that dissolves under our attention.

Sri Nisargadatta says:

The real world is beyond our thoughts and ideas; we see it through the net of our desires, divided into pleasure and pain, right and wrong, inner and outer. To see the universe as it is, you must step beyond the net. It is not hard to do so, for the net is full of holes.

As we open and empty ourselves, we come to experience an interconnectedness, the realization that all things are joined and conditioned in an interdependent arising. Each experience and event contains all others. The teacher depends on the student, the airplane depends on the sky.

When a bell rings, is it the bell we hear, the air, the sound on our ears, or is it our brain that rings? It is all of these things. As the Taoists say, "The between is ringing." The sound of the bell is here to be heard everywhere—in the eyes of every person we meet, in every tree and insect, in every breath we take. . . .

When we truly sense this interconnectedness and the emptiness out of which all beings arise [see pages 180–181], we find liberation and a spacious joy. Discovering emptiness brings a lightness of heart, a flexibility, and an ease that rests in all things. The more solidly we grasp our identity, the more solid our problems become. Once I asked a delightful old Sri Lankan meditation master to teach me the essence of Buddhism. He just laughed and said three times, "No self, no problem."

Misconceptions about selflessness and emptiness abound, and such confusions undermine genuine spiritual development. Some people believe that they can come to selflessness by struggling to get rid of their ego-centered self. Others confuse the notion of emptiness with inner feelings of apathy, unworthiness, or meaninglessness that they have carried from a painful past into spiritual practice. . . . [S]ome students use emptiness as an excuse for a withdrawal from life, saying it is all illusion, trying to make a "spiritual bypass" around life's problems. But each of these diseases of emptiness misses the true meaning of emptiness and its liberating freedom.

To try to get rid of the self, to purify, root out, or transcend all desire, anger, and centeredness, to vanquish a self that is "bad," is an old religious idea. This notion underlies the ascetic practices, such as wearing hair shirts, extreme fasting, and self-mortification, that are found in many traditions. Sometimes such practices are used skillfully, to induce altered states, but more often they only reinforce aversion. Worse, what comes with them is the notion that our body, our mind, our "ego," is somehow sinful, dirty, and deluded. "I (the good part of me) must use these techniques to get rid of the self (the lower, bad part of me)." But this can never work. It can never work because there is no self to get rid of! We are a changing process, not a fixed being. There never was a self—only our identification makes us think so. So while purification, kindness, and attention can certainly improve our habits, no amount of self-denial or self-torture can rid us of a self, for it was never there.

CHARLOTTE JOKO BECK

Impermanence

SUZUKI ROSHI SAID, "Renunciation is not giving up the things of this world, but accepting that they go away." Everything is impermanent; sooner or later everything goes away. Renunciation is a state of nonattachment, acceptance of this going away. Impermanence is, in fact, just another name for perfection. Leaves fall; debris and garbage accumulate; out of the debris come flowers, greenery, things that we think are lovely. Destruction is necessary. A good forest fire is necessary. The way we interfere with forest fires may not be a good thing. Without destruction, there could be no new life; and the wonder of life, the constant change, could not be. We must live and die. And this process is perfection itself.

All this change is not, however, what we had in mind. Our drive is not to appreciate the perfection of the universe. Our personal drive is to find a way to endure in our unchanging glory forever. That may seem ridiculous, yet that's what we're doing. And that resistance to change is not attuned with the perfection of life, which is its impermanence. If life were not impermanent, it couldn't be the wonder that it is. Still, the last thing we like is our own impermanence. Who hasn't noticed the first gray hair and thought, "Uh-oh." So a battle rages in human existence. We refuse to see the truth that's all around us. We don't really see life at all. Our attention is elsewhere. We are engaged in an unending battle with our fears about ourselves and our existence. If we want to see life we must be attentive to it. But we're not interested in doing that; we're only interested in the battle to preserve ourselves forever. And of course it's an anxious and futile battle, a battle that can't be won. The one who always wins is death, the "right-hand man" of impermanence. . . .

Intelligent practice always deals with just one thing: the fear at the base of human existence, the fear that I *am not*. And of course I am not, but the last thing I want to know is that. I am impermanence itself in a rapidly changing human form that appears solid. I fear to see what I am: an ever-changing energy field. I don't want to be that. So good practice is about fear. Fear takes the form of constantly thinking, speculating, analyzing, fantasizing. With all that activity we create a cloudy cover to keep ourselves safe in a make-believe practice. True practice is *not* safe; it's anything but safe. But we don't like that, so we obsess with our feverish efforts to achieve our version of the personal dream. Such obsessive practice is itself just another cloud between ourselves and reality. The only thing that matters is seeing with an impersonal searchlight: seeing things as they are. When the personal barrier drops away, why do we have to call it anything? We just live our lives. And when we die, we just die. No problem anywhere.

Karma

Karma—the action of body, speech, and mind—affects every aspect of our life. Actions affect both doers and those around them in unimaginable ways, and the seeds of karma shape our lives and our worlds, though different Buddhist traditions give different weight to whether the action is willed or not. In either case, through mindfulness, we become aware of the nature of these actions and can in fact change our karma.

JOSEPH GOLDSTEIN
Cause and Effect

THE LAW OF karma is one of the most important laws governing our lives. When we understand it, and live our understanding, when we act on what we know, then we experience a sense of wholeness and peace. If we live in a way that is out of harmony, ignoring the nature of things, we then experience dissonance, pain, and confusion. The law of karma is one of the fundamental natural laws through which we create these vastly different realities. It is as though we are all artists, but instead of canvas and paint, or marble or music, as our medium, our very bodies, minds, and life experience are the materials of our creative expression. A great sense of fulfillment in dharma practice comes from knowing this and from actively creating and fashioning our lives.

Karma is a Sanskrit word (*kamma* in Pali) that means "action." The law of karma refers to the law of cause and effect: that every volitional act brings about a certain result. If we act motivated by greed, hatred, or delusion, we are planting the seed of suffering; when our acts are motivated by generosity, love, or wisdom, then we are creating the karmic conditions for abundance and happiness. An analogy from the physical world illustrates this: if we plant an apple seed, the tree that grows will bear apples, not mangoes. And once the apple seed is planted, no amount of manipulation or beseeching or complaining will induce the tree to yield a mango. The only meaningful action that will produce a mango is to plant a mango seed. Karma is just such a law of nature, the law of cause and effect on the psychophysical plane.

The Buddha used the term *karma* specifically referring to volition, the intention or motive behind an action. He said that karma is volition, because it is the motivation behind the action that determines the karmic fruit. Inherent in each intention in the mind is an energy powerful enough to bring about subsequent results. When we understand that karma is based on volition, we can see the enormous responsibility we have to become conscious of the intentions that precede our actions. If we are unaware of the motives in our minds, when unskillful volitions arise we may unmindfully act on them and thus create the conditions for future suffering.

The law of karma can be understood on two levels, which indicate the vast scope of its implications in our lives. On one level, karma refers to the experience of cause and effect over a period of time. We perform an action, and sometime later we begin to experience its results. We plant a mango seed, and many years later we taste the fruit. The other level of understanding karma has to do with the quality of mind in the very moment of action. When we experience a mind state of love, there comes naturally, along with it, a feeling of openness and love that is its immediate fruit; similarly, when there are moments of greed or hatred, in addition to whatever future results will come, we also experience the painful energies that arise with those states. Our direct awareness of how the karmic law is working in each moment can be a strong motivation to develop skillful states of mind that create happiness for us in the moment, as well as produce the fruit of well-being in the future.

Another dimension of the law of karma helps in understanding how individual personalities develop. While it is true that there is no enduring entity, no unchanging self that can be called "I," it is also quite obvious that each of us is a uniquely changing and recognizable pattern of elements. This comes about because each of us has in our own way, both consciously and unconsciously, cultivated different mind states. If we cultivate lovingkindness, we experience its taste in the moment and at the same time are strengthening it as a force in the mind, making it easier for it to arise again. When we are angry, we experience the suffering of that anger as present karma and are also strengthening that particular pattern of mind. Just as we condition our bodies in different ways through exercise or lack of it, so we also condition our minds. Every mind state, thought, or emotion that we experience repeatedly becomes stronger and more habituated. Who we are as personalities is a collection of all the tendencies of mind that have been developed, the particular energy configurations we have cultivated.

We tend not to pay attention to this conditioning factor of our experience, thinking instead that once an experience has passed it is gone without residue or result. That would be like dropping a stone in water without creating any ripples. Each mind state that we experience further conditions and strengthens it. When we see how this is happening in our own minds, we begin to get an intuitive sense of something the Buddha spoke of often in his teachings, the conditionality of the six realms of existence. These six realms are the manifestations of strongly developed patterns of mind. They refer to the different realities we experience from moment to moment, and also to the actual planes of existence in which beings are reborn according to their karma.

The attitude in Western cultural conditioning toward rebirth and different realms of existence is often skeptical or disbelieving; there is a healthy strain of "Show me, I'm from Missouri" in our approach to these questions. It may be of value, though, to realize that along with all that we can verify directly in our practice, these concepts of karma and rebirth are very much part of what the Buddha taught, and that it is possible through meditative attainment to experience for oneself the truth of these teachings. For those of us with something less than perfect concentration or great psychic power, however, an attitude that helps to keep us open to possibilities beyond our present level of understanding is expressed in a phrase of the poet Coleridge: "the willing suspension of disbelief." With this attitude of mind we are trapped neither by blind belief nor blind disbelief. In this way we acknowledge what we don't yet know for ourselves and stay receptive to new levels of understanding.

According to the Buddha's teachings there are six realms or planes of existence: the four lower realms of suffering, the human realm, and the higher planes of the various heaven worlds. The lower realms are conditioned by intense anger, hatred, greed, and delusion, and when we cultivate these states, developing them as a pattern of response to situations, they become a strong force in the mind. Not only do we then experience the present karma of the painful feelings in the moment, but we also create the conditions for possible rebirth in realms of terrible suffering.

The human realm is the first of the happy planes of existence. It is said to be the most conducive for developing wisdom and compassion because of its particular mixture of pain and pleasure. In the lower realms the intensity and degree of suffering is too great for most beings to develop wholesome qualities of mind, while in the higher planes of existence everything is so blissful that there is little inspiration to practice. It is precisely the combination of pain and pleasure in the human realm that provides the best circumstances for deep understanding and realization.

We take birth as human beings conditioned by a basic attitude of generosity and nonharming. These mind states create the powerful karmic force that results in birth in this realm, and indeed, these qualities of mind reflect a true humaneness. When generosity and morality are practiced and developed even further, they condition rebirth in the deva realm, the heavenly planes of existence. In these deva worlds everything is pleasant, beings have refined bodies of light, and there are delightful sense objects on all sides.

The highest planes of conditioned existence are the brahma realms. They are characterized by great bliss, which is a happiness beyond sensual pleasure and is the result of the cultivation of a deep concentration of mind known as absorption.

These six realms are all karmically created. There is no one who judges, condemns, or elevates us to different realms, just as there is nobody who decides which mind states we are to experience in each moment. The great inspiration of the Buddha's teaching is that we must each take ultimate responsibility for the quality of our lives. Given certain volitional actions, certain results will follow. When we understand that our lives are the unfolding of karmic law that we are the heirs to our own deeds, then there grows in us a deepening sense of responsibility for how we live, the choices we make, and the actions we undertake.

People sometimes wonder whether reflecting upon the law of karma will lead to feelings of guilt for past unwholesome actions. Guilt is a manifestation of condemnation or aversion toward oneself, which does not understand the changing transformative quality of mind. It solidifies a sense of self by being nonforgiving. Understanding the law of karma leads us to reflect wisely on the skillfulness or unskillfulness of our actions. In the infinite time of our births, through all the realms of existence, we have done so many different kinds of actions, wholesome and unwholesome. In view of karmic law, guilt is an inappropriate feeling, and a rather useless burden. It simply creates more unwholesome results. Coming to an understanding of karma is the basis for a very straightforward development of the wisdom to know whether our actions will lead to happiness and freedom, or to further suffering. When we understand this, it allows us to take responsibility for past actions with an attitude of compassion, appreciating that a particular act may have been unwholesome or harmful, and strongly determining not to repeat it. Guilt is a manifestation of condemnation, wisdom an expression of sensitivity and forgiveness. . . .

It is said that on the eve of his enlightenment, the Buddha, with the power of his mind, reviewed the births and deaths of countless beings wandering throughout the cycle of existence in accordance with their karma. His great compassion was awakened when he saw all those beings wanting happiness, striving for happiness, yet performing the very actions that would lead to suffering. When we do not understand the unfolding of karmic law, when we are deluded about the nature of things, then we continually create the conditions for greater suffering for ourselves and others, even when we are wishing and hoping for peace. There are those even today who have developed the power of mind to see karmic unfolding through past and future lifetimes. But it is not necessary to be able to see our past lives in order to understand the principles of karmic law. If we pay attention and carefully observe our own lives, it can become very clear how our actions condition certain results.

The Buddha spoke often about right and wrong view with regard to the effects of one's actions. Right view is the understanding that our actions do bring results, both in the present and in the future, while wrong view denies this cause-and-effect relationship. Our culture is generally geared to the pursuit of immediate gratification of desires, and this reinforces the view that what we do will not have effects, that there is no karmic result from our actions that will come back to us. But when we step back and take a broader perspective, we begin to understand that we are the heirs of our own motives and deeds and that our lives do not unfold randomly or haphazardly. It is important to see what our motives and volitions are and to understand the results they condition.

Mindfulness plays a critical role in understanding the unfolding of karma. Two aspects of mindfulness that are particularly relevant to this are clear comprehension and suitability of purpose. Clear comprehension means paying attention to what we are doing, being fully aware of what is actually happening. When we stand up, we know we're standing; when we walk, we know we're walking. Clear comprehension of what we are doing in the moment then allows us to consider the suitability of purpose. This means knowing whether the actions are skillful or unskillful, whether or not they will bring the results that we want.

When mindfulness is weak, we have little sense of clear comprehension or suitability of purpose. Not only may we be unaware of our intentions, we often are not even paying attention to the action itself, hence we may be propelled by habitual patterns into actions that bring painful results. The deep understanding that actions condition results creates a compelling interest in what we do. We begin to pay quite meticulous attention; we begin to awaken. Not only does each action, no matter how insignificant it may seem, condition a future result, it also reconditions the mind. If a moment of anger arises in the mind and we get lost in it, we are then actually cultivating anger. If we get lost in greed, we are cultivating greed. It is like a bucket being filled with water, drop by drop. We think each drop is so tiny, so insignificant, that it doesn't matter at all. Yet drop by drop the bucket gets filled. In just this way, the mind is conditioned by each experience in every moment, and moment after moment the mind gets filled. We should have a tremendous respect for the conditioning power of the mind, not only in terms of our present experience, but also in terms of our future direction. . . .

During a visit to the United States, His Holiness the Dalai Lama gave a talk about emptiness of self and the karmic law of cause and effect. In the course of the talk, he said that given a choice between understanding karma and understanding emptiness, one should try to understand karma. To many that was surprising, because the very heart of the wisdom of Buddhism is understanding the empty, selfless, insubstantial nature of phenomena. His point of emphasis, though, is extremely important for us to grasp, because without an understanding of karma, of the effect of our actions, the aspect of the emptiness of phenomena can be used as a rationale for not taking responsibility in our lives. To think that nothing matters, that we can do anything because it's all empty anyway, is a serious misunderstanding of the teaching and a poor justification for unskillful behavior. If we are sensitive to the law of karma and become responsible for our actions and their results, then it will help us come to a genuine understanding of emptiness.

Compassion, as well as insight, arises from understanding karma. When we understand that unfair, harmful, or hateful actions rebound in suffering to the person committing them as well as to the recipient, we can respond to both with compassion rather than with anger or resentment. This in no way means that our response is weak or indecisive. In fact, seeing people act out of ignorance in ways that cause themselves or others great pain can inspire a very strong and direct response to that ignorance, but it is a response of compassion. . . .

In explaining the workings of karma, the Buddha spoke of the potency of different actions. He spoke often of the great power of generosity, explaining that an act of generosity is purified and empowered in three ways. It is purified by the giver, by the receiver, and by that which is given. The purity of mind of the one giving and of the one receiving, and the purity of the gift itself (that is, the means by which the gift came into one's possession), strengthen the karmic force of each act of generosity.

And many times more powerful than giving a gift even to the Buddha and the whole order of enlightened disciples is one moment in which the mind is fully concentrated on extending thoughts of lovingkindness toward all beings. When we genuinely open our hearts, the deep feeling of our connectedness to all beings is a tremendously effective force, which can then motivate a wide variety of skillful actions.

The Buddha went on to say that even more powerful than that moment of lovingkindness is one moment of deeply seeing the impermanent nature of phenomena. This moment of insight is so profound because it deconditions attachment in the mind and opens up the possibility of true nonattachment. When we deeply see the impermanent, ephemeral nature of the mind and body, how they are in constant flux, we develop detachment and equanimity toward the dreamlike elements of our experience. Sometimes in meditation practice when we are dealing with the pain, restlessness, boredom, and other difficulties that come up, we may lose sight of the larger context of what the practice is about. It is helpful to remember that the karmic energy generated by the repeated observation and awareness of the changing nature of things is a tremendously powerful karmic force that leads to many kinds of happiness and to freedom.

Understanding the law of karma is known as the light of the world because through this understanding we can take responsibility for our destinies and be more truly guided to greater fulfillment in our lives.

JON KABAT-ZINN

Changing Karma

I'VE HEARD ZEN masters say that daily meditation practice could turn bad karma into good karma. I always chalked this up to a quaint moralistic sales pitch. It took me years to get the point. I guess that's my karma.

Karma means that this happens because that happened. B is connected in some way to A, every effect has an antecedent cause, and every cause an effect that is its measure and its consequence, at least at the non-quantum level. Overall, when we speak of a person's karma, it means the sum total of the person's direction in life and the tenor of the things that occur around that person, caused by antecedent conditions, actions, thoughts, feelings, sense impressions, desires. Karma is often wrongly confused with the notion of a fixed destiny. It is more like an accumulation of tendencies that can lock us into particular behavior patterns, which themselves result in further accumulations of tendencies of a similar nature. So, it is easy to become imprisoned by our karma and to think that the cause always lies elsewhere—with other people and conditions beyond our control, never within ourselves. But it is not necessary to be a prisoner of old karma. It is always possible to change your karma. You can make new karma. But there is only one time that you ever have to do it. Can you guess when that might be?

Here's how mindfulness changes karma. When you sit, you are not allowing your impulses to translate into action. For the time being, at least, you are just watching them. Looking at them, you quickly see that all impulses in the mind arise and pass away, that they have a life of their own, that they are not you but just thinking, and that you do not have to be ruled by them. Not feeding or reacting to impulses, you come to understand their nature as thoughts directly. This process actually burns up destructive impulses in the fires of concentration and equanimity and non-doing. At the same time, creative insights and creative impulses are no longer squeezed out so much by the more turbulent, destructive ones. They are nourished as they are perceived and held in awareness. Mindfulness can thereby refashion the links in the chain of actions and consequences, and in doing so it unchains us, frees us, and opens up new directions for us through the moments we call life. Without mindfulness, we are all too easily stuck in the momentum coming out of the past with no clue to our own improvement, and no way out.

Our dilemma always seems to be the other person's fault, or the world's fault, so our own views and feelings are always justified. The present moment is never a new beginning because we keep it from becoming one.

How else to explain, for example, the all-too-common observation that two people who have lived their whole adult lives together, had children together, tasted success in their own realms to a degree not usually achieved, might in their later years, when by all accounts they should be enjoying the fruits of their labors, each blame the other for making life miserable, for feeling isolated, trapped in a bad dream, so mistreated and abused that anger and hurt are the fabric of each day? Karma. In one form or another, you see it over and over again in relationships gone sour or missing something fundamental from the start, the absence of which invites sadness, bitterness, hurt. Sooner or later, we are most likely to reap that which we have sown. Practice anger and isolation in a relationship for forty years, and you wind up imprisoned in anger and isolation. No big surprise. And it is hardly satisfactory to apportion blame here.

Ultimately, it is our mindlessness that imprisons us. We get better and better at being out of touch with the full range of our possibilities and more and more stuck in our cultivated-over-a-lifetime habits of not-seeing, but only reacting and blaming. . . .

If we hope to change our karma, it means we have to stop making those things happen that cloud mind and body and color our every action. It doesn't mean doing good deeds. It means knowing who you are and that you are not your karma, whatever it may be at this moment. It means aligning yourself with the way things actually are. It means seeing clearly.

Where to start? Why not with your own mind? After all, it is the instrument through which all our thoughts and feelings, impulses and perceptions are translated into actions in the world. When you stop outward activity for some time and practice being still, right there, in that moment, with that decision to sit, you are already breaking the flow of old karma and creating an entirely new and healthier karma. Herein lies the root of change, the turning point of a life lived.

The very act of stopping, of nurturing moments of nondoing, of simply watching, puts you on an entirely different footing vis-à-vis the future. How? Because it is only by being fully in this moment that any future moment might be one of greater understanding, clarity, and kindness, one less dominated by fear or hurt and more by dignity and acceptance. Only what happens now happens later. If there is no mindfulness or equanimity or compassion now, in the only time we ever have to contact it and nourish ourselves, how likely is it that it will magically appear later, under stress or duress?

The Dhammapada

The Dhammapada (Sanskrit: Dharmapada) is a collection of inspirational verses embodying the basic teachings—Dhamma (Sanskrit: Dharma)—of the Buddha found in the Theravada Pali canon. These verses in very practical ways deal with both facing everyday life in the world at the time it was written and achieving the liberation that is Nibbana (Sanskrit: Nirvana).

ACHARYA BUDDHARAKKHITA
The Dhammapada

THE DHAMMAPADA IS the best known and most widely esteemed text in the Pali Tipitaka, the sacred scriptures of Theravada Buddhism. The work is included in the Khuddaka Nikaya ("Minor Collection") of the Sutta Pitaka, but its popularity has raised it far above the single niche it occupies in the scriptures to the ranks of a world religious classic. Composed in the ancient Pali language, this slim anthology of verses constitutes a perfect compendium of the Buddha's teaching, comprising between its covers all the essential principles elaborated at length in the forty-odd volumes of the Pali Canon.

According to the Theravada Buddhist tradition, each verse in the Dhammapada was originally spoken by the Buddha in response to a particular episode. Accounts of these, along with exegeses of the verses, are preserved in the classic commentary to the work, compiled by the great scholiast Bhadantacariya Buddhaghosa in the fifth century CE on the basis of material going back to very ancient times. The contents of the verses, however, transcend the limited and particular circumstances of their origin, reaching out through the ages to various types of people in all the diverse situations of life. For the simple and unsophisticated the Dhammapada is a sympathetic counselor; for the intellectually over-burdened its clear and direct teachings inspire humility and reflection; for the earnest seeker it is a perennial source of inspiration and practical instruction. Insights that flashed into the heart of the Buddha have crys-tallized into these luminous verses of pure wisdom. As profound ex-pressions of practical spirituality, each verse is a guideline to right living. The Buddha unambiguously pointed out that whoever earnestly practices the teachings found in the Dhammapada will taste the bliss of emanci-pation.

ACHARYA BUDDHARAKKHITA, TRANS.

From The Dhammapada

1. Mind precedes all mental states. Mind is their chief; they are all mind-wrought. If with an impure mind a person speaks or acts, suffering follows him like the wheel that follows the foot of the ox.

2. Mind precedes all mental states. Mind is their chief; they are all mind-wrought. If with a pure mind a person speaks or acts, happiness follows him like his never-departing shadow.

3. "He abused me, he struck me, he overpowered me, he robbed me"— those who harbor such thoughts do not still their hatred.

4. "He abused me, he struck me, he overpowered me, he robbed me"—those who do not harbor such thoughts still their hatred.

5. Hatred is never appeased by hatred in this world; by non-hatred alone is hatred appeased. This is an Eternal Law.

6. There are those who do not realize that one day we all must die, but those who realize this settle their quarrels.

7. Just as a storm throws down a weak tree, so does *Mara* overpower the man who lives for the pursuit of pleasures, who is uncontrolled in his senses, immoderate in eating, indolent, and dissipated.

8. Just as a storm cannot throw down a rocky mountain, so *Mara* can never overpower the man who lives meditating on the impurities, who is controlled in his senses, moderate in eating, and filled with faith and earnest effort.

13. Just as the rain breaks through an ill-thatched house, even so passion penetrates an undeveloped mind.

14. Just as the rain does not break through a well-thatched house, even so passion never penetrates a well-developed mind.

19. Much though he recites the sacred texts, but acts not accordingly, that heedless man is like a cowherd who only counts the cows of others—he does not partake of the blessings of a holy life.

20. Little though he recites the sacred texts, but puts the Teaching into practice, forsaking lust, hatred, and delusion, with true wisdom and

emancipated mind, clinging to nothing in this or any other world—he, indeed, partakes of the blessings of a holy life.

42. Whatever harm an enemy may do to an enemy, or a hater to a hater, an ill-directed mind inflicts on oneself a greater harm.

43. Neither mother, father, nor any other relative can do one greater good than one's own well-directed mind.

132. One who, while himself seeking happiness, does not oppress with violence other beings who also desire happiness, will find happiness hereafter.

133. Speak not harshly to anyone; for those thus spoken to might retort. Indeed, angry speech hurts, and retaliation may overtake you.

134. If, like a broken gong, you silence yourself, you have approached *Nibbana*, for vindictiveness is no more in you.

172. He who having been heedless is heedless no more, illuminates this world like the moon freed from clouds.

173. He who by good deeds covers the evil he has done, illuminates this world like the moon freed from clouds.

190–191. He who has gone for refuge to the Buddha, his Teaching and his Order, penetrates with wisdom the Four Noble Truths—suffering, the cause of suffering, the cessation of suffering, and the Noble Eightfold Path leading to the cessation of suffering.

192. This indeed is the safe refuge, this is the refuge supreme. Having gone to such a refuge, one is released from all suffering.

246–247. One who destroys life, utters lies, takes what is not given, goes to another man's wife, and is addicted to intoxicating drinks—such a man digs up his own root even in this very world.

273. Of all paths the Eightfold Path is the best; of all truths the Four Noble Truths are the best; of all things passionlessness is the best; of men the Seeing One (the Buddha) is the best.

274. This is the only way: there is none other for the purification of insight. Tread this path, and you will bewilder *Mara*.

276. You yourselves must strive; the Buddhas only point the way. Those meditative ones who tread the path are released from the bonds of *Mara*.

277. "All conditioned things are impermanent"—when one sees this with wisdom one turns away from suffering. This is the path to purification.

278. "All conditioned things are unsatisfactory"—when one sees this with wisdom one turns away from suffering. This is the path to purification.

279. "All things are not self"—when one sees this with wisdom one turns away from suffering. This is the path to purification.

280. The idler who does not exert himself when he should, who though young and strong is full of sloth, with a mind full of vain thoughts—such an indolent man does not find the path to wisdom.

281. Watchful of speech, well controlled in mind, let a man not commit evil with the body. Let him purify these three courses of action and win the path made known by the Great Sage.

282. Wisdom springs from meditation, without meditation wisdom wanes. Having known these two paths of progress and decline, let a man so conduct himself that his wisdom may increase.

286. "Here shall I live during the rains, here in winter and summer"—thus thinks the fool. He does not realize the danger (that death might intervene).

287. As a great flood carries away a sleeping village, just so death seizes and carries away a man with a clinging mind, doting on his children and cattle.

288. For him who is assailed by death there is no protection by kinsmen. None there are to save him—no sons, nor father nor relatives.

289. Realizing this fact, let the wise man, restrained by morality, hasten to clear the path leading to *Nibbana*.

Nirvana

One of the major lessons of The Dhammapada *is how to achieve the condition called nirvana in Sanskrit, or nibbana in Pali. Although there are descriptions of the state of nirvana in this life—particularly in the Buddha's life—the Buddha discouraged speculative descriptions of what happens at death. Instead, he stressed the path to nirvana in the Fourth Noble Truth: the Eightfold Path (see pages 85–101). Thus, this book closes where it began, with the Buddha's teachings—his only teachings, he declared—on suffering and the end of suffering.*

JOHN SNELLING

Nirvana

FREEDOM FROM *TRISHNA* [Pali: *tanha*; literally, "thirst," a fundamental ache in everything that exists, a gnawing dissatisfaction with what is and a concomitant reaching out for something else] is known in Pali as nibbana, the Sanskrit equivalent of which, nirvana, has now entered English parlance. There are two kinds of nirvana:

1. That which has a residual basis

2. That which has no residual basis

The first arose in Shakyamuni Buddha as he sat beneath the bodhi tree at Bodh Gaya on the fateful night of the full moon of May; the second arose when he finally passed away at Kushinagara. In the first case a living being continued to pursue an earthly life; in the second, there was complete extinction (Parinirvana): nothing tangible remained behind.

What is nirvana? Invariably it is stressed that it cannot be grasped via sense experience or by the mind operating in terms of its usual conceptual categories. And it certainly cannot be described in words. To do so would be like trying to describe the color red to a blind person. As it lies wholly outside our normal field of experience, we can and must come to it through direct insight, and this indeed is basically what the Buddha's way is all about. However, bearing in mind that any description must be more or less inaccurate, a few tentative pointers may be given to guide us in the right general direction. The word nirvana itself possesses connotations of blowing out or extinguishing, as a flame may be blown out or extinguished once the fuel that feeds it has been exhausted. It is cool and peaceful. *Dukkha* doesn't touch it, nor the passions of greed, hatred, and ignorance. In the Buddha's own words:

Monks, there is an unborn, unoriginated, unmade and unconditioned. Were there not the unborn, unoriginated, unmade and unconditioned, there would be no escape from the born, originated, made and conditioned. Since there is the unborn, unoriginated, unmade and unconditioned, there is escape from the born, originated, made and conditioned. (Udana, VIII, 3)

Finally, even though nirvana is usually described in negative terms—it is obviously easier to say what it is *not* than what it *is*—it is never-

theless lavishly praised in the Buddhist scriptures as amounting to supreme bliss, no less.

At once, of course, the mind starts to create speculative pictures,
and stumbles into mistaken views. One classic misconception is to see
nirvana as some kind of nothingness. This is to fall prey to the mistaken
view of annihilationism (complete non-existence), which is twinned with
the equally mistaken view of eternalism (that something may exist forever). Nirvana lies beyond both existence and non-existence. Another
misconception is to imagine nirvana as a heaven where all good Buddhists
go. It is definitely not a place, nor is it "somewhere else." Paradoxi-
cally, though unconditioned itself, it only arises amid worldly conditions,
and in the case of human beings, within the human body:

> In this fathom-long body, with all its perceptions and thoughts, do I
> proclaim the world, the origin of the world, the cessation of the world
> and the path leading to the cessation of the world. (Anguttara Nikaya,
> II, 46)

The fourth noble truth defines this path to liberation by telling us
what practical steps we have to take in order to root out *trishna* and
thereby create the fertile ground in which nirvana may arise. These steps
are laid out in the teaching of the Noble Eightfold Path.

DAMIEN KEOWN

Nirvana

THIS [FOURTH NOBLE] Truth announces that when craving is removed suffering ceases and nirvana is attained. As will be recalled from the story of the Buddha's life, nirvana takes two forms: the first occurs during life and the second at death. The Buddha attained what is known as "nirvana-in-this-life" while sitting under a tree at the age of 35. At the age of 80 he passed away into "final nirvana" from which he would not be reborn.

"Nirvana" literally means "quenching" or "blowing out," in the way that the flame of a candle is blown out. But what is it that is "blown out"? Is it one's soul, one's ego, one's identity? It cannot be the soul that is blown out, since Buddhism denies that any such thing exists. Nor is it the ego or one's sense of identity that disappears, although nirvana certainly involves a radically transformed state of consciousness which is free of the obsession with "me and mine." What is extinguished, in fact, is the triple fire of greed, hatred, and delusion which leads to rebirth. Indeed, the simplest definition of nirvana-in-this-life is "the end of greed, hatred, and delusion" (*Samyutta Nikaya,* I, 38). It is clear that nirvana-in-this-life is a psychological and ethical reality, a transformed state of personality characterized by peace, deep spiritual joy, compassion, and a refined and subtle awareness. Negative mental states and emotions such as doubt, worry, anxiety, and fear are absent from the enlightened mind. Saints in many religious traditions exhibit some or all of these qualities, and ordinary people also possess them to some degree, although imperfectly developed. An enlightened person, however, such as a Buddha or an Arhat, possesses them all completely.

What becomes of such a person at death? It is in connection with final nirvana that problems of understanding arise. When the flame of craving is extinguished, rebirth ceases, and an enlightened person is not reborn. So what has happened to him? There is no clear answer to this question in the early sources. The Buddha said that asking about the whereabouts of "an enlightened one" after death is like asking where a flame goes when it is blown out. The flame, of course, has not "gone" anywhere: it is simply the process of combustion that has ceased. Removing craving and ignorance is like taking away the oxygen and fuel which a flame needs to burn. The image of the blowing out of the flame, however, should not be taken as suggesting that final nirvana is annihilation: the sources make quite clear that this would be a mistake, as would the conclusion that nirvana is the eternal existence of a personal soul.

The Buddha discouraged speculation about the nature of nirvana and emphasized instead the need to strive for its attainment. Those who asked speculative questions about nirvana he compared to a man wounded by a poisoned arrow who, rather than pulling the arrow out, persists in asking for irrelevant information about the man who fired it, such as his name and clan, how far away he was standing, and so forth (*Majjima Nikaya*, I, 426). In keeping with this reluctance on the part of the Buddha to elaborate on the question, the early sources describe nirvana in predominantly negative terms such as "the absence of desire," "the extinction of thirst," "blowing out," and "cessation." A smaller number of positive epithets are also found, including "the auspicious," "the good," "purity," "peace," "truth," and "the further shore." Certain passages seem to suggest that nirvana is a transcendent reality which is "unborn, unoriginated, uncreated and unformed" (*Udana*, 80), but it is difficult to know what interpretation to place upon such formulations. In the last analysis the nature of final nirvana remains an enigma other than to those who experience it. What we *can* be sure of, however, is that it means the end of suffering and rebirth.

The Fourth Noble Truth, that of the Path or Way (*magga*; Sanskrit: *marga*), explains how the transition from *samsara* to nirvana is to be made.

B. ALAN WALLACE

The Path/Nirvana

THE BUDDHA OFFERED no support to the view that we, as individuals or as a species, are naturally evolving toward liberation from lifetime to lifetime whether we try or not. The path of Dharma requires conscious, skillful effort. Without Dharma, each individual's continuum of awareness continues without end, moving from one dissatisfaction to the next. The Buddha was not content to reach states of awareness that bring mere temporary bliss or peace. He was seeking ultimate liberation from the cycle of existence. And this was his great discovery.

There are two Sanskrit words that have made their way into the English language, though often with their meanings somewhat misconstrued. The first of these is *samsara*. Many people are familiar with this term, though it is frequently used quite loosely. Sometimes the whole universe is referred to as samsara, but occasionally the word is used to refer more specifically to human civilization, or one's home city, job, or living conditions. To escape samsara then in this context would mean to exit from the cosmos, to go out into the wilderness, or leave one's job, or home.

Although appealing, the truth is that samsara, like so much unwanted baggage, will still accompany the traveler who "exits," for samsara can be best understood as an inner condition of existence, not a place. Samsara is the condition of being subject to the cycle of birth, aging, sickness, and death, the cycle of being propelled from one life to another by the force of one's own mental distortions and the actions conditioned by them.

Nirvana, the second of these Sanskrit terms, means final liberation from that condition of samsaric existence. It does not mean one is annihilated, blown out like a light. With the attainment of nirvana, one is no longer compelled to take birth by the force of mental distortions and tainted actions.

So one does not "go to" nirvana; it is not a place, not heaven, nor is it nothingness. Instead, liberation, or the attainment of nirvana, means a person is finally freed from the mental afflictions of confusion, attachment, and hatred. Fear and anxiety, pain and discontent are banished. According to Tibetan Buddhism, one may indeed continue to take birth, motivated by compassion for those who are bound in samsara, but this act then becomes a matter of choice, an expression of freedom, not of bondage.

Disenchantment with samsara, and the wish to attain nirvana, occur after one reflects at length on the nature of suffering and cyclic existence. This is what is meant by cultivating a spirit of emergence. However, the attainment of nirvana normally requires more than a single lifetime of spiritual practice. The task of overcoming all mental distortions, together with their latent impressions, is one that few of us are likely to complete in this life. Thus, in order to mature spiritually from this life to the next until liberation is won, it is essential to be reborn into circumstances conducive to Dharma practice. We can create such conditions for ourselves by avoiding unwholesome behavior, by devoting ourselves to the wholesome, and by dedicating our efforts to the attainment of liberation.

Meditating on the truth of suffering as it applies to ourselves is a means of cultivating a spirit of emergence. Meditating on the suffering of others leads to compassion. If our understanding of the nature of suffering is superficial, whatever compassion we feel for others may be little more than sentimentality: it arises when we see overt suffering, but as soon as that suffering is either pacified or forgotten, compassion vanishes. But as insight into the truth of suffering deepens, compassion may arise even toward those who are enjoying excellent health and prosperity. Our compassion embraces all beings who are subject to mental afflictions, all those who, while striving for happiness, create the conditions for their own misery.

Selected Glossary of Terms in Buddhism

Ananda the Buddha's personal attendant, whose remarkable memory enabled him to recite all of the Buddha's discourses

arhat (Sanskrit) a "worthy one" who attains *nirvana* at the end of this lifetime

bhikkhu (Pali) the term for a member of the Buddha's *sangha*

bodhicitta (Sanskrit) "mind of enlightenment"

bodhisattva (Sanskrit) a being destined to achieve buddhahood

Brahma-vihara (Sanskrit, Pali) the four "divine abodes": lovingkindness, compassion, sympathetic joy, and equanimity

Buddha Siddhartha Gautama (c. 563–483 BCE), Shakyamuni Buddha, the historical Buddha

buddha (Sanskrit, Pali) "awakened one," a fully enlightened being

buddhahood perfect enlightenment

Buddha-mind the mind of *not knowing*, of oneness, of complete intimacy with the interrelatedness and interpenetration of all things

conditional arising the interconnection and interdependence of all things, so that anything arising affects everything else; also called dependent origination

devas celestial beings who live in heavenly realms but are subject to rebirth

Dharma (Sanskrit; Dhamma in Pali) Buddhist teachings

dharma (Sanskrit; dhamma in Pali) means all elements, all things

Dharmakaya the unity of the Buddha's existence with all things

dukkha (Pali) the quality of dissatisfaction, discomfort, and impatience that is part of everyday life; often translated as "suffering"

Eightfold Path the Buddha's teachings on the way to end *dukkha* through *Right Action, Right Speech, Right Livelihood, Right Thought, Right View, Right Mindfulness, Right Concentration,* and *Right Effort*

emptiness the stripping away of all definitions and notions of each and every thing as having separate existence

enlightenment seeing into one's true nature and experiencing oneness with all things; being free of the delusion of a separate self

First Council the assembly called by *Mahakashyapa,* at Rajagriha, after the Buddha's death to establish the authoritative version of his teachings

First Noble Truth *dukkha* is the intrinsic nature of existence

Four Noble Truths the Buddha's fundamental teaching—that *dukkha* is the intrinsic nature of existence; that it has a cause; that it can be ended; that the method for ending *dukkha* is the *Eightfold Path*

Fourth Noble Truth the way to end *dukkha* through the *Eightfold Path*

Hinayana (Sanskrit) "lesser vehicle"; derogatory term applied to *Theravada* Buddhism by early *Mahayana* Buddhists

karma "action" or "deed," as well as the fruit of action; cause and effect

koan a paradoxical phrase or story that transcends logic, most frequently used by teachers in the *Rinzai* Zen tradition

Mahakashyapa the senior monk at the time of the Buddha's death, who with 500 *arhats* established an authoritative version of the Buddha's teachings

Mahayana the "Great Vehicle" tradition, which encompasses both Zen and Tibetan Buddhism and stresses seeking enlightenment for all beings

Mara embodiment of death or murder, often used as the manifestation of our minds

monk a renunciant who may live in a monastery; a *bhikkhu*

Nichiren founder of the thirteenth-century Japanese school of Buddhism named after him

Nirvana (Sanskrit; Pali: Nibbana) literally, "blown out"—the state of being where there is no grasping or desire for things to be different than they are

paramitas (Sanskrit) "perfections": generosity, discipline, patience, endeavor, meditative concentration, wisdom

perfections, or **six perfections** (*paramitas* in Sanskrit) generosity, discipline, patience, endeavor, meditative concentration, wisdom

Pure Land Japanese Buddhist sects that began to prosper in the tenth to fourteenth centuries

Right Concentration meditation, taking the time to "step into oneself" and really be aware of the workings of the mind and body, allowing oneself to let go and just be in great emptiness

Right Effort over and over again to strive for mindfulness, especially in meditation

Right Livelihood earning one's living according to the teachings of the Buddha

Right Mindfulness awareness during everything one does in life

Right Speech speaking in a way that causes no harm

Right Thought managing one's thoughts toward getting off the wheel of suffering and grasping

Right View understanding the world so that one can experience life with wisdom and compassion

Rinzai the Zen tradition in which there is a strong impulse to koan study and a vigorous and active style within the monasteries

samadhi (Sanskrit) concentration meditation practice

samsara (Sanskrit) "journeying," day-to-day life, the cycle of ignorance and suffering

sangha (Sanskrit) spiritual community—originally a particular group of monks, living under quite specific guidelines, but now expanded to include nuns, novitiates, lay practitioners, and sometimes all who follow a spiritual path

satori (Japanese) term used for "enlightenment" in Zen Buddhism

Second Noble Truth the cause of *dukkha* is grasping, greed, and the desire for things to be different than they are

Shakyamuni the "sage of the Shakya clan"; the historical *Buddha*

shunyata (Sanskrit) "emptiness, voidness"; having no inherently separate existence

Siddhartha Gautama the given name of the historical *Buddha*

sila (Pali) the term used primarily in Theravada Buddhism for "morality," especially *Right Speech, Right Action,* and *Right Livelihood*

skandhas (Sanskrit) the five aggregates of one's being: form, sensation, perception, mental formations, and consciousness

Soto the Zen tradition in which there is a great reverence for form and an emphasis on silent illumination or shikantaza, just sitting

sutra (Sanskrit; Pali: sutta) a Buddhist discourse

Tantra the practices of *Vajrayana* Tibetan Buddhism

Theragatha collections of enlightenment verses of the early monks

Theravada the "teachings of the elders," the oldest Buddhist tradition, which exists in the West primarily as Vipassana, or Insight Meditation, and stresses the enlightenment of the individual

Therigatha collections of enlightenment verses of the early nuns

Third Noble Truth there is an end to the cycle of wanting something, having dissatisfaction, wanting things to be different, and constantly creating *dukkha* within oneself

Three Refuges, or Three Treasures take refuge in or be one with the *Buddha*; take refuge in or be one with the *Dharma;* take refuge in or be one with the *Sangha*

Tripitaka (Sanskrit; "Three Baskets") the core of the Buddhist scriptures, comprising the Sutra Pitaka ("Discourse Basket"), the Vinaya Pitaka ("Discipline Basket"), and the Abhidharma Pitaka ("Special Teachings Basket"), codified at the *First Council*

Upali the monk who recited all the monastic rules and procedures when *Mahakashyapa* established the authorized version of the Buddha's teachings

Vajrayana (Sanskrit) "Diamond Vehicle" school of northern Indian Buddhism, today found primarily in Tibet

vihara monastery

vipassana (Pali) insight meditation

zazen literally, "seated mind"; Zen meditation

Zen from the Sanskrit *dhyanna* ("meditative absorption"), which was transliterated into *ch'an* in Chinese, then into *zenna*, or *Zen*, in Japanese; came to Japan from China toward the end of the twelfth century and became the major Japanese school of Buddhism, primarily consisting of *Rinzai* and *Soto* sects

zendo a hall where zazen is formally practiced

Contributors

STEPHEN BATCHELOR was born in Scotland and educated in England and in Buddhist monasteries in India, Korea, and Switzerland. He is a cofounder of the Buddhist-based Sharpham Community in Devon, England. A noted scholar and translator, he has written numerous books, which include *The Awakening of the West* (Parallax, 1994) and classic translations of *A Guide to the Bodhisattva's Way of Life* (Library of Tibetan Works and Archives, 1979) and Geshe Rabten's *Echoes of Voidness* (Wisdom Publications, 1983).

CHARLOTTE JOKO BECK, American Zen teacher, studied at the Los Angeles Zen Center with Maezumi Roshi, Yasutani Roshi, and Soen Roshi. In 1983 she moved to the Zen Center of San Diego, where she lives and teaches. Her books on practice include *Everyday Zen* (HarperCollins, 1989) and *Nothing Special: Living Zen* (HarperCollins, 1993).

BHIKKHU BODHI (Jeffrey Block) was born in New York City. He was ordained as a monk in Sri Lanka in 1972, and currently is the president and editor of the Buddhist Publications Society. He has published *The Middle Length Discourses of the Buddha* (Wisdom Publications, 1995), and other major Pali texts and commentaries.

BODHIDHARMA (c. 470–543) is believed to be the son of a south Indian king. After he was confirmed as the twenty-eighth patriarch in the Indian Buddhist lineage, he went by ship to China, where he became the first patriarch of Chinese Ch'an (Zen).

SYLVIA BOORSTEIN is a Vipassana teacher and retreat leader across the United States. She is a cofounding teacher, with Jack Kornfield, at the Spirit Rock Meditation Center in California and is a senior teacher at the Insight Meditation Society in Massachusetts. She is the author of *Don't Just Do Something, Sit There* (HarperCollins, 1996) and *It's Easier Than You Think* (HarperCollins, 1995).

BUDDHAGHOSA was born toward the end of the fourth century near Bodhgaya, India. After converting to Buddhism, he went to Ceylon (Sri Lanka), where he studied Theravada teachings at the Mahavihara monastery. He wrote numerous commentaries on the discourses of the Pali canon, the teachings of the Buddha, and meditation, including *The Path of Purification*.

ACHARYA BUDDHARAKKHITA, born in India, is a Buddhist monk who directs the Maha Bodhi Society center in Bangalore and is the founder of the Buddha Yoga Meditation Society in the United States. His publications include a classic translation of the early Pali canon work *The Dhammapada* (Buddhist Publication Society, 1985).

EDWARD CONZE was a pioneering British Buddhist scholar and translator who held teaching appointments in England, Germany, and the United States. His books include *Buddhism* (Penguin, 1951), *Buddhist Wisdom Books* (Penguin, 1958), and *Thirty Years of Buddhist Studies* (Penguin, 1962).

DALAI LAMA, THE FOURTEENTH (TENZIN GYATSO), is considered a living embodiment of the spiritual ideal in Tibetan Buddhism. After the Chinese invasion of Tibet in 1959, he fled to India, where he established a government in exile in Dharamsala. Since then he has traveled worldwide, teaching and conducting rituals, and his contributions to world peace were recognized in 1989 when he was awarded the Nobel Peace Prize. His many writings include *A Flash of Lightning in the Dark of Night* (Shambhala, 1994) and *A Policy of Kindness* (Snow Lion, 1990).

EIHEI DOGEN, a thirteenth-century Japanese aristocrat, experienced enlightenment in 1223 on a visit to China. Four years later, he returned to his homeland and founded the Japanese school of Soto Zen Buddhism. He is revered as the most important Japanese Zen master, and his writings are widely anthologized; a collection known as *Treasury of the Eye of the True Dharma* is the most well known.

BERNARD GLASSMAN is abbot of the Zen Community of New York and the Zen Center of Los Angeles, spiritual leader of the White Plum Sangha, founder of the Greyston Mandala, and president of the Soto Zen Buddhist Association. He is the author of *Instructions to the Cook: A Zen Master's Lessons in Living a Life That Matters* (Bell Tower, 1996).

JOSEPH GOLDSTEIN has studied Buddhism in India, Thailand, and Burma. In 1976 he cofounded, with Sharon Salzberg and Jack Kornfield, the Insight Meditation Society in Barre, Massachusetts. He has led meditation retreats and taught around the world for more than twenty years. Among his widely read books are *Insight Meditation* (Shambhala, 1993), *The Experience of Insight* (Shambhala, 1987), and, with Jack Kornfield, *Seeking the Heart of Wisdom* (Shambhala, 1987).

HENEPOLA GUNARATANA was ordained as a Buddhist monk in Sri Lanka when he was twelve years old. After missionary work in India and Malaysia and teaching in Malaysia, he came to the United States in 1968. He was president of the Buddhist Vihara Society of Washington, D.C.; and he taught at the American University, Georgetown University, and the University of Maryland. His writings on Theravada tradition have been published in Malaysia, India, Sri Lanka, and the United States, where his book *Mindfulness in Plain English* (Wisdom Publications, 1991) is widely recognized as an extraordinarily valuable introduction to insight meditation.

KELSANG GYATSO, who was born in Tibet, is a meditation master, scholar, and author of a number of books on Buddhist thought and practice, including *Meaningful to Behold* (Tharpa Publications, 1986), a commentary on Shantideva's *Guide to the Bodhisattva's Way of Life*. He is resident teacher at Manjushri Institute in England, a center for Tibetan Buddhist studies.

THICH NHAT HANH, a Vietnamese Zen Buddhist monk, founded the Van Hanh Buddhist University in Saigon, and has taught at Columbia University in New York City and the Sorbonne in Paris. For his efforts for peace, he was nominated by Martin Luther King, Jr., in 1967 for the Nobel Peace Prize. He is the author of more than seventy-five books, including a biography of the Buddha, *Old Path/ White Clouds* (Parallax, 1991); *Present Moment, Wonderful Moment* (Parallax, 1990); *Breathe! You Are Alive* (Parallax, 1988), and *Zen Keys* (Doubleday, 1974).

HUANG PO, a ninth-century proponent of the "sudden" approach to enlightenment, represents the full flowering of Ch'an (Zen) Buddhism in China. His teachings were compiled by his student scholar P'ei Hsiu.

JON KABAT-ZINN is associate professor of medicine and the founder and director of the Stress Reduction Clinic at the University of Massachusetts Medical Center. His clear and accessible teachings on Buddhist mindfulness in daily life have made his writings popular among a remarkably wide audience of Buddhists and non-Buddhists. His books include *Wherever You Go, There You Are* (Hyperion, 1994) and *Full Catastrophe Living* (Delta, 1991).

DAININ KATAGIRI trained at Soto Zen monasteries in Japan before moving to the United States in 1963. After residing at several monasteries in California, including the San Francisco Zen Center, where he assisted Shunryu Suzuki, he became the first abbot of the Minnesota Zen Center, in Minneapolis. *Returning to Silence* (Shambhala, 1988) is a collection of his teachings on meditation.

DAMIEN KEOWN, a senior lecturer in Indian religion at the University of London and a fellow of the Royal Asiatic Society, is the author of *Buddhism: A Very Short Introduction* (Oxford University Press, 1996).

AYYA KHEMA (1923–1997), who was born in Germany and emigrated to the United States at the end of World War II, was ordained as a Buddhist nun in Sri Lanka in 1979. She was active worldwide in supporting women Buddhists: She set up the International Buddhist Women's Centre in Sri Lanka; in 1987 coordinated the first international conference of Buddhist nuns; and established Sakyadhita, a worldwide Buddhist women's organization. In 1987, she was the first Buddhist ever to address the United Nations. Her numerous books include *When the Iron Eagle Flies* (Arkana, 1991) and *Being Nobody, Going Nowhere* (Wisdom Publications, 1988).

SHERAB CHÖDZIN KOHN, who has taught Buddhism throughout North America and Europe, is the editor and translator of numerous books on Buddhism and is the coeditor, with Samuel Bercholz, of *Entering the Stream: An Introduction to the Buddha and His Teachings* (Shambhala,1993).

JACK KORNFIELD was trained as a Buddhist monk in Thailand, Burma, and India. When he returned to the United States, he cofounded the Insight Meditation Society in Massachusetts and the Spirit Rock Meditation Center in California. He is recognized worldwide as an exceptional Vipassana teacher. His books include *A Path with Heart* (Bantam, 1993) and, with Joseph Goldstein, *Seeking the Heart of Wisdom* (Shambhala, 1987).

KATHLEEN MCDONALD (SANGYE KHADRO) was ordained as a Tibetan Buddhist nun in 1974, and is a teacher in the Foundation for the Preservation of the Mahayana Tradition, a worldwide organization of Buddhist teaching and meditation centers. Her guide *How to Meditate* (Wisdom Publications, 1984) covers practical aspects of her teachings on meditation.

PAT ENKYO O'HARA is a Soto Zen priest and resident teacher at the Village Zendo in New York City, where she teaches at New York University as well. She is also active in the Zen Peacemaker Order.

GESHE RABTEN was born in Tibet and studied and taught at the Sera Monastic University before his exile in 1959. He founded Tharpa Choeling Centre for Higher Buddhist Studies in Switzerland in 1979.

WALPOLA RAHULA was born and educated as a Buddhist monk in Sri Lanka and held teaching positions at universities worldwide, including the University of Calcutta and the University of Paris. He is the author of *What the Buddha Taught* (rev. ed. Grove Press, 1974), a classic study of basic teachings and texts.

PAUL REPS was an American scholar and student of comparative religions. His collection *Zen Flesh, Zen Bones* (Anchor, 1986) is a classic compilation of Zen and pre-Zen stories and koans.

SHARON SALZBERG, cofounder with Joseph Goldstein and Jack Kornfield of the Insight Meditation Society in Massachusetts, has taught meditation at Buddhist centers around the world. She is the author of the widely acclaimed books *Lovingkindness* (Shambhala, 1995) and *A Heart as Wide as the World* (Shambhala, 1997).

SHANTIDEVA, according to legend the son of a king in south India, lived in the seventh and eighth centuries as a monk. His most important surviving work is *A Guide to the Bodhisattva's Way of Life*, still used as a teaching text within Tibetan Buddhism.

SULAK SIVARAKSA is the author of *Seeds of Peace: A Buddhist Vision for Renewing Society* (Parallax, 1992).

JEAN SMITH, who practices in the Vipassana tradition, is a freelance editor and writer living in New York City. Among her publications are three books on Buddhism: *Everyday Mind: 366 Reflections on the Buddhist Path* (Riverhead, 1997), *Breath Sweeps Mind: A First Guide to Meditation Practice* (Riverhead, 1998), and *Radiant Mind: Essential Teachings and Texts* (Riverhead, 1999).

JOHN SNELLING was born in Wales and educated in England. A noted scholar and author, he was general secretary of the Buddhist Society, then editor of its widely read journal, *The Middle Way*, from 1980 to 1987. His numerous writings include the book *The Elements of Buddhism* (Elements Books, 1990).

MU SOENG SUNIM is the author of *Heart Sutra: Ancient Wisdom in the Light of Quantum Reality* (Primary Point Press).

GESHE SONAM RINCHEN is a scholar and the author of *The Thirty-seven Practices of Bodhisattvas* (Snow Lion, 1997), which was translated by Ruth Sonam.

D. T. SUZUKI was born and educated in Japan, and his teachings worldwide earned him the informal title of chief emissary of Zen Buddhism to the West. Among the numerous publications of his works is *Zen Buddhism: Selected Writings of D. T. Suzuki*, edited by William Barrett (Image Books, 1996).

SHUNRYU SUZUKI was a spiritual descendant of the thirteenth-century Zen master Dogen. He came to the United States from Japan in 1958 and founded three centers, including Zen Mountain Center, the first Zen training center outside Asia. He is respected as one of the most important Zen teachers of his time, and his core teachings are recorded in *Zen Mind, Beginner's Mind* (Weatherhill), published in 1970, a year before his death.

KOSHO UCHIYAMA was born in Tokyo and educated in Western philosophy before becoming a Soto Zen priest in 1940. He became abbot of the Antaiji, a temple and monastery near Kyoto, in 1965. He wrote more than twenty texts on Zen, including translations of Dogen's works into modern Japanese. Among his writings available in English are *Opening the Hand of Thought* (Arkana, 1993) and *Refining Your Life* (Weatherhill, 1983).

TETSUO UNNO is a minister and follower of the Jodoshinshu sect of Pure Land Buddhism.

B. ALAN WALLACE, one of the first Westerners ordained in the Tibetan Buddhist tradition, is a noted scholar, teacher, and translator. He has written several books stressing the relevance of Tibetan Buddhist teaching to contemporary life, including *Tibetan Buddhism from the Ground Up* (Wisdom Publications, 1993).

MAURICE WALSHE, British scholar and translator of Pali texts, was president of the Buddhist Society and chair of the English Sangha Trust before his retirement. Among his many publications, he is especially known for the classic translation *Thus Have I Heard: The Long Discourses of the Buddha* (Wisdom Publications, 1987).

BURTON WATSON is a scholar and translator whose translation of *The Lotus Sutra* was published by Columbia University Press.

Credits

Part I: The Buddha and Buddhism
The Buddha

John Snelling: The Teaching Career. Reprinted from *The Elements of Buddhism* by John Snelling. Copyright © 1990 by John Snelling. Reprinted with permission of Element Books, Ltd., Shaftesbury, Dorset, England.

Joseph Goldstein: The Example of the Buddha. From *Seeking the Heart of Wisdom* by Joseph Goldstein and Jack Kornfield, © 1987. Reprinted by arrangement with Shambhala Publications, Inc., Boston.

The Dalai Lama: The Buddha's Life. © Tenzin Gyatso, the Fourteenth Dalai Lama, 1995. © Geshe Thupten Jimpa, English translation, 1995. Reprinted from *The World of Tibetan Buddhism: An Overview of Its Philosophy and Practice* with permission of Wisdom Publications, 199 Elm Street, Somerville, Massachusetts 02144, USA.

Huang Po: The Real Buddha. Reprinted from *The Zen Teachings of Huang Po,* translated by John Blofeld. Used by permission of Grove/Atlantic, Inc.

Buddhism

Sherab Chödzin Kohn: A Short History of Buddhism. From *Entering the Stream* by Samuel Bercholtz and Sherab Chödzin Kohn, © 1993. Reprinted by arrangement with Shambhala Publications, Inc., Boston.

Jack Kornfield: Theravada/Vipassana Practice. From *Seeking the Heart of Wisdom* by Joseph Goldstein and Jack Kornfield, © 1987. Reprinted by arrangement with Shambhala Publications, Inc., Boston.

The Dalai Lama: Mahayana/Vajrayana Practice. From *A Flash of Lightning in the Dark* by Tenzin Gyatso, © 1994 by Association Bouddhiste des Centres de Dordogne. Reprinted by arrangement with Shambhala Publications, Inc., Boston.

D. T. Suzuki: Mahayana/Zen Practice. From *Zen Buddhism: Selected Writings of D. T. Suzuki* edited by William Barrett. Reprinted by permission.

Shunryu Suzuki: Mahayana/Zen Practice. From *Zen Mind, Beginner's Mind* by Shunryu Suzuki. Copyright © 1970 by Shunryu Suzuki. Reprinted by permission of Weatherhill, Inc.

B. Alan Wallace: Teachers/Mentors. From *Tibetan Buddhism from the Ground Up*. © B. Alan Wallace, 1993. Courtesy of Wisdom Publications, 199 Elm Street, Somerville, Massachusetts 02144, USA.

D. T. Suzuki: Teachers/Koans. From *Zen Buddhism: Selected Writings of D. T. Suzuki* edited by William Barrett. Reprinted by permission.

Part II: Teachings and Texts
The Four Noble Truths

Walpola Rahula, trans.: *The First Sermon of the Buddha*. From *What the Buddha Taught,* © 1959. Used by permission of Grove/Atlantic, Inc.

Bhikkhu Nanamoli and Bhikkhu Bodhi, trans.: *The Exposition of the Four Noble Truths.* © Bhikkhu Bodhi, 1995. Reprinted from *The Middle Length Discourses of the Buddha: A New Translation of the Majjhinia Nikaya* with permission of Wisdom Publications, 199 Elm Street, Somerville, Massachusetts 02144, USA.

Bhikkhu Bodhi: Impermanence and the Four Noble Truths. © Bhikkhu Bodhi, 1995. Reprinted from *The Middle Length Discourses of the Buddha: A New Translation of the Majjhinia Nikaya* with permission of Wisdom Publications, 199 Elm Street, Somerville, Massachusetts 02144, USA.

Walpola Rahula: Functions Regarding the Four Noble Truths. From *What the Buddha Taught,* © 1959. Used by permission of Grove/Atlantic, Inc.

Wisdom Publications, 199 Elm Street, Somerville, Massachusetts 02144, USA.

Kathleen McDonald: Tibetan Buddhist Meditation. © Wisdom Publications, 1984. Reprinted from *How to Meditate: A Practical Guide* by Kathleen McDonald with permission of Wisdom Publications, 199 Elm Street, Somerville, Massachusetts 02144, USA.

B. Alan Wallace: Tibetan Buddhist Meditation. Reprinted from *The World of Tibetan Buddhism: An Overview of Its Philosophy and Practice.* © Tenzin Gyatso, the Fourteenth Dalai Lama, 1995. © Geshe Thupten Jinpa, English translation, 1995. Courtesy of Wisdom Publications, 199 Elm Street, Somerville, Massachusetts 02144, USA.

Sharon Salzberg, trans.: *The Metta Sutta.* From *Loving-Kindness* by Sharon Salzberg, © 1995. Reprinted by arrangement with Shambhala Publications, Inc., Boston.

Sharon Salzberg: Metta Practice. Reprinted from *Inquiring Mind Newsletter,* Fall 1996.

Ayya Khema: The Heart Essence. From *When the Iron Eagle Flies,* 1991. Copyright © Ayya Khema, 1991. Reproduced by permission of Penguin Books, Ltd.

Wisdom

Editors of *Tricycle*: The Heart Sutra. Reprinted from *Tricycle: The Buddhist Review,* volume I, number 3.

Thich Nhat Hanh: The Heart of Understanding. Reprinted from *The Heart of Understanding: Commentaries on the Prajñaparamita Heart Sutra* (1988) by Thich Nhat Hanh with permission of Parallax Press, Berkeley, California.

Geshe Rabten: *The Heart Sutra.* From *Echoes of Voidness.* © Geshé Rabten and Stephen Batchelor, 1983. Courtesy of Wisdom Publications, 199 Elm Street, Somerville, MA 02144 USA.

Shunryu Suzuki: *The Prajna Paramita Sutra.* From *Zen Mind, Beginner's Mind* by Shunryu Suzuki. Copyright © 1970 by Shunryu Suzuki. Reprinted by permission of Weatherhill, Inc.

The Self

Karma

Jon Kabat-Zinn: Changing Karma. From *Wherever You Go, There You Are: Mindfulness Meditation in Everyday Life* by Jon Kabat-Zinn. Copyright © 1994 by Jon Kabat-Zinn. Reprinted with permission by Hyperion.

The Dhammapada

Acharya Buddharakkhita, trans.: *The Dhammapada*. Reprinted from *The Dhammapada,* translated by Acharya Buddharakkhita, copyright © 1985. Permission granted by the Buddhist Publication Society, Sangharaja Mawata, Kandy, Sri Lanka.

Acharya Buddharakkhita, trans.: From *The Dhammapada*. Reprinted from *The Dhammapada,* translated by Acharya Buddharakkhita, copyright © 1985. Permission granted by the Buddhist Publication Society, Sangharaja Mawata, Kandy, Sri Lanka.

Nirvana

John Snelling: Nirvana. Reprinted from *The Buddhist Handbook* by John Snelling, published in the U.S. by Inner Traditions International, Ltd., Rochester, Vermont 05767. Copyright © 1991 by John Snelling. Reprinted outside the U.S. courtesy of Century Hutchinson.

Damien Keown: Nirvana. Reprinted from *Buddhism: A Very Short Introduction* by Damien Keown, copyright © 1996. Used by permission of Oxford University Press.

B. Alan Wallace: The Path/Nirvana. From *Tibetan Buddhism from the Ground Up.* © B. Alan Wallace, 1993. Courtesy of Wisdom Publications, 199 Elm Street, Somerville, Massachusetts 02144, USA.

Index